MAPS OF UTOPIA

Maps of Utopia

H. G. Wells, Modernity, and the End of Culture

SIMON J. JAMES

*'A map of the world that does not include Utopia
is not worth even glancing at.'*

Oscar Wilde, 'The Soul of Man under Socialism'

OXFORD
UNIVERSITY PRESS

OXFORD
UNIVERSITY PRESS

Great Clarendon Street, Oxford OX2 6DP

Oxford University Press is a department of the University of Oxford.
It furthers the University's objective of excellence in research, scholarship,
and education by publishing worldwide in

Oxford New York

Auckland Cape Town Dar es Salaam Hong Kong Karachi
Kuala Lumpur Madrid Melbourne Mexico City Nairobi
New Delhi Shanghai Taipei Toronto

With offices in

Argentina Austria Brazil Chile Czech Republic France Greece
Guatemala Hungary Italy Japan Poland Portugal Singapore
South Korea Switzerland Thailand Turkey Ukraine Vietnam

Oxford is a registered trade mark of Oxford University Press
in the UK and in certain other countries

Published in the United States
by Oxford University Press Inc., New York

© Simon J. James 2012

The moral rights of the author have been asserted
Database right Oxford University Press (maker)

First published 2012

British Library Cataloguing in Publication Data

Data available

Library of Congress Cataloging in Publication Data
Library of Congress Control Number: 2011939892

Typeset by SPI Publisher Services, Pondicherry, India
Printed in Great Britain
on acid-free paper by
MPG Books Group, Bodmin and King's Lynn

ISBN 978–0–19–960659–7

1 3 5 7 9 10 8 6 4 2

For Kate, of course. And Trevor and Lenny Bob

Contents

Preface

Writing on an author with whose personal views one frequently disagrees with can produce difficulties. An author as opinionated as H. G. Wells will provoke some disagreement in almost all of his readers. As a consequence, different critical work on Wells has severally dismissed the majority of his published output, been nakedly hostile to the content of the text it discusses, sought to find a means of legitimizing his work's agenda in the present day, or even reshaped the text to promote the critic's own agenda.

I have attempted in what follows to avoid where possible unnecessary hindsight condemnation of Wells's failings, but also to suggest a small revision in the received version of the literary history of the *fin-de-siècle* and early twentieth-century periods. The period dubbed the 'Interregnum' by Raymond Williams (a critic who was nonetheless among the first to treat such writers as Gissing, Wells, and Bennett with the historical seriousness that they deserve) has only recently begun to receive the critical attention it deserves, in comparison to the high Victorian era and canonical modernism.[1] Even as staunch a Wellsian as John Hammond makes a case for the value of Wells's work on the grounds of his 'modernism', as if this, as for Conrad and James, is the means by which he might escape the backwater of 'transition' and be counted in the first rank of canonical writers.[2] Since high modernism and the birth of English Studies as a major academic discipline share an origin at roughly the same time, they share many of the same values and methodologies—Wells is thus proved 'wrong' by the canons that evolved for literary study over the twentieth century. As David Trotter has also argued, modernism is still too often used to evaluate rather than to characterize, to distinguish between those writers who are considered innovatory, and thus worthy of study, and those who aren't.[3] *Maps of Utopia* seeks to recover some of Wells's reputation in his own lifetime, as perhaps the most influential Anglophone

---

[1] Raymond Williams, *Culture and Society, 1780–1950* (Harmondsworth: Penguin, 1963), 165.

[2] J. R Hammond, *H. G. Wells and the Modern Novel* (New York: St Martin's Press, 1988). For a thoughtful discussion of this issue, see Robert L. Caserio, 'The Novel as Novel Experiment in Statement: The Anticanonical Example of H. G. Wells', in *Decolonizing Tradition: New Views of Twentieth-Century 'British' Literary Canons* (Urbana: University of Illinois Press, 1992), 88–109.

[3] David Trotter, *The English Novel in History, 1895–1920* (London: Routledge, 1993), 5.

writer of the first half of the twentieth century; but this book is primarily a literary study of Wells's aesthetics, outside of those canons and perhaps more in Wells's own terms, of what he thought what literature was, and what he thought it was for.

Literary criticism is, naturally, often preoccupied with texts which prominently feature images of reading and writing. Although Wells constantly downplayed his seriousness as a serious creative artist, he was certainly not a writer who disliked writing—on the contrary, he saw it as a vitally important task 'to make [. . .] the creative imagination embodied in English literature a fertilizing power throughout the earth'.[4] Rather, Wells believed the ways in which imaginative writing was evaluated and thought of in his own time to be misguided. Indeed, his ambition for the novel was higher even than the claims for art made by Henry James—as John R. Reed puts it, 'to identify fiction with the broadest of contexts—the history of the race'—to bring about world peace and greater happiness for every man, woman, and child both in the present and for the future.[5]

No writer can be said to have been more concerned with the future than Wells, but prophecy as a genre can only be judged by the criterion of prescience. Once it has been said that Wells predicted to a greater or lesser degree genetic engineering, the tank, aerial bombardment, the nuclear bomb, the European Union, environmentalism, the human rights movement, and the internet, what more can usefully be said, from the point of view of literary criticism? As a consequence, *Maps of Utopia* focuses mainly on those Wells texts of the greatest interest from the literary point of view (not necessarily only the fiction). While many of Wells's books possess as much literary merit as those of his more celebrated contemporaries, any study of Wells must sooner or later confront the issue that many of the books that Wells wrote are not, simply, very good. Literary value still tends to be predicated, and rightly so, on originality: the dominant mode of Wells's later work is repetition. Nonetheless, there is much that can be said about Wells's non-fictional work (and this volume makes extensive use of *Mankind in the Making* in particular). There is, perhaps, more verve in *An Englishman Looks at the World* than in *The Passionate Friends*, more wit in *A Year of Prophesying* than *Christina Alberta's Father*, more to engage the reader in *The Science of Life* than *The Secret Places of the Heart* (a novel which even Wells himself denigrated). (Later works such as *The Croquet Player* and *The Camford Visitation* do show Wells adopting a different

[4] 'The Future of the British Empire', *A Year of Prophesying* (New York: Macmillan, 1925), 61.
[5] John R. Reed, *The Natural History of H. G. Wells* (Athens: Ohio University Press, 1982), 233.

narrative mode, but Wells's very late work must lie outside of the scope of this study.) Most critical material on Wells celebrates the inventiveness of Wells's work up until 1910, and then stops short with a (not unjustified) complaint about how the output of the author's remaining thirty-six years fails to compare with what preceded it. This study does focus on the most inventive period of Wells's work, but, rather than just futilely lamenting the lack of merit of what follows, seeks to investigate the origins of the change in the nature of Wells's work—to tell a different version of the story of the supposed 'corruption' of Wells's art by his politics.

Wells began his career as a Victorian writer, and this study begins by locating the ancestries of Wells's ideas about literature in the Victorian era's post-1870 anxieties about reading fiction, and also its tradition of sage-writing by public intellectuals. The first chapter also suggests the evolutionary basis of Wells's notions about the uses or otherwise of the artistic. In considering Wells's subsequent uses and representations of artistic culture, it will be necessary slightly to violate chronology, ordering the remaining topics as follows: what Wells thinks the world might be (the scientific romances), what it actually is (the realist novels), what it should be (the utopias), and finally, what he fears it might become (the writings on war and history), closing with his collaborative cinematic project *Things to Come*. This story both begins and ends with popular media (the novel, the cinema) and with educational reform (the Education Acts, *The Outline of History*): the coexistence of entertainment and the didactic is perhaps the keynote of Wells's imagination.

Acknowledgements

Every researcher working on H. G. Wells is in the debt of Patrick Parrinder. The gratitude of this one could not be greater: Professor Parrinder has offered me many opportunities for further study of Wells, and this book could not be what it has become without his generosity and his scholarship. Steven McLean has been an unstintingly supportive comrade-in-arms throughout the time we have both been working on Wells; John S. Partington supplied valuable material throughout the process of writing, and learned commentary on a final draft. I am grateful to more members of the H. G. Wells Society than I can name, but Sylvia Hardy and John Hammond have been unfailingly encouraging and help-ful; John Clute also gave an inspirational conference presentation on *The Sea Lady*. Geoffrey Hunt supplied numerous references that I would never have encountered without his contributions, and I am most grateful to him. I would also like to acknowledge the help of the following Wells scholars: Gillian Beer, Emily Evans, David Lodge, John Sutherland, Roger Till, and the late and much-missed Michael Foot and David C. Smith. Needless to say, I am also much in the debt of the Durham students with whom I have discussed Wells, notably Paul McAdam and Yoonjoung Choi, and of my colleagues in the Department of English Studies.

Work towards completing this book was assisted by Research Leave granted by Durham University, and I was fortunate enough to be awarded a Jean 'Bud' Velde Fellowship by the Rare Book and Manuscript Library at the University of Illinois to consult one of the world's greatest literary archives. I am grateful to the friendship and learning shared at Urbana-Champaign by Chatham Ewing and Gene Rinkel, and most of all, by Dennis Sears, whom I won't embarrass by saying any more about his kindness and generosity of spirit. Durham's Institute of Advanced Study funded the learned research assistance and percipience of Tony Patterson, who has also materially shaped the contents of this volume for the better. I am very grateful to the staff of the British and Durham University Libraries; the archive.org has also provided some valuable material for referencing. My thanks are also due to Jacqueline Baker, Ariane Petit, Jo North, and Briony Ryles for seeing the book through to publication.

The early stages of my research for this project owe a great deal to the friendship and hospitality of Simon Pick and Ann Nishigaya. Simon's devotion to science fiction as an art-form worthy of serious attention has been both inspiring and illuminating and this section of my work would have been the poorer without my discussions with him. Like many born in the 1970s, my very earliest exposure to Wells's words was through Jeff Wayne's musical adaptation of *The War of the Worlds*, and for this I have to thank Douglas Cope; also my father for letting me read his copies of the *Complete Short Stories* and *The Island of Doctor Moreau* when I was at an age when he probably shouldn't. I would also like to thank Adrian Poole for returning me to an interest in Wells during study for my PhD.

Work in progress has been presented at the Universities of Durham, Salerno, Dayton, and Illinois, and at the conferences of the H. G. Wells Society. Earlier drafts of the content of this volume appear in *Consuming for Pleasure: Selected Essays on Popular Fiction*, ed. Julia Hallam and Nickianne Moody (Liverpool: Liverpool John Moores University Press, 2000); *English* 57 (2008), *H. G. Wells: Interdisciplinary Essays*, ed. Steven McLean (Newcastle: Cambridge Scholars, 2008); and *The Evolution of Literature: Legacies of Darwin in European Cultures*, ed. Nicholas Saul and Simon J. James (Amsterdam: Rodopi, 2011).

1

Of Art, Of Literature, Of Mr. H. G. Wells

The era in which H. G. Wells began his literary career was much preoccupied with the purposes and effects of reading. The Education Act of 1870 had enabled School Boards to provide all children with schooling; by 1880, Boards were required to do so. The enormous increase in the size of the public able to read and now willing to purchase printed matter consequently increased the number of books published, especially fiction. In 1873, according to Peter Keating, 516 novels for adults were published; in 1887, 762; by 1894, the number was 1,315.[1] Books were also becoming cheaper; David Vincent has evaluated the decreasing cost of Victorian reading matter thus:

> With every year that passed, more could be bought for less. A penny would buy a 250-word broadside in the 1840s, a fifty-page songbook or a 7,000-word serial by the 1860s, a 20,000-word novelette by the 1880s, and from 1896, with the appearance of Newnes' Penny Library of Famous Books, unabridged versions of classic texts.[2]

The material changes that had been wrought by the larger number of books and their greater cheapness also transformed the cultural and material practices surrounding the production of imaginative literature. The nineteenth-century *fin-de-siècle* saw the foundation of the Society of Authors, the rise of the literary agent, the beginnings of the cult of the 'bestseller', and long-running debates about the status of the writer as a professional, about international copyright and the right of an author to own his or her own work, and about censorship and the representation of

---

[1] Peter Keating, *The Haunted Study: A Social History of the English Novel, 1875–1914* (London: Secker & Warburg, 1989), 32.
[2] David Vincent, *Literacy and Popular Culture: England, 1750–1914* (Cambridge: Cambridge University Press, 1989), 211. See Douwe Draaisma, *Metaphors of Memory: A History of Ideas About the Mind* (Cambridge: Cambridge University Press, 2000), 36, on the decline on books being considered objects of value.

sexuality in literature.[3] Following such extensive changes in the nature of reading as a social practice, its scope, nature, and effect were being debated as never before.[4] Debates about material issues such as copyright and commodity value were mingled with aesthetic and ethical discussions of the use and purpose of writing and reading.[5] The hugely increased size of the reading public created by the Act generated an anxiety in literary producers over what the effects of reading might be on the newly and vastly increased audience for books. The effects of reading could now no longer be a matter of private, individual response, but of national concern, and nowhere was this debate more fiercely concentrated than on the subject of reading fiction.

The newly literate and reading public had, of course, a choice about what it might read: predominantly, it chose novels, romances, and short stories. Writing in 1893 for the *Pall Mall Gazette*, on 'The Literature of the Future', H. G. Wells wondered whether this was 'an age of literature', concluding that 'this is the age of books [...] and the books are novels'.[6] Herbert Maxwell attested in 1893 to fiction's 'immense preference [...] over other forms of literature'; George R. Humphery found only '160 solid books against 352' of fiction in his account of working-class reading habits.[7] Public libraries had long argued over whether even to admit fiction into their holdings; its popularity was confirmed when they did, making the editor of the *Pall Mall Gazette*, John Morley, worry that the

---

[3] James G. Hepburn, *The Author's Empty Purse and the Rise of the Literary Agent* (London: Oxford University Press, 1968); Nigel Cross, *The Common Writer: Life in Nineteenth-Century Grub Street* (Cambridge: Cambridge University Press, 1985); N. N. Feltes, *Literary Capital and the Late Victorian Novel* (Madison: University of Wisconsin Press, 1993); John O. Jordan and Robert L. Patten, eds, *Literature in the Market Place: Nineteenth-Century British Publishing and Reading Practices* (Cambridge: Cambridge University Press, 1995); Peter D. McDonald, *British Literary Culture and Publishing Practice, 1880–1914* (Cambridge: Cambridge University Press, 1997); P. J. Waller, *Writers, Readers and Reputations: Literary Life in Britain, 1870–1918* (Oxford: Oxford University Press, 2006).

[4] Nicholas Dames, *The Physiology of the Novel: Reading Neural Science and the Form of the Victorian Novel* (Oxford: Oxford University Press, 2007); Patrick Brantlinger, *The Reading Lesson: The Threat of Mass Literacy in Nineteenth-Century British Fiction* (Bloomington: Indiana University Press, 1998).

[5] See, for instance, Josephine Guy, 'Aesthetics, Economics and Commodity Culture: Theorizing Value in Late Nineteenth-Century Britain', *English Literature in Transition*, 42/2 (1999), 143–71; Mary Poovey, 'Forgotten Writers, Neglected Histories: Charles Reade and the Nineteenth-Century Transformation of the British Literary Field', *English Literary History*, 72/2 (2004), 433–53.

[6] 'The Literature of the Future: The Horoscope of Books', *Pall Mall Gazette*, 11 October 1893.

[7] Herbert Maxwell, 'The Craving for Fiction', *Nineteenth Century*, 33 (1893) 1046–61 (1046); George R. Humphery, 'The Reading of the Working Classes', *Nineteenth Century*, 33 (1893), 690–701 (694).

proportion of titles borrowed that were fiction, as opposed to 'solid books', had become far too high.[8]

Commentators thus worried that in the proliferation and evolution of new literary species, the fittest rather than the best might survive. If fiction is what the public wanted to read, it was felt that they should therefore do so with a definite object in mind, and should choose books of a higher and improving kind, that possess enduring merit, rather than only transitory value. Frederic Harrison, for example, fretted in 1886 that such works might prove too difficult to identify in the flood-tide of new printed matter.[9] In an address to the Working Men's College of which he was principal, MP Sir John Lubbock celebrated the cheapness and greater availability of books, and proposed a bibliography which the *Pall Mall Gazette* christened the 'Hundred Best Books'. These recommendations were subsequently adopted by a publisher's advertising campaign, a telling combination of the spread of literacy, ruling-class intervention, and commercial aptitude.[10] (Indeed, reprints of classic literature made up a significant part of the late-Victorian publishing boom.)[11]

While writers of new fiction recognized that the expanding literature industry provided greater opportunities for success for themselves as well as for booksellers, publishers, agents, and critics, not everyone was entirely happy about the increasingly visible commodification of literary production: what would be mass literacy's implications for writing's aesthetic value and durability? Thomas Henry Farrer, the Permanent Secretary to the Board of Trade, admitted to the 1875–6 Copyright Commission that there could be no 'definite or assignable relation between the money payment made to an author and the permanent value of this book'.[12] Not all writers of fiction felt that the dignity of literature was necessarily augmented by its being made available to more readers: Robert Louis Stevenson and George Gissing, amongst others, worried that the calling of the writer might be debased by the more widespread and commercialized

[8] Mary Hammond, *Reading, Publishing and the Formation of Literary Taste, 1880–1914* (Aldershot: Ashgate, 2006), 31, 34; John Morley, 'On the Study of Literature' (1887), in *Studies in Literature* (London: Macmillan, 1891), 189–228. See also Lewis C. Roberts, 'Disciplining and Disinfecting Working-Class Readers in the Victorian Public Library', *Victorian Literature and Culture*, 26 (1998), 105–32.

[9] Frederic Harrison, *The Choice of Books: And Other Literary Pieces* (London: Macmillan, 1886).

[10] John Lubbock, 'On the Pleasure of Reading', *Contemporary Review*, 49 (1886), 240–51; Feltes, *Literary Capital*, 42–8. Wells recalls the Hundred Best Books in 'What Everyone Should Read: The Reading of History', *John O'London's Weekly*, 5 May 1923.

[11] Keating, *Haunted Study*, 433.

[12] Feltes, *Literary Capital*, 62.

consumption of its products.[13] On the one hand, there had never been a better time for an artist to be a writer of fiction in English. On the other, commitment to fiction as one's chosen form of artistic vocation could mean forfeiting any claim to the prestige of 'high culture' if fiction's popularity lessened its power to confer cultural capital. Consequent debates about the value, status, purpose, and future of reading thus sought to inscribe fiction in particular with a meaning, a value, and a use, especially within the burgeoning specialized sub-industry of literary criticism.[14]

From the 1860s onwards, the novel was being considered worthy of extended literary criticism in journals such as the *Pall Mall Gazette* (founded in 1865), the *Cornhill Magazine* (1860), the *Fortnightly Review* (1865), and the *Academy* (1869).[15] W. B. Rands, writing in the *Contemporary Review* (1866) in 1880 argued that the recent rise of the novel had been so swift and extensive that literary criticism was not yet sufficiently developed to deal with it adequately:

> It may almost be said that there is now a branch of criticism specially, if not exclusively, applying to novels; and, perhaps, it may be added that the critics who cultivate this branch of work do not yet feel themselves quite up to their work. In fact, the New Fiction is a product for which the canons were not ready, and some of the best things said about it and what it foretells are little better than self-conscious talk to fill up time.[16]

For Rands, although the novel was an art-form with a clearly established lineage from the eighteenth century through Walter Scott and Charles Dickens to the present day, it was one that was above all associated with the future, with modernity, and with the increasingly rapid pace of social change.

> All this stands connected with the spread of scientific knowledge, the increase of luxury, the far-reaching aesthetic revival, and some other topic, which would be at the first glance utterly alien. There are great changes in the air, and in these the novel will play a large and increasing part.[17]

---

[13] Simon J. James, *Unsettled Accounts: Money and Narrative Form in the Novels of George Gissing* (London: Anthem, 2003), 94–5.

[14] John Gross, *The Rise and Fall of the Man of Letters: Aspects of Literary Life since 1800* (London: Weidenfeld and Nicolson, 1969).

[15] Kenneth Graham, *English Criticism of the Novel, 1865–1900* (Oxford: Clarendon Press, 1965); J. C. Olmsted, ed., *A Victorian Art of Fiction*, 3 vols (New York: Garland, 1979).

[16] W. B. Rands, writing as 'Henry Holbeach', 'The New Fiction', *Contemporary Review*, 37 (1880), 247–62 (247).

[17] Ibid., 262.

In his 1880 essay 'Copyright', Matthew Arnold had argued for the necessity of cheaper books 'as our nation grows more civilised, as a real love of reading comes to prevail more widely'.[18] Arnold's most influential contribution to the debate about reading had been the promotion of 'culture', as a remedy both for the increasing philistinism and self-interest of different classes of British society, and for the decline of religious belief as the means of regulating individual self-interest and ensuring ethical behaviour. In the series of lectures published as *Culture and Anarchy* (1867–9), Arnold argued the somewhat paradoxical case that the study of the cultural residuum constituted by the best cultural artefacts of the past would stimulate a fresh perspective on the present day:

> The whole scope of this essay is to recommend culture as the great help out of our present difficulties; culture being a pursuit of our total perfection by means of getting to know, on all the matters which most concern us, the best which has been thought and said in the world; and through this knowledge, turning a stream of fresh and free thought upon our stock notions and habits.[19]

Culture should be autonomous and dynamic, rather than static, in order to bear the burden of replacing religion as a mastering ethical principle; 'to achieve by a more secular and less arid means', according to Vincent, 'the long-held ambition of reconstructing the judgement of working-class children through the promotion of new modes of communication'.[20] Literature was thus no longer a simple leisure activity, mere gentlemanly cultivation of the mind, but a mode of communication on which the future development of the nation might depend.

Arnold himself had mixed feelings about the novel, however, and was anxious that reading fiction should not be counted as 'culture'.[21] In his essay on the eighteenth-century man of letters Joseph Joubert, Arnold quotes with approval Joubert's contention that 'fiction has no business to exist unless it is more beautiful than reality. Certainly the monstrosities of fiction may be found in the booksellers' shops; [...] but they have no place in literature', adding himself that 'those who produce them are not really men of letters'.[22] The equally influential sage John Ruskin

---

[18] 'Copyright', in *The Complete Prose Works of Matthew Arnold*, 10 vols, ed. R. H. Super (Ann Arbor: University of Michigan Press, 1974), IX, 114–36 (125).

[19] Matthew Arnold, *Culture and Anarchy and Other Writings*, ed. Stefan Collini (Cambridge: Cambridge University Press, 1993), 190.

[20] Vincent, *Literacy and Popular Culture*, 224.

[21] Ben Knights, *The Idea of the Clerisy in the Nineteenth Century* (Cambridge: Cambridge University Press, 1978), 123.

[22] Arnold, 'Joubert', *Works*, III, 183–211 (202). On the pejorative associations of the word 'fiction', see Raymond Williams, *Keywords: A Vocabulary of Culture and Society* (London: Fontana, 1988), 134–5.

diagnosed in 1881 a preference for fiction that portrayed diseased rather than healthy subjects as a new urban pathology, the consequence of a readership being deprived of regular aesthetic exposure to the natural world.[23] One of the most influential attacks on the art of the *fin-de-siècle*, and its fiction in particular, was Max Nordau's *Degeneration* (1892), first translated into English in 1895. Nordau diagnoses the degenerate artist as suffering from a pathological condition, as an egotist, prone to mysticism, as well as to realism and to impressionism. 'The fabrication of stories' is a symptom of pathological need for attention and the feeling of importance.[24] 'Our republic of letters is neither governed nor defended', warns Nordau. He argues that if society were to be:

> passively abandoned to the influences of graphomaniacal fools and their imbecile or unscrupulous bodyguard of critics, the inevitable result of such a neglect of duty would be a much more rapid and violent outspread of the mental contagion, and civilized humanity would with much greater difficulty, and much more slowly, recover from the disease of the age than it might under a strong and resolute combat with the evil.[25]

While Nordau was widely (and justifiably) derided for the hysteria of his response and the purple of his rhetoric, the tone and the angle of his attack were widely adopted in other conservative criticism, especially after Oscar Wilde's highly public downfall seemed to make explicit a pathological connection between experimental or transgressive forms of fiction and socially transgressive behaviour.[26]

The disagreements between supporters and opponents of new developments in fiction thus tended to take place on the grounds of the effect, whether beneficial or harmful, it had on its readers. Ann Mozley wondered

---

[23] John Ruskin, 'Fiction Fair and Foul', *The Works of John Ruskin*, 39 vols, ed. E. T. Cook and A. Wedderburn (London: George Allen, 1903–12), XXXIV, 265–397 (270–1).
[24] Max Nordau, *Degeneration*, ed. George L. Mosse (Lincoln: University of Nebraska Press, 1993), 26.
[25] Ibid., 534, 551–2.
[26] See for instance Hugh Stutfield, 'Tommyrotics', *Blackwood's Edinburgh Magazine*, 157 (1895), 858–67; Ed Cohen, *Talk on the Wilde Side: Toward a Genealogy of a Discourse on Male Sexualities* (New York: Routledge, 1993), 15. Wells repudiates Nordau in *Mankind in the Making* (London: Chapman and Hall, 1903): 'The less gifted portion of the educated public was greatly delighted some years ago by a work by Dr. Nordau called *Degeneration*, in which a great number of abnormal people were studied in a pseudo-scientific manner and shown to be abnormal beyond any possibility of dispute. Mostly the samples selected were men of exceptional artistic and literary power. The book was pretentious and inconsistent [...] but it did at least serve to show that if we cannot call a man stupid we may almost invariably call him mad with some show of reason. The public read the book for the sake of its abuse, applied the intended conclusion to every success that awakened its envy, and failed altogether to see how absolutely the definition of madness was destroyed' (62).

whether, 'as we view the enormous amount of novels issuing from the press, it can be said of few that any of the readers for whom they are expressly written are materially the better for them?'[27] Brian Waller Procter averred in 1884 that, 'We should read in order to know and to feel what is good, and what is evil, and to do what is good and useful.'[28] Malcolm McColl, in 'Morality in Fiction' (1891) argued that even if disavowing such for the sake of either realism or romance, an artist always displays ethical sympathies; and Henry Norman, prompted by the post-humous publication of Anthony Trollope's *Autobiography*, claimed that naturalist writings such as Zola's do not achieve their effect because of the theoretical claims to objectivity that inform them, but in spite of them:[29]

> Now life is the great school of mankind; there is nothing of life that does not teach its lesson; *experientia docet* is the tritest of proverbs. If, therefore, any novel faithfully represents life, it must necessarily teach. [...] There is no chasm between art and instruction; on the contrary, they cannot properly exist separately.[30]

Norman goes on to predict that fiction will play its part in the 'struggle of ideas' (886), but nonetheless suggests that realism will pass away as a fad since the future of storytelling lies in the romance, the story that is told purely for amusement's sake. Walter Benjamin has famously suggested that storytelling has its origins in the desire to instruct, that 'every real story [...] contains, overtly or covertly, something useful'.[31] According to Edwin M. Eigner and George J. Worth, in the Victorian period 'the demand that a novel be moral was at least as frequently made as the requirement that it should be real'.[32] '"It is extraordinary,"' muses Marcel in Vernon Lee's 'A Dialogue on Novels' (1885), '"how aesthetical questions invariably end in ethical ones when treated by English people."'[33]

[27] Ann Mozley, 'On Fiction as an Educator', *Blackwood's Magazine*, 108 (1870), 449–59 (449).
[28] Brian Waller Procter, 'On the Reading of Books', *Temple Bar*, 72 (1884), 178–86 (180).
[29] Malcolm McColl, 'Morality in Fiction', *Contemporary Review*, 60 (1891), 234–52.
[30] Henry Norman, 'Theories and Practice of Modern Fiction', *Fortnightly Review*, 34 (1883), 870–86 (886).
[31] Walter Benjamin, 'The Storyteller: Reflections on the Works of Nikolai Leskov', *Illuminations*, ed. Hannah Arendt, trans. Harry Zohn (London: Jonathan Cape, 1970), 83–109 (86). See also Lord Neaves, *On Fiction As a Means of Popular Teaching* (London: Blackwood, 1869).
[32] Edwin M. Eigner and George J. Worth, eds, *Victorian Criticism of the Novel* (Cambridge: Cambridge University Press, 1985), 7.
[33] Vernon Lee, 'A Dialogue on Novels', *Contemporary Review*, 48 (1885): 378–401 (388), in *Victorian Criticism of the Novel*, ed. Eigner and Worth, 223–37 (235).

Writers of late-Victorian fiction attempted to liberate themselves from this burden of moral responsibility in one of two ways: realists tended to claim their art as a simple mimesis of life, uninflected by didactic intention; writers of romance appealed to art's purely ludic qualities.[34] Even the romancer Sir Henry Rider Haggard, though, argued for the importance of literary merit over moral considerations, and that whatever their moral benefit, works lacking in corresponding aesthetic merit should not be published at all.[35] While the grounds for evading (or accepting) responsibility may have varied, however, no late-Victorian writer of fiction could have been unaware of the responsibility that would be attributed to them for the effect of their work on readers.

WELLS AND LITERARY DEBATES

For all of the fears of many *fin-de-siècle* commentators in the late nineteenth and early twentieth centuries over the effects of reading literature on the newly literate masses, much empirical evidence seems to suggest that literature of genuine merit did have a transformative effect on those who read it. Jonathan Rose has recently made an influential case against present-day literary critics who:

> tend to see literature as freighted with ideological baggage that may insidiously indoctrinate the unsuspecting reader. This school of criticism tells us more about the preoccupations of critics than the experience of common readers in history, which, frankly, Arnold understood far better. Far from reinscribing traditional ideologies, canonical literature tended to ignite insurrection.[36]

The young Herbert George Wells was just such a reader, for whom reading literature awakened thoughts of insurrection, and whose own subsequent writing sought to provoke similar thoughts in his readers. According to Vincent:

> The growing abandonment of 'popular' by 'polite' culture throughout early modern Europe [. . .] was founded on the assumption that the common people could make little or no use of the written word. Their subordination was both caused and measured by their relation to reading and writing. In turn the arrival of mass literacy [. . .] embodied a two-fold challenge to the

---

[34] Keating, *Haunted Study*, 344–51.
[35] Sir Henry Rider Haggard, 'About Fiction', *Contemporary Review*, 51 (1887), 172–80.
[36] Jonathan Rose, *The Intellectual Life of the British Working Classes* (New Haven: Yale University Press, 2001), 9.

identity of popular culture. The increasingly widespread employment of the new modes of communication threatened the structures of authority which kept the cultures apart, whilst the meanings attached to literacy itself, and to associated concepts such as learning, rationality, science and literature, were at the heart of the debate about the boundaries between the cultures.[37]

Wells straddled 'cultures' both in terms of social class, the 'popular' and the 'polite', and two cultures also as disciplines of knowledge, art, and science.[38] He is similarly located on the cruces of competing views on the ideological effects and counter-effects of reading literature, and of the rival claims of realism and the romance. As a teenager, Wells, seeking to improve himself, ruled 'never to read a work of fiction'; once he became a student, however, he began 'reading poetry and imaginative work with an attention to language and style that [he] had never given these aspects of literature before'.[39] Provoked by Frederic Harrison, *The Science Schools Journal*, the student periodical that Wells had co-founded, enquired in 1889, 'What Shall Be Read?', concluding that fiction 'is more comprehensive in its scope, more calculated to widen our sympathies and enlarge our views' than other kinds of writing, but also that 'prophets of an age' such as Thomas Carlyle and Ruskin should be read alongside fiction.[40] Wells's own later work would be characterized by a fiction that sought both to enlarge views and to widen sympathy for his frequently downtrodden protagonists.

Early in his writing career, Wells joined the late-Victorian debate over literature through the literary and dramatic criticism he wrote for *The Pall Mall Gazette* and *The Saturday Review*. While the older novelist would

---

[37] Vincent, *Literacy and Popular Culture*, 4–5.

[38] According to Raymond Williams, the word 'culture' is 'one of the two or three most complicated words in the English language'; the adjective 'cultural' was not used commonly to mean 'artistic' until the 1890s (*Keywords*, 92). Malcolm Bradbury evaluates culture as having 'the double meaning of referring to individual and group accomplishments in those who achieve and possess it, and to a general and impersonal provision of society' (*The Social Context of Modern Literature* [Oxford: Blackwell, 1971], 241–2). In this study, it will be used largely in its sense of referring to aesthetic practices and artefacts, as Wells does here, although given Wells's views on art's desired participation in social reconstruction, some overlap with culture as the totality of social practices will be inevitable. The *OED* definition charts a similar movement: 'refinement of mind, taste, and manners; artistic and intellectual development. Hence: the arts and other manifestations of human intellectual achievement regarded collectively' (*OED*, 6). See David Amigoni, *Colonies, Culture and Evolution: Literature, Science and Culture in Nineteenth-Century Writing* (Cambridge: Cambridge University Press, 2007), especially 11–17, also 104–41.

[39] *Experiment in Autobiography: Discoveries and Conclusions of a Very Ordinary Brain*, 2 vols (London: Gollancz, 1934), I, 167, 304.

[40] E. J. Reynolds, 'What Shall Be Read?', *Science Schools Journal*, 2 (1889), 98–108 (104).

with increasing emphasis choose to violate aesthetic canons, the younger
Wells is more concerned to defend them. What remains dominant
throughout Wells's career, however, is the importance that he places on
the essential seriousness of the enterprise of writing, even of writing fiction
(although the specific grounds of that seriousness alter over time), and on
the good that can be achieved by consumption of the right kinds of
literature.[41]

The reader implied by Wells's early critical writing is a discriminating
consumer who prides himself on having taste a cut above mass taste ('him',
since Wells is severe on books spoilt by being too feminine or too juvenile,
thus implying a reader who is adult and male). Wells recognizes that mass
public taste and critical taste are not one and the same, since post-1870
literary production is driven less by the need for social improvement than
profit. He would write in 1901's *Anticipations of the Reaction of Mechanical
and Scientific Progress Upon Human Life and Thought* that:

> A large proportion of English books are novels adapted to the minds of
> women, or of boys and superannuated business men, stories designed rather
> to allay than stimulate thought—they are the only books, indeed, that are
> profitable to publisher and author alike. [...] The present conditions of
> book production for the English reading public offer no hope of any
> immediate change in this respect.[42]

The critic's imperative duty is thus the recognition of literary merit, since
it is only innovative writers who will succeed in challenging the social
status quo.[43] (When he later began to imagine how the conditions of
literary production might be improved in his political and utopian writings, Wells also argues for the need for proper and accurate literary
criticism.)[44] Wells is confident in making judgements on literary merit
and here, as in his technological predictions, he is prophetic, championing

---

[41] See Gordon N. Ray, 'H. G. Wells Tries to Be a Novelist', in *Edwardians and Late
Victorians*, ed. Richard Ellmann (New York: Columbia University Press, 1959), 106–59.

[42] *Anticipations, The Works of H. G. Wells*, 28 vols (New York: Scribner's, 1924–8), IV,
201. For a later repetition of this view, see *The Brothers* (London: Chatto & Windus, 1938),
15. The details of the editions used of Wells's primary works will be given in the first
citation and then, for ease of reference, parenthetical references in the text will be given by
chapter and chapter division number. For a discussion of Wells, copyright, and editing, see
Patrick Parrinder, *Shadows of the Future: H. G. Wells, Science Fiction and Prophecy* (Liverpool: Liverpool University Press, 1995), xii.

[43] See Wells's letter to Conrad, *The Correspondence of H. G. Wells*, 4 vols, ed. David C.
Smith (London: Pickering & Chatto, 1998), I, 262–3.

[44] *Mankind in the Making*, 368–74. For Wells's attack on reviewers in an 1897 speech,
see Waller, *Writers, Readers and Reputations*, 119; Wells suggested in 1907 that the *New Age*
might fulfil such a function (*Correspondence*, II, 149).

Thomas Hardy, George Moore, Rudyard Kipling, and even John Buchan over the now comparatively discarded Anthony Hope, Hall Caine, and Marie Corelli. Wells seeks for the distinctive in literary production, ruling in a piece on Robert Louis Stevenson that 'the first quality of great art is sincerity [. . .], that inflexible self-conceit that is, perhaps, the essence of originality'.[45] Correspondingly, he is harshest on writing which makes no further demands on the reader than acquiescence, merely fulfilling expectations without challenging them. He is at his most vituperative when he sees a convention hardening into a cliché: Lewis Waller's high-Victorian theatricality, or Corelli's breathless mysticism.[46]

Wells's participation in the debate between realism and romance characteristically seeks a place between them. On the topic of romance, he rails at the 'popularity to-day of scores of books whose relation to life is of the slightest, and whose connexion with Art is purely accidental'.[47] Hall Caine had claimed in 1890 that romance is the true genre of idealism, that the literary artist should depict the world as it should be, rather than as he sees it: 'Not the bare actualities of life "as it is", but the glories of life as it might be; not the domination of fact, but of feeling.'[48] In an article that protests against the unreality of Victorian heroines, Wells parodies Caine as claiming that, 'If life is ugly [. . .] it is our duty to make it pleasant in fiction.'[49] Romance might provide an imaginative liberation from the constraints of the real world, but also sap the desire to alter the nature of that world—anathema to Wells's later stern adjurations for fiction to stimulate just such a desire. On the other hand, while fiction should reflect life as it is, it should not focus exclusively on the unpleasant aspects of life, a tendency for which Wells reproves naturalism. In his 1896 review of Arthur Morrison's *A Child of the Jago*, which he otherwise thinks excellent, Wells suggests that exceptional individuals might evolve to escape the environment of the Jago, and that the conditions of that environment are not an 'inheritance' but a 'contagion', and thus preventable.[50] When

---

[45] H. G. Wells, 'The Lost Stevenson', *Saturday Review*, 13 June 1896, 603–4, in *H. G. Wells's Literary Criticism*, ed. Patrick Parrinder and Robert Philmus (Brighton: Harvester; Totowa, NJ: Barnes and Noble, 1980), 102.

[46] Cf. Wells's story, 'The Sad Story of a Dramatic Critic', in *The Complete Short Stories of H. G. Wells*, ed. John Hammond (London: Dent, 1998), 243–9.

[47] 'Popular Writers and Press Critics', *Saturday Review*, 8 February 1896, 145–6, in *Literary Criticism*, 74–8 (74).

[48] Hall Caine, 'The New Watchwords of Fiction', *Contemporary Review*, 57 (1890), 479–88 (488).

[49] 'The Sawdust Doll', *Pall Mall Gazette*, 13 May 1895, 3, in *Literary Criticism*, 44–7 (44).

[50] 'A Slum Novel', *Saturday Review*, 28 November 1896, 573, in *Literary Criticism*, 115–18 (117–18).

Wells wrote realism, he never accepted the material conditions of reality depicted therein as permanent.[51] Lewisham and Kipps might struggle against existing social conditions, but the novels in which they appear seek to make the inequity of those conditions visible and thus perhaps changeable. Strict realism is too much restriction, just as romance is excess of freedom; and perhaps surprisingly, given Wells's own tendency to preach in his later fiction, he also warns here against being over-didactic at the expense of the novel's artistic effect:

> The sooner that Mr Allen realizes that he cannot adopt an art-form and make it subservient to the purposes of the pamphleteer, the better for humanity. [...] The philosopher who masquerades as a novelist, violating the condi- tions of art that his gospel may win notoriety, discredits both himself and his message, and the result is neither philosophy nor fiction.[52]

If romance is enjoyable but in no way improving, and realism too complicit in existing social conditions, then Wells implies an ideal of fiction that should combine aspects of both. He does not use the term 'novel' of one of his own books until 1900's *Love and Mr. Lewisham*, and Wells's choice of subtitles for his early romances attempts to play down their seriousness. *The Time Machine* takes the pun *An Invention* as its subtitle, *The Wheels of Chance* (1896) *A Holiday Adventure*, *The Invisible Man* (1897) *A Grotesque Romance*, and *The Sea Lady* (1902) *A Tissue of Moonshine*.[53] (Later, writing Prefaces for the 1920s Atlantic Edition, when his strain of anti-aestheticism was even stronger, Wells claimed that, 'possibly these writings, in whole or in part, are literature, but certainly [...] they are not Works of Art'.)[54] Romance, however, does allow the literary imagination to escape from imprisonment by the rules of natural- ism, a tendency for which Wells reproves Gissing and Morrison. Wells's romances are still made to engage with the real material conditions of existence by their adherence to not a naturalist, but a scientific realism, hence 'scientific romances'.

---

[51] Roslynn D. Haynes, *H. G. Wells: Discoverer of the Future: The Influence of Science on his Thought* (New York: New York University Press, 1980), 163–96. '"I want reality"', demands Graham in *When the Sleeper Wakes* (1900). '"Not realism"' (*When the Sleeper Wakes*, ed. John Lawton [London: Dent, 1994], 168). The second phrase is omitted in the revised version published as *The Sleeper Awakes* (1910).

[52] 'Mr Grant Allen's New Novel', *Saturday Review*, 14 December 1895, 785–6, in *Literary Criticism*, 61.

[53] *The Island of Doctor Moreau* is, more ominously, dubbed *A Possibility*.

[54] 'A General Introduction to the Atlantic Edition', *Works*, I, ix–xx (xi).

KICKING THE PAST TO PIECES:
WELLS'S TWO CULTURES

Writing in 1892, J. A. Symonds had argued, like Arnold, that the study of culture was not an end in itself but a preparation for life. 'In a particular sense, and in order to distinguish culture from education, it implies that this training has been consciously carried on by the individual.'[55] Symonds, however, is unusual in including science within his definition of 'culture'. He argues for the superiority of artistic culture as being more genuinely disinterested, while science is limited by being more narrowly functional, but also that science should nonetheless be liberally tolerated and not despised by its counterpart. Presciently, Symonds foresees a division between these 'two cultures' of the arts and the sciences: 'for the future it is probable that there will always be two differently constituted orders of minds, the one inclining to the purely humanistic, and the other to the purely scientific side of culture' (109).

Wells's authority for his career-long pronouncements on the role that art should play in society is founded less on an implicit sense of the artist as unacknowledged legislator than explicitly on his scientific education. This professional training is the fundamental difference between both Wells's predecessors as a prophetic writer, even John Stuart Mill and Herbert Spencer, and his contemporaries as a novelist, such as James, Gissing, and Kipling. Wells was arguably both the first writer in the canon of English Literature to have been trained as a pure scientist (a word not in use until the late nineteenth century), but also, according to Roslynn D. Haynes, 'the last great literary writer to have been so strongly influenced by science'.[56] In *Mankind in the Making* (1903), Wells argues for the benefits of a synthesis of the artistic and literary imaginations.

> For the lack of a sufficient literature we specialize into inco-ordinated classes. A number of new social types are developing, ignorant of each other, ignorant almost of themselves, full of mutual suspicions and mutual misunderstandings, narrow, limited, and dangerously incapable of intelligent collective action in the face of crises. [. . .] Each thinks parochially in his own limits, and, except for his specialty, is an illiterate man. It is absolutely necessary to the progress of our civilization that these isolations should be

---

[55] J. A. Symonds, 'Culture: Its Meaning and Uses', *New Review*, 7 (1892), 105–15 (106). See 'Literature and Science', in Arnold, *Works*, X, 53–73; C. P. Snow, *The Two Cultures and The Two Cultures: A Second Look*, ed. Stefan Collini (Cambridge: Cambridge University Press, 1993).

[56] Haynes, *H. G. Wells*, ix, 1.

overcome, that the community should become aware of itself collectively and should think as a whole. And the only thing that can overcome these isolations and put the mass of intelligent men upon a common basis of understanding, is an abundant and almost universally influential contemporary literature. (*Mankind in the Making*, ch. 10)

Science for Wells is not an essentially disinterested practice, but in a more Huxleyan fashion, should be fundamentally instrumental, a form of thinking that is a spur to doing. So too Wells's notion of artistic production ultimately places it at the service of a larger purpose. '"Science left the gentleman's mansion long ago; literature must follow it,"' rules Reginald Bliss in *Boon* (1914).[57] Wells's rhetoric against the over-idealization of high aesthetic culture becomes more and more vituperative throughout his career, and this assault might be seen as a kind of revenge by scientific culture on the arts. John Morley had predicted that, 'After the severity with which science was for so many ages treated by literature, we cannot wonder that science now retaliates, now mightily exalts herself, and thrusts literature down into the lower place.'[58] While Wells's early romances can show scientists as dangerous or eccentric, by the 1930s, Wells was making his retaliation explicit:

> The self-love of the ignorant has demanded that the man of science, in play and story, should be caricatured, ridiculed, and misrepresented. From Laputa to the Pickwick Club, British Literature, for example, spits and jeers at its greater sister, and to devote a life to science and the service of truth is still to renounce most of the common glories and satisfactions of life for a hard and exalted mistress.[59]

In *Mankind in the Making*, Wells stakes a claim for the superiority of the scientific way of seeing over the artistic. Wells argues that the post-Romantic notion of nature does not expand mankind's vision of the environment, but can inhibit its scope:

> One would think that no human being would ever discover there was any such thing as "nature" were it not for the schoolmaster—and quotation from Wordsworth. And this nature, as they present it, is really not nature at all, but a factitious admiration for certain isolated aspects of the universe conventionally regarded as "natural." [...] Trees, rivers, flowers, birds, stars—are, and have been for many centuries Nature—so are ploughed fields—really the most artificial of all things [...]. A grassy old embankment

---

[57] *Boon, The Mind of the Race, The Wild Asses of the Devil, and the Last Trump* (London: Fisher Unwin, 1915), 87.

[58] Morley, 'Literature', 199–200.

[59] *The Science of Life*, 2 vols (New York: Doubleday, 1931), I, 19.

to protect low-lying fields is Nature, and so is all the mass of apparatus about a water-mill; a new embankment to store an urban water supply, though it may be one mass of splendid weeds, is artificial, and ugly. A wooden windmill is Nature and beautiful, a sky-sign atrocious. [. . .] Vesuvius, for example, is grand and beautiful, its smell of underground railway most impressive, its night effect stupendous, but the glowing cinder heaps of Burslem, the wonders of the Black Country sunset, the wonderful fire-shot nightfall of the Five Towns, these things are horrid and offensive and vulgar beyond the powers of scholastic language. (*Mankind in the Making*, ch. 5)

Because of the oppressiveness of the topos of 'Nature', a schoolgirl carrying a cut flower expensively obtained from a botanical garden fails to perceive it as a biological specimen that is part of a wider ecology, blind both to the beauty and to the larger meanings of the urban environment that she actually inhabits.[60] 'Even the sense of beauty may be clouded and betray', Wells warns in *First and Last Things* (1908).[61] Wells himself is happy to murder romantic tropes to dissect them, as in, for example, the scientific deconstruction of figurative images of stars and starlight in the opening chapters of *The War of the Worlds* (1898).

Wells's aesthetic increasingly demonstrates hostility to over-adherence to the high aesthetic culture of the past if such culture has ceased to address aspects of the present and the future. To provide an extended example: after the First World War, Wells took upon himself the task of writing the non-fictional textbooks that would educate the citizens of the post-war world in which such wars would no longer occur (see chapter 5). He recruited collaborators to assist in areas where he did not trust his own knowledge, and in the serial parts of the *Outline of History* (1919), allowed them to dissent in footnotes with judgements he makes in the main text. (In *Anticipations*, ch. 8, n. 49, Wells laments that copyright restrictions prevent controversial books from being published in this way.) The classicist Gilbert Murray and the historian Philip Guedella take issue with Wells's deprecation of eighteenth-century art for its isolation from the wider world:

a dullness, a tarnish, came over the intellectual life of the land with [George I]'s coming, the poetry, painting, architecture, and imaginative literature of later eighteenth-century England is immeasurably below that of the seventeenth century,

But Sir Joshua Reynolds, Hogarth, Gray, Gibbon, for instance!—G.M.

---

[60] Cf. Theodor Adorno, 'Natural Beauty', in *Aesthetic Theory*, ed. Gretel Adorno and Rolf Tiedemann, trans. Robert Hullot-Kentor (London: Continuum, 2004), 81–103.
[61] *First and Last Things: A Confession of Faith and Rule of Life* (London: Archibald Constable, 1908), 63.

And the golden age of the great cabinet makers!—P.G.

Exactly! Culture taking refuge in the portraits, libraries and households of a few rich people. No national culture in the court, nor among the commonalty; a steady decay.—H.G.W.[62]

Wells and the political scientist Ernest Barker similarly dispute the success of a typical early Victorian education in preparing statesmen to govern:

The great Oxford school of *Literae Humaniores*, which means a serious study of Ancient Philosophy and Ancient History, was already thirty years old in Gladstone's time, and was a really serious training in solid philosophy and solid history. It was all the more serious, as every candidate for Honours had to take *two* schools, and to offer Mathematics as well as *Literae Humaniores*. Both Peel (about 1810) and Gladstone (about 1830) took these two schools and both gained Firsts in both. [. . .] Men with such a training were genuinely and nobly trained for statesmanship.—E.B.

　　With no knowledge of ethnology, no vision of history as a whole, misconceiving the record of geology, ignorant of the elementary ideas of biological science, of modern political, social, and economic science and modern thought and literature!—H.G.W. (*Outline*, ch. 39, 7)

The dialogue runs for more than two columns before Wells despairingly concludes that Gladstone lived:

in a luminous and blinding cloud. That cloud, which I call his ignorance, my two editors call his wonderful and abounding culture. It was a culture that wrapped about and adorned the great goddess Reality. But, indeed, she is not to be adorned but stripped. She ceases to be herself or to bless her votary unless she is faced stark and fearlessly.—H.G.W. (ch. 39, 7)[63]

Wells's ideal of modern education is essentially scientific, and for him classical education comes to stand for the very worst of art's failure to engage with lived reality. I have evaluated the significance of Wells's friendship with George Gissing elsewhere, but it is worth noting that Gissing came to personify for Wells both the restrictions of literary naturalism and of over-reverence towards aesthetic relics of a no longer relevant past.[64] The two-cultural difference between them was thrown

---

[62]　H. G. Wells et al., *The Outline of History: Being A Plain History of Life and Mankind*, 2 vols (London: Newnes, 1919), II, 545.

[63]　Cf. *In the Days of the Comet*, *Works*, X, 245–6.

[64]　Simon J. James, 'The Truth About Gissing: Reassessing the Literary Friendship of George Gissing and H. G. Wells', in *H. G. Wells's Fin-de-Siècle: Twenty-First Century Reflections on the Early H. G. Wells*, ed. John S. Partington (Frankfurt: Peter Lang, 2007), 85–100.

into sharp relief by their shared visit to Rome in 1898.[65] When confronted with over-reverence for the past, Wells tended to over-emphasize his philistine iconoclasm, for example writing to Gissing before the holiday:

> I'm not coming to Rome a sight seeing. I don't care a triturated damn for all the blessed oil paintings in the world and precious little for the sculpture, and I'm not going to be made to go and see places I shouldn't go to see if I lived in Rome.[66]

In Wells's autobiography, Gissing is remembered at that time as 'an extraordinary blend of a damaged joy-loving human being hampered by inherited gentility and a classical education [...] at the back of my mind I thought him horribly miseducated and he hardly troubled to hide from me his opinion that I was absolutely illiterate.'[67] Wells enjoyed Rome, exhilarated by the aesthetic spectacle of its ruins, but was bemused and irritated by Gissing's reverence for antiquity, a reverence that he diagnoses as a consequence of Gissing's education having been classical, rather than scientific:[68]

> Through Gissing I was confirmed in my suspicions that this orthodox classical training which was once so powerful an antiseptic against [...] ancient superstitions, is now no longer a city of refuge from barbaric predispositions. It has become a vast collection of monumental masonry, a pale cemetery in a twilight, through which new conceptions hurry apologetically on their way to town, finding neither home nor sustenance there. [...] It has ceased to be a field of education.[69]

The scientific metaphor of 'antiseptic' confirms the nature of Wells's difference from the Victorian ideal of autonomous culture: scientific terminology is often used by Wells to express his own side of an argument, and theological language to characterize the other. In a characteristically splenetic exchange with George Bernard Shaw years later, Wells opposed Shaw's scheme for preserving Rome's treasures from the Second World War:

---

[65] Patrick Parrinder, 'The Roman Spring of George Gissing and H.G. Wells', *Gissing Newsletter*, 21/3 (1985), 1–12; see the note in *The Collected Letters of George Gissing*, ed. Pierre Coustillas, Paul F. Mattheisen, and Arthur C. Young, 9 vols (Athens: Ohio University Press, 1990–97), VII, 74–5.

[66] Letter to Gissing, 22 January 1898, *George Gissing and H. G. Wells: Their Friendship and Correspondence*, ed. Royal A. Gettmann (London: Rupert Hart-Davis, 1961), 77.

[67] *Autobiography*, II, 571, 569.

[68] Rosalind Dobbs, 'Biographical Sketches', unpublished MS held in the library of the London School of Economics; Parrinder, *Shadows*, 71–2.

[69] *Autobiography*, II, 572.

I *detest* Rome. I dont care if all the treasures in the world are ground to powder. (This is between ourselves.) I want to see humanity de-cultivated and making a fresh start. Culture is merely the ownership of stale piddle. Mantegna, Brahms, my Tang horse, St Paul's Cathedral, I rank a little higher than the lavender-smelling correspondence of my nicer great-aunts. I'd like to keep them but not if they lead to idolatry.[70]

Wells's evaluation of culture, and especially the artistic and literary culture of the past, is strongly inflected by a requirement for it to serve the needs of the present and the future. The traditional notion of high literary culture depends on a canon: for contemporary writing to be judged worthy of the serious attention of literary criticism, it is habitually evaluated against writing from the past.[71] Wells, however, disagrees. Unlike those of most Victorian literary writers, his canon privileges contemporary writing over that of past ages. By 1903, more than a generation on from the Education Act, Wells protests that the mission of culture has already lost touch with what its intended converts actually prefer to read. Criticism's function should be to guide readers within the literary over-production of the present time towards whatever would actually benefit them the most:

> Why not base the literary education of people upon the literature they read instead of upon literature that they are scarcely more in touch with than with Chinese metaphysics? A few carefully chosen pages of contemporary rubbish, read with a running comment, a few carefully chosen pages of what is, comparatively, not rubbish, a little lucid discussion of effects and probabilities, would do more to quicken the literary sense of the average person than all the sham enthusiasm about Marlowe and Spenser that was ever concocted. [...] Without a real and popular criticism of contemporary work as a preliminary and basis, the criticism and circulation of the classics is quite manifestly vain. (*Mankind in the Making*, ch. 10)[72]

For Wells, literature plays such a large part in the construction of a better world that mistaken submission to an archaic hierarchy of Great Books

---

[70] Letter to Shaw, 22 April 1941, *Bernard Shaw and H.G. Wells: Selected Correspondence of Bernard Shaw*, ed. J. Percy Smith (Toronto: University of Toronto Press, 1995), 195–6. See also *The Future in America: A Search After Realities* (London: Chapman and Hall, 1906), 326. '"Ask any cultivated person who tells the truth whether he'd rather see Leonardo's Monna Lisa destroyed or half a dozen babies ... "', poses Uncle Robert in *Babes in the Darkling Wood* (London: Secker & Warburg, 1940), 317. Wells was still continuing the argument in the chapter 'The Art Treasures of Rome' in his final, uncompleted book *Exasperations* (Illinois Collection).

[71] Matthew Arnold, 'On the Modern Element in Literature', *Works*, I, 18–37 (20–1). Cf. Arnold Bennett, *Literary Taste: How to Form it, with Detailed Instructions for Collecting a Complete Library of English Literature* (London: Hodder, 1916), 32–3.

[72] See also 'Modern Reviewing', *Adelphi*, 5 (1923), 150–1.

threatens not only the future development of writing, but of the entire human race. Too much attention given to writing from past generations risks the possibility that the literature of the future will become degenerate or even extinct. Wells worried that, permitted an over-privileged afterlife, high literary culture would become ossified rather than dynamic, not a practice but a relic. Wells rejects the notion of art and culture as something autonomous from society in favour of a literature that must serve as a means of improving, even perfecting society. If Arnold's mission for art to replace religious belief as the means of national regeneration becomes a mere Puritanism or dogmatism, literature risks the same historical fall into obsolescence as Wells saw the Church suffering after Darwin—inspiring not critical thinking but submission to an archaic literary hierarchy of decreasingly relevant artefacts. The satire *Boon*, for instance, imagines a future in which:

> "The classics were still bought by habit, as people who have lost faith will still go to church; but it is only necessary to examine some surviving volume of this period to mark the coruscation of printer's errors, the sheets bound in upside down or accidentally not inked in printing or transferred from some sister classic in the same series, to realize that these volumes were mere receipts for the tribute paid by the pockets of stupidity to the ancient prestige of thought [...]
>
> Preparations were made for the erection of a richly decorative memorial in London to preserve the memory of Shakespeare, an English Taj Mahal; an Academy of uncreative literature was established [...] and it seemed but the matter of a few years before the goal of a complete and final mental quiet would be attained by the whole English-speaking community [...]" (*Boon*, ch. 3, 1)

Rather than revere such antiquities, Wells vowed instead to 'kick the past to pieces' if that is what was required to establish the new republic.[73]

A WINDOW ON HENRY JAMES

Given the antagonistic nature of Wells's imagination, the nature of his aesthetics became most clearly defined in his debates about fiction with the most articulate and influential novelist-critic of the late nineteenth- and early twentieth-century period, Henry James. While Arnold saw the novel as the slightest of artistic productions, James was the pre-eminent advocate in English literary culture of fiction as the most serious and

[73] *A Modern Utopia*, *Works*, IX, 318.

important kind of writing. In his essay 'The Future of the Novel' (1899), James was excited by the prospect of readers' devotion to this one form of writing above all others, of whom 'it is not too much to say [. . .] that they live in a great measure by the immediate aid of the novel'. Given its popularity, the novel's future might be a bright one:

> In the flare of railway bookstalls, in the shop-fronts of most book-sellers, especially the provincial, in the advertisements of the weekly newspapers, and in fifty places besides, this testimony to the general preference triumphs, yielding a good-natured corner at most to a bunch of treatises on athletics or sport, or a patch of theology old and new.[74]

Nonetheless, James too was concerned that ease in the novel's consumption might be to the detriment of the care taken in its production. Lampooned by Oscar Wilde for writing 'fiction as if it were a painful duty', no novelist took more seriously the task of establishing the cultural value of writing fiction than James.[75] James's contribution to the late-Victorian debate over the uses of fiction was his essay for *Longman's Magazine* 'The Art of Fiction' (1884). In this essay, James argues both for freedom of scope in fiction's subject matter, and that the novel's claims for seriousness as a high cultural artefact rest on the significance of its aesthetic form. James's emphasis on form overrides any concerns about the moral effect of a novel's content, or the consequences of reading pleasure:

> 'Art,' in our Protestant communities, where so many things have got so strangely twisted about, is supposed, in certain circles, to have some vaguely injurious effect upon those who make it an important consideration, who let it weigh in the balance. It is assumed to be opposed in some mysterious manner to morality, to amusement, to instruction. [. . .] Literature should be either instructive or amusing, and there is in many minds an impression that these artistic preoccupations, the search for form, contribute to neither end, interfere indeed with both.[76]

James shows concern in places about the cheapness and easy availability of fiction, but makes these his grounds for the seriousness of the practice of novel criticism: since the novel is so popular, then the practice of evaluating it must be worthy of sustained effort.

---

[74] Henry James, 'The Future of the Novel', in *Literary Criticism: Essays on Literature, American Writers, English Writers*, ed. Leon Edel and Mark Wilson (New York: Library of America, 1984), 100–10 (101). See Trotter, *English Novel in History*, 25.

[75] Oscar Wilde, 'The Decay of Lying', in *The Complete Works of Oscar Wilde*, 4 vols, ed. Josephine M. Guy (Oxford: Clarendon Press, 2007), IV, 73–103 (77).

[76] 'The Art of Fiction', *Longman's Magazine*, 1884, in *Literary Criticism: Essays on Literature*, 44–65 (47–8).

James's essay had been written in response to a lecture, also titled 'The Art of Fiction', given by the bestselling novelist Walter Besant to the Royal Institution.[77] James insisted on the novel's independence from the more pragmatic social use assigned by Besant: 'I should directly reverse Mr. Besant's remark, and say not that the English novel has a purpose, but that it has a diffidence.'[78] (Indeed, critic and novelist Julia Wedgewood exempted James from the Victorian debate about the ethical benefits of reading fiction, since he 'cannot be accused of trying to make a single reader wiser or better by his writings'.)[79] James chides Besant for counselling that a writer should write only from personal experience, finding 'rather chilling' Besant's advice that '"a writer whose friends and personal experiences belong to the lower middle-class should carefully avoid introducing his characters into Society"'.[80] Wells would boldly do just this in novels such as *Kipps* (1905) and *Tono-Bungay* (1909); his work received energetic if qualified support from James.

Wells's first glimpse of the older writer was seeing him booed at his curtain call on the first night of James's play *Guy Domville* in 1895 (an event perhaps overworked in subsequent psychobiographical readings of James's *oeuvre*), when Wells was the dramatic critic for the *Pall Mall Gazette*.[81] Three years later, when Wells was living at Sandgate and James at Rye, the two writers became friends. James's tone in his letters to Wells is eager to please, usually cordial, at best genial, even mildly flirtatious, sometimes disavowing the importance of the letter itself in favour of anticipating a face-to-face encounter instead.[82] In its early stages, the correspondence skirts around the writers' differences in aesthetics, but these become progressively clearer in James's responses as the nature of Wells's output becomes more openly didactic. James adopts a pose of *de haut en bas* that a simultaneous

---

[77] For a useful comparison of the two pieces, see John Goode, 'The Art of Fiction: Walter Besant and Henry James', in *Tradition and Tolerance in Nineteenth-Century Fiction*, ed. David Howard, John Lucas, and John Goode (London: Routledge & Kegan Paul, 1966), 243–81.

[78] 'Art of Fiction', 63.

[79] Julia Wedgewood, 'Contemporary Records: I – Fiction', *Contemporary Review*, 50 (1886), 897–905 (899).

[80] 'Art of Fiction', 51.

[81] Leon Edel, *The Life of Henry James*, 2 vols (Harmondsworth: Penguin, 1977), II, 141–3.

[82] See for instance the letter of 5 August 1898, in *Henry James and H. G. Wells: A Record of Their Friendship, their Debate on the Art of Fiction, and their Quarrel*, ed. Leon Edel and Gordon N. Ray (London: Rupert Hart-Davis, 1959), 77–8. For a perceptive reading of images of sexuality in the correspondence, *Autobiography*, *Boon* and 1927's *Meanwhile* (which is subtitled *The Picture of a Lady*), see Janet Gabler-Hover, 'H. G. Wells's and Henry James's Two Ladies', in *The Critical Response to H. G. Wells*, ed. William J. Scheick (Westport, CT: Greenwood Press, 1995), 145–64.

self-deprecation can only partly ironize: 'I am beastly critical—but you are in a still higher degree wonderful. I re-write you, much, as I read—which is the highest tribute my damned impertinence can pay an author.'[83] (Improbably, 1901's *The First Men in the Moon* elicits the half-serious suggestion that the two authors should collaborate.) James's habitual response to Wells's work is to praise its vividness, often in imagery of the body or of the natural, while at the same time faintly belittling its formal artistry.[84] *Love and Mr. Lewisham* is 'a bloody little chunk of life, of no small substance'; *Anticipations* 'a charming exhibition of complete freedom of mind'; *Mankind in the Making* 'a record of a romantic adventure of which You are the Hero'; each of *Twelve Stories and a Dream* 'a substantial coloured sweet or bonbon'.[85] James faults both Wells's characterization—Kipps is 'not so much a masterpiece as a mere born gem'; *Ann Veronica* (1909) 'wants clearness and *nuances*'—and narrative mode—*The New Machiavelli* (1910), while 'so alive and kicking and sprawling', lacks detachment.[86] James tends to be more generous to the utopian and political works, an area where, unlike Wells, he feels that he has less of a stake (although he finds *The Future in America* 'too *loud*').[87] *In the Days of the Comet* (1906) brings the pronouncement that, 'I don't find your work [. . .] as projected an artistic fact, quite, as it is my habit to yearn to find suchlike'; by the time of *Marriage* (1912), James confesses to reading Wells 'with a complete abdication of all those "principles of criticism," canons of form, preconceptions of felicity, references to the idea of method or the sacred laws of composition'.[88]

Since James burned most of the letters Wells sent to him, it is impossible to know in what terms Wells defended his own work: although Wells did admit the lack of 'finish' in *The Passionate Friends* (1913), compared to James's more polished work.[89] Wells is generous to James's novels—having achieved a much greater commercial success very early in his career,

[83] Letter of 20 June 1901, *James and Wells*, 63; cf. 81–2 and 173. Wells would later claim to find 'nothing to resent in that'. 'Introduction', *The Country of the Blind* (London: Golden Cockerel Press, 1939), 5–8 (7).

[84] This is noted by Christine Devine, who also calls attention to Edel and Ray's privileging of James's higher class status in their commentary on the correspondence. Christine Devine, *Class in Turn-of-the Century Novels of Gissing, James, Hardy and Wells* (Aldershot: Ashgate, 2005), 111–33.

[85] *James and Wells*, 67, 75, 94, 94.

[86] Ibid., 105, 123, 128.

[87] Ibid., 115. James, in a letter to Gissing, expressed his regret that Wells 'is so launched in the paths of prophecy & of the reconstruction of society'. *The Collected Letters of George Gissing*, IX, 42.

[88] *James and Wells*, 111, 166.

[89] Edel, *The Life of Henry James*, II, 762–3. In 1900, Wells defended and praised James in the *Morning Post* and later chose *The Golden Bowl* as his book of the year for *The Bookman* (*Correspondence*, I, 362–3, II, 130).

a fact ruefully acknowledged by James, he could afford to be—but as Wells grew in self-confidence he was decreasingly inclined to tolerate James's lofty patronizing of work that he saw increasingly of importance not only to literature, but to the future of humanity. In his 1914 essay for the first number of the new *Times Literary Supplement*, 'The Younger Generation' (1914), James reproves Wells and Bennett, as he had earlier realists such as Balzac, for 'more attestations of the presence of material than of an interest in the use of it'.[90] Seeing this as a personal attack, and also enraged by what he saw as the literary establishment's ignoring of a book on James by Wells's lover Rebecca West, Wells added to the draft of his dialogue-novel *Boon* the chapter 'Of Art, Of Literature, of Mr. Henry James'.[91]

According to Leon Edel and Gordon N. Ray, Wells had been trying to write this novel since 1901, adding to it in 1905, and again in 1909, while being excoriated by the reading public for the sex-novel *Ann Veronica*. Wells used the titles 'Of A Book Unwritten' and *The Anatomy of Frustration* elsewhere, but either might have served for *Boon*, which tries as hard as any artefact of twentieth-century literature not to be a coherent text at all.[92] It presents itself as the literary remains of a writer whom the Great War has hastened to a premature death, then edited by another hack writer, the full title being: *Boon, The Mind of the Race, The Wild Asses of the Devil and The Last Trump: Being a First Selection from the Literary Remains of George Boon, Appropriate to the Times, Prepared for Publication by Reginald Bliss, Author of 'The Cousins of Charlotte Brontë,' 'A Child's History of the Crystal Palace,' 'Firelight Rambles,' 'Edible Fungi,' 'Whales in Captivity,' and Other Works, with An Ambiguous Introduction by H. G. Wells.*[93] *Boon* attempts to make an art-form of iconoclasm, not only affronting James personally, in its portrayal of him, but also theoretically, by attempting to dispense with formal constraints altogether. *Boon* presents itself as a remnant, and is, like much contemporaneous modernist fiction, highly fragmented, composed of various dialogic, dissolving, different voices. The text is highly metafictional and even self-condemnatory: Bliss repeatedly deplores both the fissiparous nature and poor literary

---

[90] 'The Younger Generation', *The Times Literary Supplement* 19 March, 133–4 and 2 April 1914, 137–58, in *James and Wells*, 178–215 (190). Cf. James's comments on Balzac in *Literary Criticism: French Writers, Other European Writers, The Prefaces to the New York Edition*, ed. Leon Edel (New York: Library of America, 1984), 67, 96.

[91] See letters to Hugh Walpole, *Correspondence*, II, 535–6 and to the *New Statesman*, IV, 396.

[92] Walpole described *Boon* as a 'mad incoherent thing with much cleverness'— see Rupert Hart-Davis, *Hugh Walpole: A Biography* (London, Macmillan, 1952), 144.

[93] For the second edition in 1920, Wells added '(*Who is in Truth the Author of the Entire Book*)'.

quality of the manuscript he is reproducing, wondering if it is even worth
reading, let alone publishing.

Taking as its avowed model W. H. Mallock's *The New Republic* (1877),
the text shows various author-personae discussing different aesthetic
points of view during 'the profound decadence of letters at the opening
of the Twentieth Century' (*Boon*, ch. 3, 1). The fact that war has broken
out proves both the failure of the Victorian conception of literature (as
typified by the list of Bliss's other works) to do its duty towards civilization, and the need instead for a kind of writing that is '"something
tremendously comprehensive, something that pierces always down towards the core of things, something that carries and changes all the
activities of the race"' (*Boon*, ch. 4, 3). This need arises from a lacuna
within the world in which the text is produced: as in the earlier *Tono-
Bungay*, literary form is deliberately fragmented because society is so
fragmented.

In *Boon*'s fourth chapter, Wells famously pastiches James himself,
unkindly representing James's prose style as if it were his speaking
voice.[94] Boon imagines a James novel entitled 'The Spoils of Mr. Blandish',
in which the hero is looking for a house that meets his imaginary mental
standards of aesthetic perfection. Blandish succeeds in finding such a
house, but living in it finds himself haunted by an indefinable 'spirit'.
The spirit turns out, prosaically and punningly, to be antique brandy;
Blandish makes obscure plans to sell the brandy, only to discover at the end
that his butler has drunk it all. Energy that is exerted solely in the aesthetic
sphere, here Blandish's quest for a house beautiful, will be wholly unrecu-
perated, an argument given further emphasis in Wells's famous image of
James himself as a 'leviathan retrieving pebbles [. . .] a magnificent but
painful hippopotamus resolved at any cost, even at the cost of its dignity,
upon picking up a pea' (*Boon*, ch. 4, 3).[95] Owing something to the plots
of such James stories as 'The Spoils of Poynton' (1897) or 'The Jolly
Corner' (1908), Wells's burlesque empties James's image of the 'house of
fiction' of significance, the two writers sharing a fondness for architectural

---

[94] Rebecca West notes the alteration in James's prose style once he had started dictating
his work thus: 'Then he would take this draft in his hand and would dictate it all over again
with what he intended to be enlightening additions, but which, since the mere act of talking
set all his family on to something quite different from the art of letters, made [*The Golden
Bowl*] less and less of a novel.' Rebecca West, *Henry James* (London: Nisbet, 1916),
113–14.

[95] West also accuses James of, while satirizing aesthetes in tales such as 'The Author of
Beltraffio', being an aesthete himself (*James*, 78–84). Wells claimed, somewhat disingenu-
ously, in the *Daily News* the detraction to be 'of the method, not the man' (*Correspondence*,
II, 445).

images of writing.[96] Rebecca West's book on James had denigrated *The Awkward Age* thus: 'With sentences vast as the granite blocks of the Pyramids and a scene that would have made a site for a capital he set about constructing a story the size of a hen-house.'[97] The house of fiction becomes transformed into Wells's favourite image for pointless artistic effort, an empty temple: 'a church lit but without a congregation to distract you, with every light and line focussed on the high altar. And on the altar, very reverently placed, intensely there, is a dead kitten, an egg-shell, a bit of string' (*Boon*, ch. 4, 3).[98]

James, naturally enough, was hurt, responding that *Boon*:

> has naturally not filled me with a fond elation. It is difficult of course for a writer to put himself fully in the place of another writer who finds him extraordinarily futile and void, and who is moved to publish that to the world—and I think the case isn't easier when he happens to have enjoyed the other writer enormously, from far back; because there has then grown up the habit of taking some common meeting-ground between them for granted, and the falling away of this is like the collapse of a bridge which made communication possible.[99]

That Wells's objections had hit home is shown in James's incorporation of images of emptiness and of architecture. James claims in conclusion that 'the fine thing about the fictional form to me is that it opens such widely different windows of attention; but that is why I like the window so to frame the play and the process!'[100] Such a claim was at least slightly disingenuous: as only a reader, James was certainly eager to try the view from other windows, but as a critic and a novelist still more so to assert the superiority of his own point of view. (In 'The Younger Generation', Wells is teased for having 'as many windows as an agent who has bought up the lot of the most eligible to retail').[101] Wells responded that, 'I have a natural horror of dignity, finish and perfection, a horror little enhanced by theory.' He apologetically described *Boon* as 'just a waste-paper basket. Some of it was written before I left my house at Sandgate, and it was while

---

[96] Cecile Mazzucco, *A Form Foredoomed to Looseness: Henry James's Preoccupation with the Gender of Fiction* (New York: Lang, 2002), 137–8.

[97] West, *James*, 107.

[98] 'Bricks ceased to be literature after Babylon', Wells laments in the essay 'The Philosopher's Public Library', *An Englishman Looks at the World: Being a Series of Unrestrained Remarks upon Contemporary Matters* (London: Cassell, 1914), 170–4 (170). See also Wells's late short story 'The Pearl of Love' (1925), in which the quest for aesthetic perfection in building a tomb corrupts its actual purpose (*Short Stories*, 625–8).

[99] *James and Wells*, 261.

[100] Ibid., 263.

[101] Ibid., 190. Wells may well have been especially stung by the mention of 'retail'.

I was turning over some old papers that I came upon it, found it expressive and went on with it.' James riposted that 'your comparison of the novel to a waste paper basket strikes me as the reverse of felicitous, for what one throws into that receptacle is exactly what one *doesn't* commit to publicity and make the affirmation of one's estimate of one's contemporaries by', adding the now famous affirmation that 'it is art that *makes* life, makes interest, makes importance, for our consideration and application of these things, and I know of no substitute whatever for the force and beauty of its process'. Wells replied: 'When you say "it is art that *makes* life, makes interest, makes importance," I can only read sense into it by assuming that you are using "art" for every conscious human activity. I use the word for a conscious attainment that is technical and special.'[102]

The correspondence terminates there; parts of it were published following James's death in Percy Lubbock's 1920 edition of James's *Letters*, and Wells expanded in his 1934 *Autobiography* upon the nature of the dispute.[103] In addressing the question of 'Whether I am a Novelist', Wells chooses to do so by revisiting his disagreement with James, and in doing so produces the clearest definition in the final phase of his career of 'the possible use of the novel as an aid to conduct' (*Autobiography*, ch. 7, 5). Once again, Wells re-adapts an architectural metaphor.

> One could not be in a room with [Henry James] for ten minutes without realising the importance he attached to the dignity of this art of his. But I was disposed to regard a novel as about as much an art form as a marketplace or a boulevard. You went by it on your various occasions. (*Autobiography*, ch. 7, 5)[104]

Wells's definition of the novel is in fact closer here to admitting that the house of fiction has a choice of windows than James's had ever been.

---

[102] Ibid., 263–4, 265, 267, 266. See Ross Posnock, *The Trial of Curiosity: Henry James, William James and the Challenge of Modernity* (New York: Oxford University Press, 1991), 187–8.

[103] Wells was not happy about the publication of this correspondence: see the letter to Arnold Bennett: *Correspondence*, III, 5. He would also have been able to see in Lubbock's edition such further Jamesian *lèse-majesté* as his description to his brother William of *Kipps* as 'really magnificent', but *A Modern Utopia* as 'even more remarkable for other things than for his characteristic cheek', and to Edmund Gosse of the 'weakness and looseness, the utter going by the board of any real self-respect of composition and of expression' in, presumably, *Marriage* (*The Letters of Henry James*, ed. Percy Lubbock, 2 vols [London: Macmillan, 1920], II, 45, 259).

[104] Hallery, one of Wells's author-personae in *Boon*, wants to move literature away from 'something that has to do with leisure and cultivated people and books and shaded lamps', wanting to 'drag in not only cathedrals and sanctuaries, but sky-signs and hoardings' (*Boon*, 158).

James's collocation of the window frame with the picture frame crystallizes James's own ideal of the relationship between life and art.

> The house of fiction has in short not one window, but a million—a number of possible windows not to be reckoned, rather; every one of which has been pierced, or is still pierceable, in its vast front, by the need of the individual vision and by the pressure of the individual will. [. . .] At each of them stands a figure with a pair of eyes, or at least with a field-glass, which forms, again and again, for observation, a unique instrument, insuring to the person making use of it an impression distinct from every other. He and his neighbours are watching the same show, but one seeing more where the other sees less. [. . .] The spreading field, the human scene, is the 'choice of subject'; the pierced aperture, either broad or balconied or slit-like and low-browed, is the 'literary form'; but they are, singly or together, as nothing without the posted presence of the watcher—without, in other words, the consciousness of the artist.[105]

In this image, for Wells, both the observer/artist and the frame/form are too static: Wells's ideal of the novel is dynamic, with both observer and frame permitted the freedom to move.[106] The quality that James most consistently praises in Wells's work is that of 'life'—even the denigrated *Marriage*, for example, is 'more convulsed with life and more brimming with blood than any it is given me nowadays to meet'.[107] For Wells, James's interest in 'life' in an art that is over-mediated by form underrates the importance of actually 'living' in the real world.[108] ' "Bare verbs he rarely tolerates," ' accuses Boon (ch. 4, 3). James's aesthetic certainties are grounded in a belief in the solidity of social structures, a belief that Wells did not share:

> The important point which I tried to argue with Henry James was that the novel of completely consistent characterization arranged beautifully in a story and painted deep and round and solid, no more exhausts the possibilities of the novel, than the art of Velazquez exhausts the possibilities of the painted picture. [. . .]

---

[105] 'Preface to *The Portrait of a Lady*', *European Writers and the Prefaces*, 1070–85 (1075). Cf. *The Portrait of a Lady* (New York: Riverside Press, 1882), 320–30, and the often quoted geometrical images in the Preface to *Roderick Hudson*, ibid., 1039–52 (1041).

[106] James complained of Wells in 'The Younger Generation' that 'the more he knows and knows [. . .] the greater is our impression of his holding it good enough for us [. . .] that he shall but turn out his mind and its contents upon us by any free familiar gesture and as from a high window forever open' (*James and Wells*, 190).

[107] Ibid., 168.

[108] James makes a similar accusation of Wells's writing in a letter to Mrs Humphry Ward on 24 October 1912: 'so much talent with so little art, so much life with (so to speak) so little living!' *Letters*, ed. Lubbock, II, 275.

Throughout the broad smooth flow of nineteenth-century life in Great Britain, the art of fiction floated on this same assumption of social fixity. The Novel in English was produced in an atmosphere of security for the entertainment of secure people who liked to feel established and safe for good. Its standards were established within that apparently permanent frame and the criticism of it began to be irritated and perplexed when, through a new instability, the splintering frame began to get into the picture.

I suppose for a time I was the outstanding instance among writers of fiction in English of the frame getting into the picture.[109]

James had claimed in 'The Future of the Novel' that 'the novel is of all pictures the most comprehensive and the most elastic. It will stretch anywhere—it will take in absolutely anything', but his aesthetic in fact requires tremendous restraint, even sacrifice.[110] What James constructs as economy, Wells sees as constriction. 'Literature is for the most part history or history at one remove, and what is culture but a mould of interpretation into which new things are thrust, a collection of standards, a sort of bed of Procrustes, to which all new expressions must be lopped or stretched?' he demands in *The Discovery of the Future* (1902).[111] Wells's writings on the novel increasingly insist instead on scope in both form and content.

Darko Suvin declares the contest between the allegorical Wells and individualistic James 'a draw', but in subsequent versions of specifically literary history, James has tended to have the ascendancy (aided, in no small part, by Wells's undeniable personal insensitivity).[112] Even *Time Magazine*, when putting Wells on its cover in 1926, titled the text that followed, 'All Brains, Little Heart', ruling that 'in *Boon*, his wicked attack on Henry James, he may have been assaulting in James what was missing in himself: infinite care and moral responsibility'.[113] James was a theorist

---

[109] *Autobiography*, II, pp. 493–5. Cf.: '"James has never discovered that a novel isn't a picture . . . That life isn't a studio . . . He wants a novel to be simply and completely *done*. He wants it to have a unity, he demands homogeneity"' (*Boon*, 101–2). See also letter to 'Mark Benney', *Correspondence*, IV, 272–3.

[110] 'The Future of the Novel', 102.

[111] *The Discovery of the Future: With The Common Sense of World Peace and The Human Adventure*, ed. Patrick Parrinder (London: PNL Press for the H. G. Wells Society, 1989), 23.

[112] Darko Suvin, *Metamorphoses of Science Fiction: On the Poetics and History of a Literary Genre* (New Haven, Yale University Press, 1979), 49n; David Lodge, '*Tono-Bungay* and the Condition of England', in *H. G. Wells: A Collection of Critical Essays*, ed. Bernard Bergonzi (Englewood Cliffs, NJ: Prentice-Hall, 1976), 110–39 (110–11); David C. Smith, *H. G. Wells: Desperately Mortal—A Biography* (New Haven: Yale University Press, 1986), 171. Cf. Mark R. Hillegas, *The Future as Nightmare: H. G. Wells and the Anti-Utopians* (New York: Oxford University Press, 1967), 5–7; Michael Sherborne, *H. G. Wells: Another Kind of Life* (London: Peter Owen, 2010), 231.

[113] *Time Magazine*, 20 September 1926. http://www.time.com/time/covers/0,16641,19260920,00.html [accessed 30 September 2011].

crucial both to the New Criticism in the United States and to F. R. Leavis and *Scrutiny* in the United Kingdom.[114] (Indeed Mark Schorer's famous New Critical deprecation of *Tono-Bungay* is strongly reminiscent of James's misgivings over Balzac's over-'inclusiveness'.)[115] As university departments of English Literature began to be founded in the 1920s and 30s, James's concern with significant form and moral seriousness exerted a profound influence over the formation of academic canons of judgement and value, to the detriment of the side of the argument that Wells, still alive, was happy to continue, in the *Autobiography* and else-where.[116] In the 1920s, Wells wrote a caption for a National Portrait Gallery postcard of James which in draft form reminded that 'he ventured upon the stage and was routed by the gallery'; Wells's own copy of his notes contains the handwritten addition, 'Keep this, to recall the crime.'[117] As late as 1943, in answer to a letter from Herbert Read, Wells asserted that, 'believe me, Henry James deserved it'.[118]

Wells's ideal of writing is not exclusive, like the traditional process of canon definition, but capacious and instrumental, like the Victorian ideal of scientific enquiry: capable of including romance and realism, the fantastic and the real, optimism and pessimism, idealism and materialism, art and science, liberty and authority, anarchism and authoritarianism, the popular and the polite, the philistine and the aesthetic. While as a young critic Wells may have argued for certain standards to be maintained, later on as a politically engaged novelist he claimed the right to break them, especially in such wilfully discursive novels as *Tono-Bungay* and *The World of William Clissold: A Novel from a New Angle* (1926).[119]

Wells's prophetic writing became increasingly strident and monologic as it claims the freedom to guide, even enforce, the responses of his readers. He attempted to fuse the dominant traditions of Victorian

---

[114] Leavis judges that Shaw and Wells 'have missed, or are incapable of, the education that can be got through "humane letters"'. 'The Literary Mind', in *For Continuity* (Cambridge: Minority Press, 1933), 47–67 (63). Wells, in turn, burlesques Leavis as Trumber in his novella *The Camford Visitation* (London: Methuen, 1937), 15–17.

[115] Mark Schorer, 'Technique as Discovery', *Hudson Review*, 1/1 (1948), 67–87; see Daniel Born, *The Birth of Liberal Guilt in the English Novel: Charles Dickens to H. G. Wells* (Chapel Hill: University of North Caroline Press, 1995), 144–9.

[116] Terry Eagleton, *Literary Theory: An Introduction* (Oxford Blackwell, 1983), 33–5. Bradbury does make a claim for the value of Wells's formal experimentation (Bradbury, *Social Context*, xxxii, 28).

[117] 'Art and Life: Postcard Biographies from the National Gallery', *Independent on Sunday*, 23 February 1997, http://www.independent.co.uk/arts-entertainment/books/art–life-postcard-biographies-from-the-national-portrait-gallery-1280306.html [accessed 7 January 2011]; Illinois Collection.

[118] Letter of 30 July 1943, *Correspondence*, IV, 421.

[119] See Parrinder and Philmus's 'Introduction', *Literary Criticism*, 1–18.

prose writing: romance, the realist novel, and social commentary. He saw himself as not only in the fictional tradition of Dickens and Balzac, but also the prophetic and moralizing tradition of Carlyle, Arnold, Ruskin, and Mill. Wells constructed the role of writer as not only that of a novelist but also in the tradition of the public moralist, a self-elected member of the early twentieth-century clerisy.[120] Wells's project is Arnoldian in seeing his writing as a means to national regeneration and social betterment, especially as orchestrated by the state, through education above all; it departs from Arnold in making art the servant of social improvement rather than the first-hand source of the values by which society is to be improved. Oscar Wilde, according to Ben Knights, 'both springs from and is an answer to Arnold'.[121] Wilde's younger contemporary, Wells also springs from Arnold, but he has a different answer, abjuring the aesthete's creative irresponsibility for an iconoclasm that seeks to destroy in order to replace or improve. Wells took from the Romantic tradition the belief that the aesthetic sense has, in Linda Dowling's words, 'a power of agency in the world, not simply to register beauty in a passive way, but to suggest a vital means of altering social reality'.[122] He shared with his Victorian forebears the urging of the pressing need for better education, and fear of national crisis if his warnings were ignored, and with his Edwardian and modernist contemporaries a vital sense of literary production springing from social crisis. Wells's is avowedly a literature of offence, which, like Chesterton's and Shaw's, constitutes writing as resistance, as speaking truth to power.[123]

In 1911, Wells gave a talk to the Times Book Club on 'The Scope of the Novel', subsequently rewritten as 'The Contemporary Novel' for *An Englishman Looks at the World* (1914). In the address, Wells makes bold claims for the required participation of art, and of the novel in particular, in the coming necessary reorganization of the social and intellectual world. The novel as an art-form is inherently, he argues, a 'powerful instrument of moral suggestion', and no established idea should be exempt from being

---

[120] These terms are drawn from Stefan Collini, *Public Moralists: Political Thought and Intellectual Life in Britain, 1850–1930* (Oxford: Clarendon Press, 1991) and Knights, *Clerisy*.

[121] Knights, *Clerisy*, 127. For Wells compared to Arnold during his own lifetime, see Van Wyck Brooks, *The World of H. G. Wells* (New York: Mitchell Kennerley, 1915), 14–18 and Stuart Pratt Sherman, *On Contemporary Literature* (New York: Henry Holt, 1917), 52–66.

[122] Linda C. Dowling, *The Vulgarization of Art: The Victorians and Aesthetic Democracy* (Charlottesville: University of Virginia Press, 1996), 20.

[123] William Bellamy, *The Novels of Wells, Bennett and Galsworthy* (London: Routledge & Kegan Paul, 1971), 22.

addressed and criticized by it.[124] He defended this 'inclusiveness' as necessary to 'have all life within the scope of the novel' so that the novel will function as a radical critique of existing structures of authority.

> I consider the novel an important and necessary thing indeed in that complicated system of uneasy adjustments and readjustments which is modern civilisation. I make very high and wide claims for it. In many directions I do not think we can get along without it. [...] The novel has inseparable moral consequences. It leaves impressions, not simply of things seen but of acts judged and made attractive or unattractive. [...] And I do not mean merely that the novel is unavoidably charged with the representation of this wide and wonderful conflict. It is a necessary part of the conflict. [...] You see now the scope of the claim I am making for the novel; it is to be the social mediator, the vehicle of understanding, the instrument of self-examination, the parade of morals and the exchange of manners, the factory of customs, the criticism of laws and institutions and of social dogmas and ideas. It is to be the home confessional, the initiator of knowledge, the seed of fruitful self-questioning.[125]

This study does not propose that Wells was antipathetic to fiction as a significant form of art; rather, Wells believed that 'for three thousand years and more the Book has been becoming more and more the evident salvation of man'.[126] Mill, one predecessor as a sage-writer, famously wrote to the Secretary of the Neophyte Writers' Society that he 'set no value whatever on writing for its own sake & have much less respect for the literary craftsman than for the manual labourer except so far as he uses his powers in promoting what I consider true & just'.[127] Wells may have shared some of Mill's general uneasiness towards the purely creative

---

[124] 'The Contemporary Novel', *An Englishman Looks at the World*, 148–69 (159).

[125] Ibid., 159, 148, 158, 167–8.

[126] *Mankind in the Making*, 357; see also Wells's defence of *In the Days of the Comet* to the *Daily Mail*, 15 September 1906, *Correspondence*, II, 104–5. Here I place a higher importance on the aesthetic for Wells than do the editors of his *Early Writings*, who argue that 'when Wells tried to reconcile mechanistic selection with the existence of the human aesthetic sensibility, he could make sense of the latter only as an epiphenomenon (perhaps following Huxley's lead): he speculated that although Man's subtler mental appreciations are biologically useless in themselves, they may be necessary concomitants of biologically utile evolutionary structures. As "inevitably involved" "bye products", the suffering entailed in their evolution would not be needless. Wells thereby arrived at what he evidently regarded as the hopeful view that the "spiritual" and the "nobler" attributes of man were evolved on the principle that "you cannot make a hay-cart that will refuse to carry roses."' *H. G. Wells: Early Writings in Science and Science Fiction*, ed. Robert M. Philmus and David Y. Hughes (Berkeley: University of California Press, 1975), 183. See Wells's 'Bye-Products in Evolution', *Saturday Review*, 79, 2 February 1895, 155–6, in *Early Writings*, 203–5.

[127] *The Collected Works of John Stuart Mill*, 33 vols., ed. Francis E. Mineka and Dwight N. Lindley (Toronto: University of Toronto Press; London: Routledge, 1972), XIV: *The Later Letters of John Stuart Mill, 1849–1873*, 205.

writer, but he also possessed 'a passionate belief in the power of words to stir the imagination'.[128] The efforts that he made to shape novels such as *Love and Mr. Lewisham*, and the ferocity of his aesthetic disputes with James, Joseph Conrad, and Shaw show how seriously Wells took the practice of artistic production, and his own vocation as a writer.[129] He wrote to the *Daily Mail* in 1906 that 'I do seek, industriously and habitually, for the truth and beauty of things. [...] My work is literature or nothing.'[130] Although this statement is followed by an admission of the difficulties caused by authors having to write for money, Wells's definition of his role might provide a model for the role of the writer of the future:

> It is, indeed, possible to certain gifted and exceptional persons that they should not only see acutely, but abstract and express again what they have seen. Such people are artists—a different kind of people from schoolmasters altogether. Into all sorts of places, where people have failed to see, comes the artist like a light. The artist cannot create nor can he determine the observation of other men, but he can, at any rate, help and inspire it. (*Mankind in the Making*, ch. 5)

Many of Wells's novels possess unarguable literary value: Wells was acclaimed as a genius on the publication of *The Time Machine*, and continues to be so in the present day.[131] As the editors of his *Literary Criticism* have argued: 'Wells would of course deny that he undervalued literature. Rather, from his earliest reviews through to the *Autobiography* he argues both for literature's vital importance, and for the writer's freedom to break rules.'[132] Wells's mockery of the products of the imagination and of some types of fiction especially is not unique to his *oeuvre*; arguably this trait goes back in the novel as far as the novel itself, even to *Don Quixote*. Patrick Brantlinger argues that:

> The inscription of anti-novel attitudes within novels is so common that it can be understood as a defining feature of the genre; accordingly, any

[128] Norman and Jeanne MacKenzie, *The Life of H. G. Wells: The Time Traveller* (London: Hogarth Press, 1987), 40. On Wells's tastes in the arts, see Smith, *Desperately Mortal*, 173–4.

[129] 'The Labour Unrest', *An Englishman Looks at the World*, 43–94 (63). Knights, *Clerisy*, 7, also 15. Bernard Loing, '*Love and Mr. Lewisham*: Foundations and Sources for a First Social Novel', in *H. G. Wells: Interdisciplinary Essays*, ed. Steven McLean (Newcastle: Cambridge Scholars Press, 2008), 76–85 (76–8); Linda Dryden, 'H. G. Wells and Joseph Conrad: A Literary Friendship', *Wellsian*, 28 (2005), 2–13.

[130] *Correspondence*, II, 362–3, 112.

[131] Unsigned review, 'A Man of Genius', *Review of Reviews*, March 1895, 11, 263; *H. G. Wells: The Critical Heritage*, ed. Patrick Parrinder (London: Routledge & Kegan Paul, 1972), 33; Smith, *Desperately Mortal*, 48.

[132] See Parrinder and Philmus, 'Introduction', *Literary Criticism*, 12–14, also 178–88.

fictional narrative which does not somehow criticize, parody, belittle, or otherwise deconstruct itself is probably not a novel.[133]

The danger and the destruction of writing is also an especially common topos in twentieth-century dystopian and utopian fictions: D-503's betrayal by his own diary in Yevgeny Zamyatin's *We* (1921, translated 1924), and Winston's by his in George Orwell's *Nineteen Eighty-Four* (1949), the futility of Shakespeare and the triumph of mass over high culture in Aldous Huxley's anti-Wellsian dystopia *Brave New World* (1932), the burning of books in Ray Bradbury's *Fahrenheit 451* (1953), the pathological disintegration of language in Neal Stephenson's *Snow Crash* (1992), the withering away of art under different conditions of sexual selection in Margaret Atwood's *Oryx and Crake* (2003).

Wells never downplayed the importance of art: his target is reverence of art for its own sake: feckless bohemians from Alec in the 1888 short story 'The Devotee of Art' to *Kipps*'s Coote to Ann Veronica's Manning to Christina Alberta's father to Bulpington are repeated targets within the fiction.[134] His work contains persistent slighting references to artworks being valued for nothing more than their own canonicity, rather than for their instrumental value, and numerous images of artistic culture vandalized, defaced, or destroyed. In Wells's short story, 'The Lost Inheritance' (1897), a will hidden inside a book is lost since the book is forever unopened, not even considered of enough worth to wrap butter.[135] Almost every scientific romance contains an image of a physically damaged text or artefact, notably *The Time Machine*'s image of the decay of all the world's books in the deserted museum of green porcelain, or, in *The War of the Worlds*:

> I followed them to my study, and found lying on my writing-table still, with the selenite paper weight upon it, the sheet of work I had left on the afternoon of the opening of the cylinder. For a space I stood reading over my abandoned arguments. It was a paper on the probable development of Moral Ideas with the development of the civilising process; and the last sentence was the opening of a prophecy: "In about two hundred years," I had written, "we may expect—" The sentence ended abruptly. I remembered my inability to fix my mind that morning, scarcely a month gone by, and how

---

[133] Brantlinger, *Reading Lesson*, 2.
[134] Reed, *Natural History of H. G. Wells*, 192–4; Peter Kemp, *H. G. Wells and the Culminating Ape* (New York: St. Martin's Press, 1982), 157; W. Warren Wagar, *H. G. Wells and the World State* (New Haven: Yale University Press, 1961), 239. One might think also of *The First Men in the Moon*'s Bedford, Holderness in *Love and Mr. Lewisham*, Aubrey Vair ('In the Modern Vein', 1894), and Egbert Craddock Cummins in 'The Sad Story of a Dramatic Critic' (1895).
[135] *Short Stories*, 237–42.

I had broken off to get my *Daily Chronicle* from the newsboy. I remembered how I went down to the garden gate as he came along, and how I had listened to his odd story of "Men from Mars."[136]

In this romance, the Artilleryman envisions the Martians sweeping away the Royal Academy of Arts, and humanity taking underground science books from the British Museum, but not novels or poetry. Wells's scenario for the film *Things to Come* imagines 'Oxford University in ruins and the Bodleian Library in ruins'; *Russia in the Shadows* (1920) a future apocalypse in which 'Mr. Galsworthy and Mr. Bennett will have to do what they can to salvage the art treasures of Mayfair.'[137] The future history *The World Set Free* (1912) imagines a war which results in the following fantasy:

> Within these areas perished museums, cathedrals, palaces, libraries, galleries of masterpieces, and a vast accumulation of human achievement, whose charred remains lie buried, a legacy of curious material that only future generations may hope to examine.[138]

Once war had actually broken out, in 1944, Wells wrote a newspaper article which claimed:

> In this world carnival of evil absurdities one of the wildest freaks of silliness is the fuss being made about the art treasures of North Italy.
> In all that region, except for manuscripts, which are easily hidden away, there is not a single art treasure that cannot be completely destroyed without the slightest diminution of man's inheritance of beauty.[139]

As late as his 1943 'My Auto-Obituary', Wells refers to 'that mighty literary mausoleum, the Reading Room (long since deserted) of the British Museum in London'.[140] When Wells uses such phrases as 'the language of Shakespeare and Herrick', the tone is almost always ironic.[141] Emerson is described as one of those 'dead Americans whose names are better treasured than their thoughts'.[142] 'Life is too short for many admirable things,' Wells wrote as early as 1896, 'for chess, and for the unravelling of

[136] *The War of the Worlds*, ed. Patrick Parrinder (London: Penguin, 2005), 176.
[137] *Two Film Scenarios: Things to Come; Man Who Could Work Miracles* (London: Cresset, 1940), 39; *Russia in the Shadows* (London: Hodder & Stoughton, 1920), 55.
[138] *The World Set Free*, *Works*, XXI, 178.
[139] 'Hard Facts about Art Treasures', *Sunday Dispatch*, 5 March 1944, Illinois Collection.
[140] 'My Auto-Obituary', *The Strand Magazine* 104a (1943), 45–7, in *H. G. Wells: Interviews and Recollections*, ed. J. R. Hammond (Totowa, NJ: Barnes and Noble, 1980), 117–19 (117).
[141] *Marriage*, *Works*, XV, 44–6.
[142] *The Future in America*, 237.

the *Faerie Queen*.'[143] Even when invited to address the Shakespeare Association on Shakespeare Day 1917, Wells cautioned against 'recommending Shakespeare as though he were a medicine', choosing to stress instead the international unity of English speakers as a means to effective communication.[144] In 1939, he declared to J. B. Priestley that, 'I am the sort of man who would edit *Hamlet*.'[145] In 1944, Wells listed authors he enjoyed reading such as Sterne, Dickens, and Austen but warned that the evolution of language means that the canon must evolve, too, and some of its species become extinct:

> No literature is permanent, because no language is permanent; all literature is journalism and will pass away in this changing world. Language will change, ideas will change, there are no immortal works, and I count all "classics" dead and bores. We impose them on the innocent, who are overawed to confess how little they enjoy them. Even Chaucer [...] is dead now, an affair for study and paraphrase, and epic and lyric poetry mere raw material for rebelliously disrespectful allusions from such lively spirits as have been subjected to them.[146]

Frequently, reading as an activity dramatized within the text fails to lift characters such as Hoopdriver, Lewisham, Kipps, or Polly out of the circumstances that oppress them, and can even sap their will to do so. For Wells, such attacks on high culture may indeed be iconoclasm, but not for mere iconoclasm's sake—more a warning of the consequences for humanity and art if the increasingly dire prognostications of his writing were to be ignored.

---

[143] 'Review of *The Well at the World's End*', *Saturday Review*, 17 October 1896, 413–15, in *Literary Criticism*, 111–13 (113). Cf. *The Bulpington of Blup* (London: Hutchinson, 1932), 27.

[144] *Shakespeare Day: Report of Meeting, Organised by the Shakespeare Association, Held at King's College, University of London, on 3 May 1917, to Promote an Annual Shakespeare Day in the Schools and Other Institutions* (London: Chatto & Windus, [1918]), 26–30 (26). See Wells's defence of his omission of Shakespeare from the *Outline of History* in *Shaw and Wells*, 115–16.

[145] *Correspondence*, IV, 220.

[146] '"Auxiliary" Languages and the Present Inadequacy of Human Speech and Symbols', *'42 to '44: A Contemporary Memoir upon the Human Behaviour during the Crisis of the World Revolution* (London: Secker & Warburg, 1944), 137–45 (144). Cf.: 'The writer confesses his profound disbelief in any perfect or permanent work of art. [...] There will come a time for every work of art when it will have served its purpose and be bereft of its last rag of significance.' 'General Introduction to the Atlantic Edition', xviii.

2

The History of the Future

The Scientific Romances

H. G. Wells was not the first English writer to produce fantastic fiction, but his pre-eminent success in the genre owes much to the way in which he melds with the fantastic material details of the actual. Joseph Conrad dubbed him a 'Realist of the Fantastic'; Arnold Bennett judged that *The First Men in the Moon* presented 'in the guise of the romance [...] a serious criticism of the real'.[1] Wells does not violate the perceived laws of reality merely to give greater imaginative liberty to the scope of his narrative, but to comment on and address something in the actual world. In the 1921 Preface to *The War in the Air* (1908), Wells refers to his romances as 'fantasias of possibility'; in the Preface to 1934's *Seven Famous Novels*, he confesses a desire 'to domesticate the impossible hypothesis'.[2] In the *Autobiography*, he added:

> I had realised that the more impossible the story I had to tell, the more ordinary must be the setting, and the circumstances in which I now set the Time Traveller were all that I could imagine of solid, upper-middle-class comfort.[3]

Wells's scientific romances distort perceived reality in order to address something that he seeks to change within it. Science fiction, according to Darko Suvin, is 'wiser than the world it speaks to: the presence of the fantastic indicates not a departure from reality, but a perspective facing in from outside it'.[4] Fredric Jameson also claims that 'one of the most

---

[1] Letter to Wells, 4 December 1898, in *Critical Heritage*, ed. Parrinder, 60; *Cosmopolitan Magazine*, 33 (1902), 465–71, reprinted in *Arnold Bennett and H. G. Wells: A Record of a Personal and a Literary Friendship*, ed. Harris Wilson (London: Rupert Hart-Davis, 1960), 260–76 (266). See also the unsigned review of *The War of the Worlds* in the *Academy*, 29 January 1898, 121–2, *Critical Heritage*, ed. Parrinder, 70–4.

[2] *Seven Famous Novels* (New York: Knopf, 1934), quoted in H. G. Wells, *The Time Machine: An Invention*, ed. Nicholas Ruddick (Peterborough, ON: Broadview Press, 2001), 252–4 (253).

[3] *Autobiography*, II, 516. Cf. Suvin, *Metamorphoses*, 36, 80.

[4] Suvin, *Metamorphoses*, 36.

significant potentialities of SF as a form is precisely this capacity to provide something like an experimental variation on our own empirical universe'. This kind of fantastic fiction seeks 'to defamiliarize and restructure our experience of our own *present*'.[5] *Gulliver's Travels*, for example, turns 'extreme anti-utopian despair into a critique of the anti-utopian world which it mirrors. The more passionate and precise Swift's negation, the more clearly the necessity for new worlds of humaneness appears before the reader.'[6] Far from being escapist fantasy, therefore, Wells's scientific romances also seek to provide their readers with, in Thomas Adorno's phrase, 'negative knowledge of the actual world', to set them in a dialectical relationship with their surroundings and thus be encouraged to alter these surroundings for the better.[7]

Like many of the best writers of the *fin-de-siècle* such as Gissing, Stevenson, Conrad, and James, Wells often ironizes, and even subverts the genre to which an individual work might loosely belong, here that of the romance.[8] If readers of a romance expect imaginative freedom from actual material concerns, such expectations will be frustrated, thus putting Wells's romances into an antithetical or ironic relationship with genre, a relationship that asserts the author's individuality from literary convention.[9] Choosing to write romance gives Wells access to a larger reading public than more hermetic (and less read) kinds of literary fiction; ironizing the genre, however, keeps his writing from complicity with the existing ideological status quo ante that it seeks to modify, a fault diagnosed by Wells in other kinds of romance.[10] The generic reversals of Wells's early romances show a desire to thwart the expectations of their implied reader. *The Time Machine* and *The Wheels of Chance* parody the conventions of the imperial and the chivalric romance, respectively, in order to undermine the ideologies of colonial domination and heroic

---

[5] Fredric Jameson, *Archaeologies of the Future: The Desire Called Utopia and Other Science Fictions* (London: Verso, 2005), 270, 286.

[6] Suvin, *Metamorphoses*, 111.

[7] Theodor Adorno, 'Reconciliation Under Duress', in *Aesthetics and Politics*, ed. Fredric Jameson (London: Verso, 1977), 151–76 (160).

[8] Susan Jones, 'Into the Twentieth Century: Imperial Romance from Haggard to Buchan', in *A Companion to Romance: From Classical to Contemporary*, ed. Corinne Saunders (Malden: Blackwell, 2004), 406–23 (408–9); on Conrad, see Fredric Jameson, *The Political Unconscious: Narrative as a Socially Symbolic Act* (London: Methuen, 1981), 207.

[9] See Winnie Chan, *The Economy of the Short Story in British Periodicals of the 1890s* (London: Routledge, 2007), 50. See Wells's anonymously published sarcastic review of Percy Russell's *How to Write Fiction: A Practical Study of Technique*, 'The Secrets of the Short Story', *Saturday Review*, 80 (1895), 693.

[10] *The Sea Lady: A Tissue of Moonshine*, *Works*, V, 603–7.

autonomy that underlie them.[11] *Tono-Bungay*, *The New Machiavelli* (1911), and even *Love and Mr. Lewisham* refuse the narrative arc of self-improvement common in the Victorian *Bildungsroman* and repeatedly imply a reader who is expecting a kind of book quite different from what these texts actually turn out to be. The later novels insist still more emphatically that lived experience cannot be contained within formal structures of language. 'Life is so much fuller than any book can be,' claims *The Passionate Friends*; 'Life is always more complicated than any account or representation of it can be' (*The Dream*, 1924).[12] Mr Blettsworthy (*Mr. Blettsworthy on Rampole Island*, 1928), like George Ponderevo in *Tono-Bungay*, acknowledges both the reader's expectations and his own incapacity to match them:

> Since my memories have to be told in fragments, given like peeps into a book opened here and there, the reader may even be a little incredulous of some of the things I have to tell. He would prefer, but then I equally would prefer, a story continuous in every detail.[13]

The refusal of generic expectation is key to the didactic effect of Wells's fantastic fiction in particular. The counter-real elements that they depict contradict what the reader believes to be the case about the world in which they live not only counterfactually but also ideologically. Repeatedly, the fantastic requires protagonists to re-evaluate or reject a presupposition about the world they inhabit.[14] Many of Wells's books are concerned with contradicting received wisdom: the Time Traveller, for example, claims that '"the geometry [...] they taught you at school is founded on a misconception"', that there are four dimensions, not three, that time can be travelled in as freely as the others, that humanity is not indubitably progressing towards an indefinite future but might in fact be degenerating.[15]

Darko Suvin argues that science fiction is the 'literature of cognitive estrangement [...] whose main formal device is an imaginative framework

---

[11] See throughout Yoonjoung Choi, 'Real Romance Came Out of Dreamland into Life: H. G. Wells as a Romancer' (PhD, Durham University, 2007).

[12] *The Passionate Friends*, Works, XVIII, 379; *The Dream*, Works, XXVIII, 365.

[13] *Mr. Blettsworthy on Rampole Island* (London: Ernest Benn, 1928), 136–7.

[14] Tzvetan Todorov, *The Fantastic: A Structural Approach to Literary Genre*, trans. Richard Howard (Ithaca: Cornell University Press, 1975), 25, 31–2.

[15] *The Time Machine: An Invention*, ed. Patrick Parrinder (London: Penguin, 2005), 3. Cf. 'The point is that you teach things at school as proofs the world is round that are no more proofs than they are poetry'; 'The Flat Earth Again', *Pall Mall Gazette*, 2 April 1894, *Early Writings*, 32–5 (34). Cf. also the predecessor to *The Time Machine*, 'The Chronic Argonauts', *Science Schools Journal*, April, May, and June 1888, in Bernard Bergonzi, *The Early H. G. Wells: A Study of the Scientific Romances* (Manchester: Manchester University Press, 1961), 187–214 (209–11).

alternative to the author's empirical environment', adding that the principle of Wells's science fiction in particular is *'mutation of scientific into aesthetic cognition'*.[16] The scientific mode that is most important to Wells's early scientific romances is, of course, evolutionary theory. For Wells, Darwin's formulation of the theory of evolution warned of the impermanence of the status quo, and Wells's fiction and non-fiction writings insist repeatedly on the same message. The irruption of the fantastic into an otherwise realistically, sometimes pseudo-scientifically, narrated fictional world is a reminder of futurity: that the indefinite passing of history will repeatedly confront humanity with contingencies that it does not have sufficient knowledge to confront, contingencies that will threaten or displace its misguided faith in its own evolutionary security.

In *The Origin of Species*, Darwin had prophesied, somewhat disingenuously, that:

> Judging from the past, we may safely infer that not one living species will transmit its unaltered likeness to a distinct futurity. And of the species now living very few will transmit progeny of any kind to a far distant futurity [...]. We can so far take a prophetic glance into futurity as to foretell that it will be the common and widely spread species [...] which will ultimately prevail and procreate new and dominant species. [...] Hence, we may look with some confidence to a secure future of great length. And as natural selection works solely by and for the good of each being, all corporeal and mental endowments will tend to progress towards perfection. Thus, from the war of nature, from famine and death, the most exalted object which we are capable of conceiving, namely, the production of the higher animals, directly follows. There is grandeur in this view of life [...] that, whilst this planet has gone circling on according to the fixed law of gravity, from so simple a beginning endless forms most beautiful and most wonderful have been, and are being evolved.[17]

The generation of readers that followed the *Origin*'s first publication, however, correctly realized that in Darwin's own terms, organisms and species are not rewarded intrinsically for complexity, beauty, or intelligence, but only as far as these qualities are favourable for natural or sexual

---

[16] Suvin, *Metamorphoses*, 4, 7–8, and 'A Grammar of Form and a Criticism of Fact: *The Time Machine* as a Structural Model for Science Fiction', in *H. G. Wells and Modern Science Fiction*, ed. Darko Suvin and Robert M. Philmus (Lewisburg: Bucknell University Press; London: Associated University Presses, 1977), 90–115 (101). Cf. Wells's 1938 Australian radio broadcast 'Fiction About the Future', *Literary Criticism*, ed. Parrinder and Philmus, 246–51.

[17] Charles Darwin, *On the Origin of Species by Means of Natural Selection, or the Preservation of Favoured Races in the Struggle for Life*, ed. Gillian Beer (Oxford: Oxford University Press, 1996), 395–6.

selection.[18] Biological evolution thus provides Wells with a framework for challenging the epistemological authority of mankind's supposed dominion in nature; the combination of science with the literary fantastic also provides him with the imaginative liberty to assail the authority of language to describe the world.[19] As Kathryn Hume has observed:

> Science has also made it hard for us to ignore the illusory nature of our sense data; art may help us experience the stoniness of the stone—in Shklovsky's phrase—but that experience may seem meaningless when we remember that the stoniness is an illusion. The stone consists of empty space, a tiny proportion of which is occupied by atoms, and they, in turn, prove to be only a form of energy, whatever that might be.[20]

The inadequacy of representation is a persistent theme of Wells's fantastic writing, and in spite of literary criticism having been somewhat over-preoccupied in recent years with signification's intrinsic unreliability, this particular aspect of Wells's writing is worthy of more attention.[21] The nature of fantastic writing calls the fidelity of language into question: the language of the text must represent not only something the reader has never seen but something that they believe to be actually impossible. In Wells's fantastic writing, the reader is confronted with something that is unreal in order to challenge or unsettle their views of the real, as the Time Traveller does to his audience, as Prendick his posthumous readership's, as Griffin does Kemp's. These texts seek to disrupt complacency, to make the

---

[18] See William Greenslade, *Degeneration, Culture and the Novel: 1880–1940* (Cambridge: Cambridge University Press, 1994); Daniel Pick, *Faces of Degeneration: A European Disorder c.1948–c.1919* (Cambridge: Cambridge University Press, 1989).

[19] John Glendening, *The Evolutionary Imagination in Late-Victorian Novels: An Entangled Bank* (Aldershot: Ashgate, 2007), 55–7. Cf. *Babes in the Darkling Wood*, 53, 209.

[20] Kathryn Hume, *Fantasy and Mimesis: Responses to Reality in Western Literature* (London: Methuen, 1984), 45. I am grateful to Dr Paul McAdam for drawing this passage to my attention.

[21] See Sylvia Hardy's inspirational 'Wells the Post-Structuralist', *H. G. Wells's Fin-de-Siècle*, ed. Partington, 113–25 and two further excellent essays, 'A Story of the Days to Come: H. G. Wells and the Language of Science Fiction', *Language and Literature*, 12/3 (2003), 199–212 and 'H. G. Wells and William James: A Pragmatic Approach', in *Interdisciplinary Essays*, ed. McLean, 130–46 (136–7). Also Michael Fried, 'Impressionist Monsters: *The Island of Doctor Moreau*', in *Frankenstein: Creation and Monstrosity*, ed. Stephen Bann (London: Reaktion, 1994), 95–112 (111–12); Timothy Christensen, 'The Bestial Mark of Race in *The Island of Doctor Moreau*', *Criticism*, 46/4 (2004), 575–95 (584); Larry W. Caldwell, 'Time at the End of its Tether: H. G. Wells and the Subversion of Master Narrative', in *H. G. Wells's Perennial Time Machine: Selected Essays from the Centenary Conference 'The Time Machine: Past, Present and Future' Imperial College, London July 26–29, 1995*, ed. George Slusser, Patrick Parrinder, and Danièle Chatelain (Athens: University of Georgia Press, 2001), 137–49.

reader perceive that of which the 'presentation', in the Time Traveller's words, is 'below the threshold' (*Time Machine*, ch. 1).

Wells's 1903 lecture to the Oxford Philosophical Society 'The Scepticism of the Instrument', published in *Mind* in 1904, calls into question the capacity of language as it exists to characterize accurately a lived experience that is in a constant state of flux.[22] (Haynes suggests that Wells's theory of language drew confidence from Darwin's dissolution of the epistemological category of the species in the *Origin*.)[23] The claim, therefore, is that language can never be more than generalization; adopting Herbert Spencer's terms, Wells warns in *Mankind in the Making* that 'we move from homogeneous to heterogeneous conditions, and we must beware of every generalization we make'.[24] Wells's 1907 personal 'Credo' begins with the following statements:

1. I believe that I possess a mind of limited capacity and an essential if sometimes only slight inaccuracy and that I am thereby debarred from any final knowledge, any knowledge of permanent and ultimate things.

2. I see the Universe in a state of flux, all Being as I conceive it is becoming.[25]

First and Last Things, Wells's experimental book on metaphysics, develops his critique of the linguistic structures available to humanity to qualify experience. Since even the signs of the perceptual world are not reliable, and 'the human mind possesses a limited capacity to make sense of reality', the signification of language should not be granted too great a credence:[26]

The senses seem surer than they are.
The thinking mind seems clearer than it is and is more positive than it ought to be.
The world of fact is not what it appears to be. [...]

[22] *Works*, IX, 335–54; see also letter to the *Daily Mail*, *Correspondence*, II, 285. Wells's thesis was later developed by Stuart Chase, whose *The Tyranny of Words* (London: Methuen, 1938), Wells cites approvingly in *Science and the World-Mind* (London: New Europe, 1942). See also *Babes in the Darkling Wood*, 132, *'42 to '44*, 139.
[23] Haynes, *H. G. Wells*, 36–7.
[24] *Mankind in the Making*, 116. Wells's early essay 'The Rediscovery of the Unique' was originally titled '"The Fallacy of the Common Noun"' (*Early Writings*, 22). Cf. *The Work, Wealth and Happiness of Mankind* (London: Heinemann, 1932), 65.
[25] *Correspondence*, II, 362–3, 198.
[26] Steven McLean, *The Early Fiction of H. G. Wells: Fantasies of Science* (Basingstoke: Palgrave Macmillan, 2009), 157.

We must needs use language, but we must use it always with the thought in our minds of its unreal exactness, its habitual deflection from fact.[27]

This argument recurs throughout Wells's subsequent writings, especially those on language and philosophy. In *The Open Conspiracy* (1928), he asserts:

Human thought is still very much confused by the imperfection of the words and other symbols it employs and the consequences of this confused thinking are much more serious and extensive than is commonly realized. We still see the world through a mist of words; it is only the things immediately about us that are plain fact. Through symbols, and especially through words, man has raised himself above the level of the ape and come to a considerable mastery over his universe. But every step in his mental ascent has involved entanglement with these symbols and words he was using; they were at once helpful and very dangerous and misleading. A great part of our affairs, social, political, intellectual, is in a perplexing and dangerous state to-day because of our loose, uncritical, slovenly use of words.[28]

First and Last Things concerns itself largely with arguing, pre-Wittgenstein, that problems of mind are fundamentally problems of language. Wells had been influenced by philosopher Alfred Sidgwick, who countered traditional accounts of formal logic by drawing attention to the imperfections of its linguistic categories: 'indefiniteness is not merely an occasional incident of descriptive language, but is a fundamental quality of it'.[29] Repeatedly, Wells's writing, especially in his fantastic texts, questions language's capacity to formulate accurately its own referent. *The War of the Worlds* famously opens with the words 'no one would have believed' (*The War of the Worlds*, bk 1, ch. 1). Trafford in *Marriage* (1912) complains that '"we've no language yet for religious truth or meta-physical truth"' and plans a book called 'The Limits of Language as a Means of Expression'.[30] The narrator of *The Time Machine* repeatedly apologizes for the insufficiency of his own discourse:[31]

In writing it down I feel with only too much keenness the inadequacy of pen and ink—and, above all, my own inadequacy—to express its quality. You

[27] *First and Last Things*, 12, 30.
[28] *The Open Conspiracy: H. G. Wells on World Revolution*, ed. W. Warren Wagar (Westport, CT: Praeger, 2002), 56.
[29] Alfred Sidgwick, *The Use of Words in Reasoning* (London: Black, 1901), 359. Wells refers to Sidgwick as well as to Christoph Sigwart in 'The So-Called Science of Sociology' (1909), *An Englishman Looks at the World*, 192–206 (192).
[30] *Marriage*, Works, XV, 553.
[31] See Bruce David Sommerville, '*The Time Machine*: A Chronological and Scientific Revision', *Wellsian*, 17 (1994), 11–29.

read, I will suppose, attentively enough; but you cannot see the speaker's white, sincere face in the bright circle of the little lamp, nor hear the intonation of his voice. You cannot know how his expression followed the turns of his story! (*Time Machine*, ch. 2)

Wells's scepticism towards language, and written language in particular, is at its most pronounced in his representation of newspapers.[32] Newspapers possess a stronger epistemological claim than novels to represent facts, and should be, Wells claims, 'by far the most important vehicle of ideas at the present time', but are exposed as also being fictions, merely constructed narratives whose discourse fails to capture adequately the nature of their plot.[33] Wells's later social writing attacks newspapers for being more concerned to generate profit than to represent truth: 'The normal news-paper is a sheet of advertisements, with articles written to attract, amuse and interest customers, provided they do nothing to detract from the primary purpose of putting goods over to the reader.'[34] The concern for profit above all else is prefigured in *The War of the Worlds*:[35]

As my brother hesitated on the door-step, he saw another news vender approaching, and got a paper forthwith. The man was running away with the rest, and selling his papers for a shilling each as he ran—a grotesque mingling of profit and panic. (*War of the Worlds*, bk 1, ch. 14)

The incapacity of newspapers to record history faithfully constitutes further evidence for Wells's mistrust of written language, or at least of writing in the form in which it exists at the present states of history and of biological evolution. Even the truth of such long-held judgements as the view that the sun revolves around the earth had been eventually over-turned by scientific progress: the hasty and compressed judgements on history forced into print by newspaper deadlines are still more woefully inexact, and may even be dangerously misleading.[36] The *St James's Gazette* mistakenly reports the Invisible Man's irruption as 'An Entire Village in Sussex Goes Mad'.[37] Repeatedly, the narrator of *The War of the Worlds* interrupts his own narration to correct the press's inaccurate rendition at

---

[32] See *Anticipations*, 138–44.

[33] *New Worlds for Old* (London: Archibald Constable, 1908), 286; *The Work, Wealth and Happiness of Mankind*, 154–6.

[34] *Phoenix: A Summary of the Inescapable Conditions of World Reorganisation* (London: Secker & Warburg, 1942), 133. In *When the Sleeper Wakes*, books are replaced by audio cylinders and newspapers by 'babble machines'.

[35] *What is Coming: A Forecast of Things After the War* (London: Cassell, 1916), 106.

[36] A 1917 letter to an unknown correspondent suggests that 'penalisation of deliberate falsehood in advertisement in the press [...] is absolutely essential to the health of democracy'. *Correspondence*, II, 515.

[37] *The Invisible Man*, ed. Patrick Parrinder (London: Penguin, 2005), 86.

the time of the same events (and also to criticize the 'the ill-imagined efforts of artists', *War of the Worlds*, bk 2, ch. 2). Even this narrator's own published work is now made subject to revision from the new perspective created by the text's fantastic elements: 'before the Martian invasion, as an occasional reader here or there may remember, I had written with some little vehemence against the telepathic theory' (*War of the Worlds*, bk 2, ch. 2); in *The Invisible Man*, Kemp's mind in his study, too, 'had travelled into a remote speculation of social conditions of the future' (*Invisible Man*, ch. 17) before his beliefs are disrupted by Griffin's abrupt violation of existing social conditions.[38]

Periodicals are frequent adjuncts to the plots of the scientific romances themselves: many of the Time Traveller's guests are connected by their professions to the press. '"Story!" cried the Editor', who offers the Time Traveller a '"shilling a line for a verbatim note"' (*Time Machine*, ch. 2). The Time Traveller checks the date of his return to the present by the *Pall Mall Gazette*; the narrator is invited to occupy himself while waiting for the Time Traveller's never-fulfilled return by reading a magazine. (In the *New Review* serialization of the novel, the narrator takes up a copy of the *New Review* itself.)[39] Even in the remote setting of *The Island of Doctor Moreau* (1896), Prendick makes a mental connection with the sensational London press:

> 'The Moreau Horrors!' The phrase drifted loose in my mind for a moment, and then I saw it in red lettering on a little buff-coloured pamphlet, to read which made one shiver and creep. [...] A journalist obtained access to his laboratory in the capacity of laboratory-assistant, with the deliberate intention of making sensational exposures; and by the help of a shocking accident (if it was an accident), his gruesome pamphlet became notorious. On the day of its publication a wretched dog, flayed and otherwise mutilated, escaped from Moreau's house. It was in the silly season, and a prominent editor, a cousin of the temporary laboratory-assistant, appealed to the conscience of the nation. It was not the first time that conscience has turned against the methods of research.[40]

The texts' scepticism towards written language naturally extends inwards to the language employed by the texts themselves. 'Mere abstractions' (*Time Machine*, ch. 1) such as the language of mathematics, the Time Traveller argues, have no actual existence; the Sea Lady sceptically

---

[38] Frank McConnell, *The Science Fiction of H. G. Wells* (New York: Oxford University Press, 1981), 125–6.

[39] Bernard Bergonzi, 'The Publication of *The Time Machine* 1894–5', *Review of English Studies*, NS 11 (1960), 42–51 (50).

[40] *The Island of Doctor Moreau*, ed. Patrick Parrinder (London: Penguin, 2005), 34.

dismisses even the elements themselves as figments of scientists' imagination.[41] The apparent mimesis of an alternate reality by Wells's scientific romances in particular can only ever be partial, since language has not yet evolved sufficiently to characterize that which has previously been outside experience. By disclosing itself as fantastic, the text declares itself as necessarily a fragment.[42] 'It was as if the real was a mere veil to the fantastic, and here was the fantastic poking through,' observes the narrator in 'The Apple' (1896).[43]

In his early scientific romances, Wells makes frequent use of unreliable narratees and narrators.[44] *The Time Machine*'s narrator is cautious in his approval of the Time's Traveller's embedded narrative, but the Time Traveller's audiences, especially the first, almost entirely fail to grasp the implications of the possibility of time travel.[45] The Very Young Man imagines speaking Greek with Homer, or investing money in the present and collecting it in the future: given Wells's hostility both to classical education and to financial speculation, such a reaction is a very disappointing one.

The implied reader's or auditor's credulity is never taken for granted, however. The Time Traveller is 'one of those men who are too clever to be believed' and he even at one point suspects that 'my intellect had tricked me' (*Time Machine*, ch. 2, ch. 3). *The Time Machine* deliberately courts disbelief, as do many of Wells's short stories; according to Haynes, Wells

---

[41] On Wells and Kurt Gödel's notion of 'unsolvability', see McConnell, *Science Fiction*, 66.

[42] McLean, *Early Fiction*, 72.

[43] *Short Stories*, 152–8 (155).

[44] Glendening persuasively outlines the case that Prendick's narration is not scientifically verifiable and may be all hallucination (*Entangled Bank*, 44–6).

[45] Peter Edgerly Firchow, *Modern Utopian Fictions: From H. G. Wells to Iris Murdoch* (Washington, DC: Catholic University Press of America, 2007), 21. For a plausible alternative view, see David J. Lake, 'Wells's Time Traveller: An Unreliable Narrator', *Extrapolation*, 22/2 (1981), 117–26. In the manuscript held at Illinois, the narrator explicitly addresses this issue: 'It is of course possible that this is simply the story of a hoax. Yet a man must be informed with a singular passion for deception to go to the pains the Time Traveller took to perfect his story, if it is only a story, and to abandon his exceedingly comfortable position to confirm it. By such a fabrication he had nothing to gain & much to lose. And had he merely thirsted after lying there were a thousand good lies less troublesome that he might have dealt out to us. For my own part I believe that things happened as he described them; that the machine he showed us was what he declared it to be, & that he did actually stand under the black skies of the Last Days & witness the dark eclipse of the dying sun. At the risk of becoming a bye-word for credulity, I assert this. The things he told us were no doubt almost incredible, but if he was not sincere in the telling of them, then I have never seen sincerity. I who heard the story, & saw the machine, believe. To expect the reader to believe, however, is a different matter' (Illinois Collection, TT-195–6). The Time Traveller himself avers, 'Most of it will sound like lying. So be it. It's true—every word of it, nonetheless' (TT-221).

'demands assent by apparently discouraging it'.[46] Narrators continually undermine their own authority to impart discourse responsibly: 'It is quite impossible to say whether this thing really happened' ('The Temptation of Harringay', 1895); 'Whether the story of Gottfried Plattner is to be credited or not, is a pretty question in the value of evidence. [...] I have resisted, I believe successfully, the natural disposition of a writer of fiction to dress up incidents of this sort' ('The Plattner Story', 1896); 'I heard this story in a fragmentary state' ('The Empire of the Ants', 1905).[47] Wells's fantastic stories, therefore, can only be grasped in parts.

FISHY TALE: *THE SEA LADY*

The Sea Lady (1902) neatly epitomizes Wells's scepticism towards the authority or reliability of social and linguistic forms. Wells chooses as his narrator not a character who has personally experienced the events related, but a professional writer who has interviewed witnesses to them. The narration is thus indirect even to flaunting its own pathological unreliability: 'such previous landings of mermaids as have been recorded, have all a flavour of doubt [...] just precisely what happened after that has been the most impossible thing to disinter'.[48] Repeatedly, the narrator questions the validity of his own assertions and even his own professionalism as a writer, neglecting, for instance, to obtain an account of Adeline's feelings: since 'the normal ruthlessness of the literary calling has deserted me. I have not ventured to touch them' (*Sea Lady*, ch. 1, 1). One important witness, the lady's maid Parker, rebuffs the narrator's approaches, and her experiences of the narrated events are therefore inaccessible to the novel's discourse except from the outside. The journalists who appear as minor characters are baffled in their attempts to filter the circumstances of the Sea Lady's appearance through the press; Melville, the narrator's cousin and his principal witness, even struggles to believe things that are supposed to have actually happened to him.

  The Sea Lady is a fantastic narrative that, unlike most fantastic literature, does not seek to overcome the reader's incredulity towards the truth

[46] Bergonzi, *Early H. G. Wells*, 43.
[47] *Short Stories*, 37–41 (37), 101–15 (101, 115), 585–97 (596).
[48] *The Sea Lady*, 313, 477. See William J. Scheick, 'The De-Forming In-Struction of Wells's *The Wonderful Visit* and *The Sea Lady*', *English Literature in Transition 1880–1920*, 30/4 (1987), 397–409 (402). In 'A Tissue of Moonshine: The Mechanics of Deception in The Sea Lady', *The Wellsian: Selected Essays on H. G. Wells*, ed. John S. Partington (Haren: Equilibris, 2003), 123–30, Bruce Sommerville concludes that the narration is so unreliable that there is no mermaid's tail at all, and that Undine is in fact a human adventuress.

of the events described; instead, rather like Bram Stoker's *Dracula* (1897), it presents its case in the form of fragments for the implied reader to interpret or disbelieve as they choose.[49] 'Verisimilitude has been my watchword rather than the true affidavit style' (*Sea Lady*, ch. 3, 1). The fantastic device of the mermaid reveals the incapacity both of social conventions to adjust to experience that lies beyond their own narrow scope, and of the conventions of literature to represent such experience. By repeatedly calling attention to its own narrative incapacity, 'this painfully disinterred story' (*Sea Lady*, ch 7, 1) seeks to downplay the epistemological consequences of its own fantastic nature. A monster, according to Diderot, is 'a being whose continued existence is incompatible with the existing order of things'; 'Gothic', adds Judith Halberstam, 'is the breakdown of genre and the crisis occasioned by the inability to "tell," meaning both the inability to narrate and the inability to categorize.'[50] The Sea Lady's tail is a purposefully Gothic excrescence, a bodily assertion of the inaptness of existing discourse to contain the range of experiences that consciousness might be asked to process.

This romance's resistance to the coding of language is expressed in its continual preoccupation not only with its own narrativity, but also its own textuality. As in *The Time Machine*, a number of the characters in the novel are identified with the press; Lady Ponting Mallow mistakenly addresses Melville as 'Milvain', the name of the untrustworthy journalist in Gissing's *New Grub Street*.[51] Chatteris claims he does not 'believe for a moment in this idea of girls building themselves on heroines in fiction' (*Sea Lady*, ch. 5, 3), but both the female antagonists of *The Sea Lady* appear to be substantially composed out of text. Adeline tries to adopt Mrs Humphry Ward's eponymous heroine Marcella as an intertextual model for her own identity but is unsuccessful in doing so: even the fantastic mermaid is more 'real' than Adeline's narcissistic self-misidentification with the imaginary heroine of a by now somewhat outdated novel: '"She's a mass of fancies and vanities. She gets everything out of books. She gets

---

[49] Cf. 'In all the mass of material of which the record is composed, there is hardly one authentic document. [. . .] We could hardly ask any one, even did we wish to, to accept these as proofs of so wild a story.' 'Mina's Afterword', Bram Stoker, *Dracula*, ed. Glennis Byron (Peterborough, ON: Broadview, 1998), 420.

[50] Diderot, *Élements de physiologie*, quoted in Steven Connor, *Dumbstruck: A Cultural History of Ventriloquism* (Oxford: Oxford University Press, 2000), 207; Judith Halberstam, *Skin Shows: Gothic Horror and the Technology of Monsters* (Durham, OH: Duke University Press, 1995), 23. Linda Dryden identifies Griffin as a Gothic monster in *The Modern Gothic and Literary Doubles: Stevenson, Wilde and Wells* (Basingstoke: Palgrave Macmillan, 2003), 173.

[51] Milvain is also the name of a newspaperman in *The Passionate Friends*, 304.

herself out of a book. You can see her doing it here"' (*Sea Lady*, ch. 6, 3).[52] The Sea Lady herself is an 'extremely well-read person' (*Sea Lady*, ch. 2, 1), and has also modelled her land persona on her reading. 'It must have been from the common latter-day novel and the newspaper that the Sea Lady derived her ideas of human life and sentiment and the inspiration of her visit' (*Sea Lady*, ch. 2, 1).

The undersea world constructs its idea of the upper world from 'saturated books and drowned scraps of paper' (*Sea Lady*, ch. 2, 2), inaccurately picturing an entire culture from fragments of its mass media. As noted in chapter 1, Wells would dispute with James over whether the 'waste-paper basket' of *Boon* ought to have been published. For James, inferior work must be consigned to the dustbin of history; for Wells, *Boon*'s eventual, supposedly posthumous, publication proved the possibility of a kind of recycling. In *The Sea Lady*, the books jettisoned overboard by one society become the basis of literature for another, since, lacking the capacity to use ink underwater, the sea people can only ever consume literature, not produce it. *Tono-Bungay* is prefigured in the capsizing of a ship, but here the dangerous cargo is not radioactive quap but *The Encyclopaedia Britannica*, books, and newspapers, which infect the sea world. This mimics James's fears of mass literacy's threat to high literary culture: 'the flood at present swells and swells, threatening the whole field of letters, as would often seem, with submersion'.[53] The sea people thus constitute a kind of literary underclass:

> They form indeed a distinct reading public, and additions to their vast submerged library that circulates for ever with the tides, are now pretty systematically sought. [. . .] There is always a dropping and blowing over-board of novels and magazines from most passenger-carrying vessels some-times, but these are not as a rule valuable additions—a deliberate shying overboard. [. . .] From the sea beaches of holiday resorts, moreover, the lighter sorts of literature are occasionally getting blown out to sea. And so soon as the Booms of our great Popular Novelists are over, Melville assured me, the libraries find it convenient to cast such surplus copies of their current works as the hospitals and prisons cannot take, below high-water mark. [. . .] There is a particularly fine collection of English work, it seems, in the English Channel; practically the whole of the Tauchnitz Library is there, thrown overboard by conscientious or timid travellers returning from the Continent, and there was for a time a similar source of supply of American

---

[52] Aunt Plessington has the same, even more outdated, ambition for Marjorie in *Marriage* (92); in the typescript, Adeline also models her life on Ward's *Eleanor* (Illinois Collection, SD-5; see also SD-347). See John R. Reed, 'H. G. Wells and Mrs. Humphry Ward', in *Critical Response*, ed. Scheick, 99–110.
[53] James, 'The Future of the Novel', 100.

reprints in the Mersey, but that has fallen off in recent years. And the Deep
Sea Mission for Fishermen has now for some years been raining down tracts
and giving a particularly elevated tone of thought to the extensive shallows of
the North Sea. (*Sea Lady*, ch. 2, 1)

The fiction boom, the rise of holiday reading, the cult of the bestseller, *fin-
de-siècle* censorship, international copyright, even religious publishing all
flow into Wells's literalized tide of post-1870 reading matter. Ease of
production has led to over-production, over-production to surplus, and
surplus leaves waste. The undersea people are unable to discriminate
between good writing and bad; even on dry land reading is more likely
to mislead than to inspire. Victorian literary culture has become literally a
relic, *Sir George Tressady*, *The Times*, and *Punch* failing to inspire or to
amuse, just heavy and useless objects like the 'inkpot of solid brass and
[...] paper-weight of lead' (*Sea Lady*, ch. 6, 5) that weigh the latter down
in Chatteris's club. Melville, searching for a simile for the metaphysical
'union of souls' which Undine fails to understand, lands upon '"sometimes it's like leaving cards by footmen—a substitute for the real presence"' (*Sea Lady*, ch. 6, 2), a further image of the impalpability of writing
compared to the substance of the real. Chatteris laments the 'insufficiency
of the cultivated life' in general to fit within the scope of his imagination:[54]

> "A few old engravings—good, I suppose—a little luxury in furniture and
> flowers, a few things that come within your means. Art—in moderation, and
> a few kindly acts of the pleasanter sort, a certain respect for truth; duty—also
> in moderation. Eh? It's just that even balance that I cannot contrive. I cannot
> sit down to the oatmeal of this daily life and wash it down with a temperate
> draught of beauty and water. Art! ... I suppose I'm one of the unfit—for the
> civilised stage." (*Sea Lady*, ch. 7, 5)

To an extent all of Wells's romances, and *The Sea Lady* in particular,
dramatize the uses and misuses of the imagination—the aesthetic, political, narcissistic, even scientific imaginations. The uses available to Chatteris in conventional Edwardian society are rejected for the more somatic
'better dreams' offered by the Sea Lady herself. She is both a more
successful freethinking New Woman than Adeline (even learning to
smoke cigarettes), and at the same time an articulate and self-conscious
noble savage. Disguising her tail beneath the bourgeois covering of an
antimacassar, she is sufficiently 'other' to see through and deconstruct
social mores, objecting in particular to social propriety's enforcing of rules

---

[54] The phrase is taken from Wells's review of Gissing's *The Whirlpool*: 'The Novels of
Mr George Gissing', *Contemporary Review*, 72 (1897), 192–210, *Literary Criticism*, 144–55
(154).

about uncomfortable clothing in hot weather. Clothing symbolizes civilization throughout Wells's writing, as it often does in English fiction from *Robinson Crusoe* onwards; Thomas Carlyle's Dr Teufelsdröckh asserts that 'Society is founded upon Cloth.'[55] Wells, however, shares Carlyle's scepticism towards the accuracy of the external social meanings presented by clothes. The discarding of clothing is consequently a common image for liberation in Wells's work. As the Time Traveller and Prendick in *The Island of Doctor Moreau* become more decivilized, their clothing becomes more ragged; in *Tono-Bungay* George's 'doubts and disbeliefs' slip from him 'like a loosely fitting garment'; when Undine returns to the sea at the close of the novel, her wrap is left behind on the beach.[56]

Adeline, the would-be New Woman, believes herself to be unconventional, but to Chatteris, she actually represents forced interpellation into his allotted social role: ' "You have defined things—very clearly. You have made it clear to him what you expect him to do. [. . .] She is—she has an air of being natural. [. . .] That is what I think she is for him, she is the Great Outside" ' (*Sea Lady*, ch 7, 3). Undine's fantastic presence allows Chatteris to puncture the veil of the perceived world, to step outside the Symbolic Order, his flight into the sea at the novel's close an escape into an ecstatic pre-Oedipal, fluid state of being unbounded by language or by cultural norms—or, at least, into an Ideal unfettered by the Real.[57]

THE DEATH OF THE BOOK: *THE TIME MACHINE*

Among the authors that Wells credits in his autobiography for his early intellectual awakening is Thomas Carlyle.[58] Carlyle's brand of philosophical idealism seeks to disrupt the reader's view of the perceived material world by drawing attention to a greater reality that lies beyond even the most apparent fundamentals of belief:

But deepest of all illusory Appearances, for hiding Wonder, as for many other ends, are your two grand fundamental world-enveloping Appearances, SPACE and TIME. [. . .] In vain, while here on Earth, shall you endeavor to

---

[55] Thomas Carlyle, *Sartor Resartus: The Life and Opinions of Herr Teufelsdröckh in Three Books*, ed. Roger L. Tarr and Mark Engel (Berkeley: University of California Press, 2000), 40.

[56] *Tono-Bungay*, ed. Patrick Parrinder (London: Penguin, 2005), 366.

[57] Wells, perhaps, intended to leave the ending somewhat vague, writing to his agent J. B. Pinker in late 1900, 'I've found out a way of settling that Sea Lady without either souls or anything calculated to bring a blush to the cheek of H[ubert] B[land]' (Letter, November–December 1900, Illinois Collection).

[58] *Autobiography*, I, 241.

strip them off; you can, at best, but rend them asunder for moments, and look through.

The narrator of *Sartor Resartus* wishes for Fortunatus's magical hat that would allow him to annihilate both space and time:

> "To clap on your felt, and, simply by wishing that you were Any*where*, straightway to be *There*! Next to clap on your other felt, and, simply by wishing that you were Any*when*, straightway to be *Then*! [...]
>
> "Or thinkest thou it were impossible, unimaginable? Is the Past annihilated, then, or only past; is the Future non-extant, or only future? Those mystic faculties of thine, Memory and Hope, already answer: already through those mystic avenues, thou the Earth-blinded summonest both Past and Future, and communest with them, though as yet darkly, and with mute beckonings. The curtains of Yesterday drop down, the curtains of To-Morrow roll up; but Yesterday and To-morrow both *are*. Pierce through the Time-element, glance into the Eternal.[59]

Repeatedly in Wells's scientific romances, the fantastic makes perception relative: that which the implied reader or narratee believes to be objectively true proves to be only partial or even inaccurate. *The Time Machine* dramatizes a crisis of intelligibility: unlike Oedipus, in whose limping steps he follows, the Time Traveller is slow to interpret the riddle of the Sphinx.[60] As Patrick Parrinder has noted, the Time Traveller does not, as a more careful scientist ought, gradually assemble facts and then present his conclusions, but stumbles four times from an inaccurate synthesis to a less inaccurate one.[61] The Time Traveller also interrupts his narrative with critical parentheses to indicate subsequently discovered inaccuracies: 'Afterwards I found I had got only a half-truth—or only a glimpse of one facet of the truth. [...] It was an obvious conclusion, but it was absolutely wrong. [...] This, I must warn you, was my theory at the time. [...] My explanation may be absolutely wrong. I still think it is the most plausible one' (*Time Machine*, ch. 4, ch. 5). So self-conscious is the narration, it is almost as if the Time Traveller knows that he is in a book, and knows how far he is failing to conform to the expectations of its genre—'I had no convenient cicerone in the pattern of the Utopian

---

[59] Carlyle, *Sartor Resartus*, 191–2.

[60] David Ketterer, 'Oedipus as Time-Traveller', *Science Fiction Studies*, 9 (1982), 340–1; Firchow, *Modern Utopian Fictions*, 26; Parrinder, *Shadows*, 21.

[61] Patrick Parrinder, *H. G. Wells* (Edinburgh: Oliver & Boyd, 1970), 19–20. Cf. 'Of course it is hard for me now to say how much I saw at that time, because my impressions were corrected by subsequent observation'; 'Cavor was continually making corrections in his previous accounts of the Selenites as fresh facts flowed in upon him to modify his conclusions' (*The First Men in the Moon*, ed. Patrick Parrinder (London: Penguin, 2005), 71–2, 180).

books' (*Time Machine*, ch. 5).[62] (In the *National Observer* text, he protests, 'I am a traveller, and I tell you a traveller's tale. I am not an annotated
edition of myself.')[63] He admits the lack of comprehensiveness in his
knowledge of the future, and at the end of his narrative invites his
audience to aestheticize their response, to:

> "take it as a lie—or a prophecy. [. . .] Consider I have been speculating upon
> the destinies of our race until I have hatched this fiction. Treat my assertion
> of its truth as a mere stroke of art to enhance its interest." (*Time Machine*,
> ch. 12)[64]

Victorian writing, especially scientific discourse, was fond of Galileo's
image of nature as a book. Wells himself uses the image in his very first
book, 1893's *A Text Book of Biology*, a text in which are narrated:

> the triumphs of survival, the tragedy of death and extinction, the tragi-
> comedy of degradation and inheritance, the gruesome lesson of parasitism,
> and the political satire of colonial organisms. Zoology is, indeed a philosophy
> and a literature to those who can read its symbols.[65]

The popularity of this trope in the nineteenth century is perhaps due to its
recurrence in *Sartor Resartus*:

> "We speak of the Volume of Nature: and truly a Volume it is,—whose
> Author and Writer is God. To read it! Dost thou, does man, so much as well
> know the Alphabet thereof? With its Words, Sentences, and grand descrip-
> tive Pages, poetical and philosophical, spread out through Solar Systems, and
> Thousands of Years, we shall not try thee. It is a Volume written in celestial
> hieroglyphs, in the true Sacred-writing; of which even Prophets are happy
> that they can read here a line and there a line. As for your Institutes, and
> Academies of Science, they strive bravely; and, from amid the thick-crowded,
> inextricably intertwisted hieroglyphic writing, pick out, by dextrous combin-
> ation, some Letters in the vulgar Character, and therefrom put together this
> and the other economic Recipe, of high avail in Practice. That Nature is
> more than some boundless Volume of such Recipes, or huge, well-nigh
> inexhaustible Domestic-Cookery Book, of which the whole secret will in this
> manner one day evolve itself, the fewest dream."[66]

---

[62] Chan, *Economy of the Short Story*, 34.
[63] *Early Writings*, 85.
[64] Haynes, *H. G. Wells*, 226–7.
[65] H. G. Wells, *A Text-Book of Biology*, 2 vols (London: Clive, 1893), I: *Vertebrates*, 131.
[66] Carlyle, *Sartor Resartus*, 189–90. The image also recurs in Winwood Reade's *The Martyrdom of Man*, a book which greatly influenced Wells. 'But it is when we open the Book of Nature, that book inscribed in blood and tears; it is when we study the laws regulating life, the laws productive of development—that we see plainly how illusive is this theory that God is Love. In all things there is cruel, profligate, and abandoned waste.' *The Martyrdom of Man*, 15th edn (London: Kegan Paul, Trench, Trubner, 1896), 519–20.

The same metaphor is adopted both by Charles Lyell in *Principles of Geology* (1830–3), whose reimagining of time was crucial to Darwin's formulation of evolution, and then by Darwin himself in the *Origin*:

> For my part, following out Lyell's metaphor, I look at the geological record, as a history of the world imperfectly kept, and written in a changing dialect; of this history we possess the last volume alone, relating only to two or three countries. Of this volume, only here and there a short chapter has been preserved, and of each page, only here and there a few lines. Each word of the slowly-changing language, being more or less different in the interrupted succession of chapters, may represent the apparently abruptly changed forms of life.[67]

For Carlyle, the book of nature cannot be fully read because mankind has not yet developed the esoteric knowledge required to do so. The Time Traveller is just such a Carlylean academician, a palaeontologist seeking for the history of his own present in the records held by the future.[68] In Darwin's development of the metaphor, however, the fragmentary nature of the reading is the fault of the text, not of the reader: the whole story may not have been fully written down and time has erased some of the writing for ever. According to Patrick Brantlinger, 'the world–book equation discloses the insufficiency of all language to represent the nontextual, nonverbal real, and therefore also the failure of book-learning or literacy to read the great book of the world'.[69] The Time Traveller may be an intellectual in his own time, but not only has the environment of the future relativized his specialist knowledge into virtual illiteracy, but he does not even have a coherent text to read:

> Suppose you found an inscription, with sentences here and there in excellent plain English, and interpolated therewith, others made up of words, of letters even, absolutely unknown to you? Well, on the third day of my visit, that was how the world of Eight Hundred and Two Thousand Seven Hundred and One presented itself to me! (*Time Machine*, ch. 5)

Metaphors of light as knowledge and darkness as ignorance are also very common in Western culture.[70] This metaphor is especially prevalent in Wells, who, Richard Hauer Costa suggests, was himself afraid of the

---

[67] Darwin, *Origin*, 251.

[68] Patrick Parrinder, 'History in the Science Fiction of H. G. Wells', *Cycnos*, 22/2 (2004), http://revel.unice.fr/cycnos/document.html?id=428 [accessed 25 January 2011].

[69] Brantlinger, *Reading Lesson*, 5.

[70] Simon Goldhill, *Reading Greek Tragedy* (Cambridge: Cambridge University Press, 1986), 218; Peter Morton, *The Vital Science: Biology and the Literary Imagination, 1860–1900* (London: Allen & Unwin, 1984), 103.

dark.[71] A number of Wells's short stories, such as 'Through a Window' (1894), 'In the Avu Observatory' (1894), 'The Remarkable Case of Davidson's Eyes' (1895), and 'The Crystal Egg' (1897) display a preoccupation with light and with vision, or take place in partial or complete darkness.[72] The powers of vision possessed by Wells's early narrators are frequently circumscribed, particularly in *The First Men in the Moon*: 'we saw it all through a thick bent glass, distorting it as things are distorted by a lens, acute only in the centre of the picture, and very bright there, and towards the edges magnified and unreal'.[73] The frame narrative of *The Time Machine* is related in semi-darkness, hinting at the possible use of hypnosis or conjuring in the disappearance of the model time machine.[74] (Lagune insists on darkness for the fraudulent seance in *Love and Mr. Lewisham*.) Both of *The Time Machine*'s narrators admit to limits to how much they can see of the events described.[75] Watching the model disappear, the frame narrator notes 'an odd twinkling appearance about this bar, as if it were somewhat unreal' (*Time Machine*, ch. 1). Admitting his inability to complete his narration of the plot since he lacks the knowledge of the Time Traveller's final destination, this narrator confesses that 'to me the future is still black and blank—is a vast ignorance, lit at a few casual places by the memory of his story' (*Time Machine*, ch. 12). Paradoxically, in 802,701, the Time Traveller is initially deluded by what he sees in daylight, but his knowledge becomes clearer at dusk when the Morlocks emerge above ground. (The Morlocks' larger retinas allow them to see in the dark; Moreau's Beast People are less civilized after nightfall.) Consequently, the basic Promethean technology of fire, produced by the handful of matches in the Time Traveller's coat pocket, proves crucial in the Time Traveller's quest to see, and read, the future correctly. *Sartor Resartus* opens thus:

> Considering our present advanced state of culture, and how the Torch of Science has now been brandished and borne about, with more or less effect,

---

[71] Richard Hauer Costa, *H. G. Wells* (Boston: Twayne, 1967), 68.

[72] Parrinder, *Shadows*, 121; Michael Draper, *H.G. Wells* (London: Macmillan, 1987), 39; Keith Williams, 'Alien Gaze: Postcolonial Vision and *The War of the Worlds*', in *Interdisciplinary Essays*, ed. McLean, 49–73 (49); Brett Davidson, '*The War of the Worlds* Considered as a Modern Myth', *Wellsian*, 28 (2005), 39–50 (44).

[73] *The First Men in the Moon*, 74. Cf. the alienated perspective of the railway traveller as described by Michel de Certeau, 'Railway Navigation and Incarceration', *The Practice of Everyday Life*, trans. Steven Rendall (Berkeley: University of California Press, 1984), 111–14.

[74] Keith Williams, *H. G. Wells, Modernity and the Movies* (Liverpool: Liverpool University Press, 2007), 16, 45.

[75] Robert Crossley, 'Taking it as a Story: The Beautiful Lie of *The Time Machine*', in *Perennial Time Machine*, ed. Slusser et al., 12–26 (12–17).

for five thousand years and upwards; how, in these times especially, not only the Torch still burns, and perhaps more fiercely than ever, but innumerable Rush-lights, and Sulphur-matches, kindled thereat, are also glancing in every direction, so that not the smallest cranny or dog-hole in Nature or Art can remain unilluminated.[76]

In an often-quoted passage from his essay 'The Rediscovery of the Unique' (1891), Wells warns that 'Science is a match that man has just got alight.'[77] The Time Traveller believes that his scientific knowledge will give him the power literally to see into the future. Instead, his journey into man's evolutionary twilight is illuminated not by Carlyle's torch but only by a single match. He discovers how little he, and humanity, actually know: as Patrick Parrinder extends Wells's metaphor, 'science is a match that man has just struck to reveal—more darkness'.[78] The ending of the Time Traveller's narrative also takes place in semi-darkness and silence:

The darkness grew apace; a cold wind began to blow in freshening gusts from the east, and the showering white flakes in the air increased in number. From the edge of the sea came a ripple and whisper. Beyond these lifeless sounds the world was silent. Silent? It would be hard to convey the stillness of it. All the sounds of man, the bleating of sheep, the cries of birds, the hum of insects, the stir that makes the background of our lives—all that was over. As the darkness thickened, the eddying flakes grew more abundant, dancing before my eyes; and the cold of the air more intense. At last, one by one, swiftly, one after the other, the white peaks of the distant hills vanished into blackness. The breeze rose to a moaning wind. I saw the black central shadow of the eclipse sweeping towards me. In another moment the pale stars alone were visible. All else was rayless obscurity. The sky was absolutely black. (*Time Machine*, ch. 11)[79]

The Time Machine's engagement with Victorian science draws not only on biology's reimagining of human physiology, but also geology's expansion of the Victorian sense of time, which relativizes perception still

<hr />

[76] Carlyle, *Sartor Resartus*, 3.

[77] 'The Rediscovery of the Unique', *Fortnightly Review*, 56 (1891), 106–11 (111), *Early Writings*, 22–31 (30). Cf. 'Thus when it is asked whether we know Reality, the only possible answer seems to be that we do not know how much or how little we know it' (Sidgwick, *Use of Words*, 229).

[78] Patrick Parrinder, '*The Time Machine*: H. G. Wells's Journey through Death', in *Wellsian: Selected Essays*, ed. Partington, 31–43 (35).

[79] Cf.: 'But when I go among snows and desolations [...] I think very much of the Night of this World—the time when our sun will be red and dull, and air and water will lie frozen together in a common snowfield where now the forests of the tropics are steaming ... I think very much of that, and whether it is indeed God's purpose that our kind should end, and the cities we have built, the books we have written, all that we have given substance and a form, should lie dead beneath the snows' (*A Modern Utopia*, *Works*, IX, 272).

further.[80] In narrative theory from Aristotle onwards, discrete 'events' are made into a 'plot' by connections of both time and causality.[81] Time travel radically destabilizes both of these elements, as the enormous scale of geological time makes local causal connections appear tiny and inconsequential. Lyell's version of the 'book of nature' speculates towards a new fantastic genre of narrative reshaped by this new understanding of temporality:

> How fatal every errour as to the quantity of time must prove to the introduction of rational views concerning the state of things in former ages, may be conceived by supposing that the annals of the civil and military transactions of a great nation were perused under the impression that they occurred in a period of one hundred instead of two thousand years. Such a portion of history would immediately assume the air of a romance; the events would seem devoid of credibility, and inconsistent with the present course of human affairs. A crowd of incidents would follow each other in thick succession. Armies and fleets would appear to be assembled only to be destroyed, and cities built merely to fall in ruins.
>
> In the vast interval of time which may really have elapsed [...] one or more races of organic beings may have passed away, and yet have left behind [...] no trace of their existence. The imagination is as much perplexed by such errors as to time, as it would be if we could annihilate space, and by some power, such as we read of in tales of enchantment, could transfer a person who had laid himself down to sleep.[82]

Awakening in the future, the Time Traveller at last reads the evidence of the book of the world correctly, realizing that mankind has evolved into two separate species, that 'this bleached, obscene, nocturnal Thing, which had flashed before me, was also heir to all the ages' (*Time Machine*, ch. 5). The allusion to 'Locksley Hall' (1842) shows how far history has failed to reward Tennyson's faith that technological progress will bring about

---

[80] Gillian Beer, '"The Death of the Sun": Victorian Solar Physics and Solar Myth', in *The Sun is God: Painting, Literature and Mythology*, ed. J. B. Bullen (Oxford: Clarendon Press, 1989), 159–80. See also Wells's 1901 short story 'The New Accelerator' (*Short Stories*, 487–97).

[81] Aristotle, *Poetics*, Section 3, B, iv, in *Classical Literary Criticism*, ed. D. A. Russell and Michael Winterbottom, trans. M. E. Hubbard (Oxford: Oxford University Press, 1989), 51–90 (62–3); E. M. Forster, *Aspects of the Novel* (Harmondsworth: Penguin, 1962), 93–4.

[82] Charles Lyell, *The Principles of Geology*, ed. Martin Rudwick, 3 vols (Chicago: University of Chicago Press, 1990), I, 78–9, 159–60; Jonathan Smith, *Fact and Feeling: Baconian Science and the Nineteenth-Century Literary Imagination* (Madison: University of Wisconsin Press, 1994), 93; Stephen Jay Gould, *Time's Arrow, Time's Cycle: Myth and Metaphor in the Discovery of Geological Time* (Cambridge, MA: Harvard University Press, 1987), 85–6.

enlightened world government.[83] The Eloi and the Morlocks show not only humanity's physical shape degenerating, but also mental life and civilization as a whole; and natural selection has shown as little respect to the cultural corpus inherited from previous generations as it has to the morphology of the human form. The Time Traveller 'had always anticipated that the people of the year Eight Hundred and Two Thousand odd would be incredibly in front of us in knowledge, art, everything. Then one of them suddenly asked me a question that showed him to be on the intellectual level of one of our five-year-old children' (*Time Machine*, ch. 4). The explorations of Victorian philologists into the science of language revealed language also to have a history, even an evolutionary history, thus revealing its nature to be contingent, rather than permanent.[84] If the Eloi no longer possess any abstract nouns, the Time Traveller worries whether the abstractions represented by those nouns can still be said to exist. His 'confident anticipations of a profoundly grave and intellectual posterity' (*Time Machine*, ch. 4) are displaced by the evolutionary awareness that natural selection has eliminated parts of speech, books, art—anything that is no longer of any advantage. The Time Traveller is troubled by how little affected the Eloi are the day after the Morlock attack. They have no memory; with no memory they have no capacity for art, and the cultural residuum has become fossilized into the 'ancient monument of an intellectual age' (*Time Machine*, ch. 8) that is the Palace of Green Porcelain.[85] Darwin's notion of beauty in *The Descent of Man* places the aesthetic as a by-product of the reproductive imperative: if art is a kind of display, beauty is ultimately a matter of sexual selection:

> When, however, it is said that the lower animals have a sense of beauty, it must not be supposed that such sense is comparable with that of a cultivated man, with his multiform and complex associated ideas. A more just comparison would be between the taste for the beautiful in animals, and that in the lowest savages, who admire and deck themselves with any brilliant, glittering, or curious object.[86]

[83] Cf. *The Shape of Things to Come: The Ultimate Revolution* (London: Hutchinson & Co., 1936), 36. Joseph Carroll also finds an allusion to *In Memoriam* in *The Time Machine* in *Evolution and Literary Theory* (Columbia: University of Missouri Press, 1995), 314.

[84] See, for instance, Max Müller, *Lectures on the Science of Language: Delivered at the Royal Institution of Great Britain on April, May and June, 1861*, 2nd rev. edn, 2 vols (London: Longman, 1862), I, 386.

[85] In the *National Observer* text of *The Time Machine*, the Time Traveller despairingly adds, 'What need for education when there is no struggle for life? What need of books, or what need of stimulus to creative effort?' (*Early Writings*, 77).

[86] Charles Darwin, *The Descent of Man, and Selection in Relation to Sex*, ed. James Moore and Adrian Desmond (London: Penguin, 2004), 246. See also 208 and Darwin's thoughts on different kinds of aesthetic pleasure in the 'M Notebook', in *Metaphysics, Materialism*

For the Eloi, however, even the taste for the beautiful now plays no part in reproduction. 'In all the differences of texture and bearing that now mark off the sexes from each other, these people of the future were alike. And the children seemed to my eyes to be but the miniatures of their parents' (*Time Machine*, ch. 4).[87] Since the Eloi have substituted the harsh testing of sexual selection for constantly 'making love in a half-playful fashion' (*Time Machine*, ch. 5), there is no longer any need for such selective adaptations as aesthetic beauty: hence the disappearance of aesthetic production, and 'the dream of the human intellect [. . .] had committed suicide' (ch. 10).

If Darwin's surmises about the evolutionary purpose of language and of artistic culture are correct, once a species reaches a fatal equilibrium, there is little purpose for either.[88] In 802,701, as mankind degenerates, its grip on language is surrendered. In 1994, Steven Pinker hypothesized:

> I would guess that most other human 'cultural' practices (competitive sports, narrative literature, landscape design, ballet), no matter how much they seem like arbitrary outcomes of a Borgesian lottery, are clever technologies we have invented to exercise and stimulate mental modules that were originally designed for specific adaptive functions.[89]

Such *Homo sapiens* cultural practices are clearly no longer of use to the Eloi. The Time Traveller, attempting 'a Carlyle-like scorn of this wretched aristocracy in decay' (ch. 7), classifies the Eloi as the descendants of aristocrats or effete bourgeois on whom the proletarian-descended Morlocks take grisly class revenge. The Eloi are described as possessing 'Dresden-china' features not only for their actual pallor and fragility, but also for the association with class privilege and conspicuous

---

and the Evolution of Mind: Early Writings of Charles Darwin*, ed. Paul H. Barrett and Howard E. Gruber (Chicago: Chicago University Press, 1980), 6–45 (11–13). Cf. Wells, *The Science of Life*, II, 1390, 1416–32.

[87] 'Angry Old Buffer' lamented of New Women and Aesthetes in 'Sexomania':

> A New Fear My Bosom Vexes
> To-morrow there may be no Sexes!
> Unless, to save all Pother,
> Each One Becomes the Other

Punch, 27 April 1895, 203. See Linda Dowling, 'The Decadent and the New Woman in the 1890s', *Nineteenth-Century Fiction*, 33/4 (1979), 434–53.

[88] *Mankind in the Making*, 113.

[89] Steven Pinker, *The Language Instinct: The New Science of Language and Mind* (London: Penguin, 2000), 473. For Pinker's assault on the high cultural canons of his own time, see *The Blank Slate: The Modern Denial of Human Nature* (London: Allen Lane, 2002), 401–7.

consumption.[90] The class of the Eloi associates them with high culture: descended from the 'Haves, pursuing pleasure and comfort and beauty' (*Time Machine*, ch. 5), hyper-evolved Wildean aesthetes (a type later parodied as effete, underdeveloped, and sexless 'Pinky-Dinkys' in *The New Machiavelli*), or inhabitants of William Morris's Nowhere without the need to work.[91] (As Linda Dowling notes, Morris's Nowhere produces no literature, and seems distrustful of it, thus also implying its eventual extinction.)[92] The Time Traveller speculates that as mankind has become so over-civilized and comfortable that there is no need to compete, its need for the evolutionary adaptation that is art has atrophied like its physical strength. The 'beautiful futility' (*Time Machine*, ch. 7) celebrated by aestheticism eventually proves an evolutionary liability: 'The little people displayed no vestige of a creative tendency. There were no shops, no workshops, no sign of importations among them' (*Time Machine*, ch. 5). The pursuit of pleasure without social responsibility leads to 'intellectual degradation' (ch. 7). Herbert Spencer had warned that under conditions of too much leisure:

> Every powerful spring of action is destroyed—acuteness of intellect is not wanted—force of moral feeling is never called for—the higher powers of his mind are deprived of their natural exercise, and a gradual deterioration of

---

[90] John Glendening's thought-provoking reading of *The Time Machine* makes a connection with Wilde's famous fondness for his blue and white china: 'The Track of the Sphinx: H. G. Wells, The Modern Universe, and the Decay of Aestheticism', *Victorians Institute Journal*, 32 (2004), 129–66 (140). In a version of 'The Chronic Argonauts' that no longer survives, 'art and literature are cultivated in a very dilettante manner' by the Eloi's ancestors (Bergonzi, *Early H. G. Wells*, 38).

[91] *The New Machiavelli*, ed. Simon J. James (London: Penguin, 2005), 86. On Morris, see Wells's 'The Past and the Great State', in H. G. Wells et al., *The Great State: Essays in Construction* (London: Harper, 1912), 1–46 (18–19, 38–9). See also Steven McLean's note in the Penguin edition of *The Time Machine*, 100–1; Stephen Derry, 'The Time Traveller's Utopian Books and his Reading of the Future', *Foundation*, 65 (1998), 16–24; Tony Fitzpatrick, 'William Morris, Socialist Romanticism and the Early Fiction of H. G. Wells', *Wellsian*, 32 (2009), 36–53; Gowan Dawson, *Darwin, Literature and Victorian Responsibility* (Cambridge: Cambridge University Press, 2007), 216; Dan Smith, 'Wells' First Utopia: Materiality and Portent', http://www.slashseconds.org/issues/002/003/articles/dsmith/index.php, [accessed 25 January 2011]. In the *National Observer* text, the Time Traveller speculates, 'Since this time-journey of mine, I have fancied that there is such a split going on even now in English society, a split that began some two hundred and fifty years ago or more. I do not mean any split between working people and rich [. . .] but between the sombre, mechanically industrious, arithmetical, inartistic type, the type of the Puritan and the American millionaire and the pleasure-loving, witty, and graceful type that gives us our clever artists, our actors and writers, some of our gentry, and many an elegant rogue. Conceive such types drifting away from one another each into its own direction' (*Early Writings*, 86). See also the diagram on 46 of 'The Past and the Great State'.

[92] Dowling, *Vulgarization of Art*, 70.

character must ensue. Take away the demand for exertion, and you will ensure inactivity. Induce inactivity, and you will soon have degradation.[93]

The Time Traveller's Promethean quest into the future finds not new additions to the corpus of human knowledge, but iterated images of forgetting: the enigma that is the Sphinx and the unreadable contents of the Palace of Green Porcelain. As the text battles complacency it seeks to disappoint: the society of the future is to be less, not more, sophisticated, than the late nineteenth century. Pinker adds that:

Although language is an instinct, written language is not. [...] Most societies have lacked written language, and those that have it inherited it or borrowed it from one of the inventors. Children must be taught to read or write in laborious lessons [...] and people do not uniformly succeed.[94]

The childlike Eloi have no one to teach them to read, and time has obliterated writing both from the metaphorical book of nature, and literally from the world itself:

The brown and charred rags that hung from the sides of it, I presently recognized as the decaying vestiges of books. They had long since dropped to pieces, and every semblance of print had left them. But here and there were warped boards and cracked metallic clasps that told the tale well enough. Had I been a literary man I might, perhaps, have moralized upon the futility of all ambition. But as it was, the thing that struck me with keenest force was the enormous waste of labour to which this sombre wilderness of rotting paper testified. At the time I will confess that I thought chiefly of the *Philosophical Transactions* and my own seventeen papers upon physical optics. (*Time Machine*, ch. 8)

This is an unsettlingly self-conscious moment to find within the pages of a book, a technology proclaiming its own obsolescence. The late-Victorian cultural elite had worried that the proliferation of cheap books would make literature valueless; here, no longer possessing any evolutionary value, all literature and other monuments of culture have indeed been discarded. Art, then, that does not serve a purpose greater than being merely beautiful for its own sake will prove an evolutionary disadvantage.[95] The lack of a place for cultural memory in the Darwinian narrative

---

[93] Herbert Spencer, Letter IX, 'The Proper Sphere of Government', in *Political Writings*, ed. John Offer (Cambridge: Cambridge University Press, 1994), 1–57 (49).

[94] Pinker, *Language Instinct*, 199. See also Walter J. Ong, *Orality and Literacy: The Technologizing of the Word* (London: Routledge, 1988), 28–9, 171–2.

[95] The history of applying a Darwinian understanding to literary criticism is summarized in Joseph Carroll, *Literary Darwinism: Evolution, Human Nature, and Literature* (New York: Routledge, 2004), vii–xxii. See also John Holmes, 'Victorian Evolutionary Criticism and the Perils of Consilience', in *The Evolution of Literature: Legacies of Charles Darwin in*

of man's progression establishes the scientific grounds for Wells's attack on the canons of the purely aesthetic. In 1874, the future poet laureate Alfred Austin had wondered whether the reader should ask more of imaginative literature than only enjoyment, and feared that too many books now being published possessed too little value:

> We entertain the profoundest veneration for works of the imagination, and we hope we should be the last to under-estimate their value. But we venerate and value them on one condition: that they raise man not only from the slough of despond, but from the mire of selfish aims, of ignoble desires, cynical beliefs and purely material views of existence.[96]

Austin proposes semi-seriously that unless the quality of superabundant printed matter improves, man's future would be improved by printing being suspended for ten years:

> Let reading continue to be a part of his life, but a subsidiary part to thinking, seeing, observing, and energising. [...] That such reading as at present prevails has, by reason both of its quality and quantity, led to a deterioration of the human species, physically, mentally, and morally, we entertain no doubt; nor do we see how, unless the vicious habit be somehow corrected, the race can escape from being ultimately divided into two sections, the members of one of which will be little removed from invalids, and the members of the other scarcely distinguishable from *cretins*.[97]

Although it is hardly likely that the seven-year-old Wells had read it, Austin's prophecy presciently connects anxieties over mass literacy with fears of the kind of cultural apocalypse dramatized by *The Time Machine*.[98] The Time Traveller hopes to find a future library but the only books that still exist in 802,701 are found in (Jameson's term) the 'prophetic archaeology' of an abandoned museum alongside 'old

---

European Cultures, ed. Simon J. James and Nicholas Saul (Amsterdam: Rodopi, 2011, 101–12).

[96] Alfred Austin, 'The Vice of Reading', *Temple Bar*, 42 (1874), 251–7 (252).

[97] Ibid., 257.

[98] Wells revisits the issue of class and evolutionary degeneration in *The Soul of a Bishop* (1917): '"There's an incurable misunderstanding between the modern employer and the modern employed," the chief labour spokesman said, speaking in a broad accent that completely hid from him and the bishop and every one the fact that he was by far the best-read man of the party. "Disraeli called them the Two Nations, but that was long ago. Now it's a case of two species. Machinery has made them into different species. The employer lives away from his work-people, marries a wife foreign, out of a county family or suchlike, trains his children from their very birth in a different manner. Why, the growth curve is different for the two species. They haven't even a common speech between them. [...] We're the Morlocks. Coming up. It isn't our fault that we've differentiated."' *The Soul of a Bishop*, *Works*, XXV, 31–2. Cf. *Babes in the Darkling Wood*, 365.

Phoenician decorations' (*Time Machine*, ch. 4) and the relics of other extinct species who have also lost the struggle for existence.[99]

The identity of the Time Traveller himself also degenerates in the environment of a less complex social organization, becoming sufficiently decivilized to fight Morlocks and to deface a museum exhibit by writing his name on it.[100] A common axiom in late nineteenth-century adventure fiction is that the line between civilization and barbarism is much thinner than is commonly believed to be the case.[101] Wells finds the idea of throwing off the restraints of civilization powerfully appealing (the scientific romances are very fond of the adverb 'incontinently'), especially since his evolutionism makes no 'civilized' cultural prohibition indelibly taboo. In an essay written for the *Fortnightly Review* two years later, Wells would claim that:

Civilisation is not material. If, in a night, this artificial, this impalpable mental factor of every human being in the world could be destroyed, the day thereafter would dawn, indeed, upon our cities, our railways, our mighty weapons of warfare, and on our factories and machinery, but it would dawn no more upon a civilised world. And one has instead a grotesque picture of the suddenly barbaric people wandering out into the streets [. . .] turning their attention to such recondite weapons as a modern city affords—all for the loss of a few ideas and a subtle trick of thinking.[102]

Insisting on the need, therefore, for a 'real and conscious apparatus of education and modern suggestion', Wells argues that since morals are evolutionary, they have to alter over time. Wells's scientific romances evaluate culture and morals as a function of biology, only as enduring as biological reality will allow them to be. Matthew Arnold, in 'Dover Beach' (1867) had listened anxiously to the withdrawing roar of the 'Sea of Faith'.[103] The Time Traveller too, at the time of the end of life on

[99] Jameson, *Archaeologies*, 99. On the significance of this motif in science fiction, see Robert Crossley, 'In the Palace of Green Porcelain: Artefacts from the Museum of Science Fiction', in *Fictional Space: Essays on Contemporary Science Fiction*, ed. Tom Shippey (Oxford: Blackwell, 1991), 76–103.

[100] See Richard Pearson, 'Primitive Modernity: H. G. Wells and the Prehistoric Man of the 1890s', *Yearbook of English Studies*, 37/1 (2007), 58–74.

[101] Daniel Bivona, *Desire and Contradiction: Imperial Visions and Domestic Debates in Victorian Literature* (Manchester: Manchester University Press, 1990), 76–80. Cf. Wells's 1938 novella *The Croquet Player*, ed. John Hammond (Nottingham: Trent Editions, 1998), 40–1.

[102] 'Morals and Civilisation', *Fortnightly Review*, 61 (1897), 263–8, *Early Writings*, 220–8 (221).

[103] Matthew Arnold, 'Dover Beach,' *The Poems of Matthew Arnold*, ed. Kenneth Allott (London: Longman, 1965), 240–2.

earth, thousands of years after not only religion but also Arnold's vaunted panacea of culture have both long since withdrawn, listens to the sea:

> The machine was standing on a sloping beach. [...] There were no breakers and no waves, for not a breath of wind was stirring. Only a slight oily swell rose and fell like a gentle breathing, and showed that the eternal sea was still moving and living. (*Time Machine*, ch. 11)

Biology, the parent, must dominate over, and even ironize, culture.

THE SAVAGE IN PURSUIT OF THE TAME: *THE ISLAND OF DOCTOR MOREAU*

Early in his career, Wells tends to be pessimistic in his fiction and optimistic in his non-fiction (later, the tendency reverses).[104] Even the essays in *Select Conversations with an Uncle* (1895) and *Certain Personal Matters* (1897), which predate the more extended political work, tend to emphasize meliorations of the human condition, rather than warning of the ways in which it might decline; the latter begins with the words 'the world mends'.[105] *The Island of Doctor Moreau*, on the other hand, further blurs the barrier between civilization and barbarism by dissolving the barrier between the human and the animal. The story begins with a struggle for existence in the very narrowly circumscribed environment of a lifeboat, a struggle which has decivilized its inhabitants into threatened cannibalism. Like the Time Traveller, Prendick eventually reverts to savagery when his survival is threatened. (Also, like the Time Traveller, and Arnold's poetic persona, he is forced to confront the truth of the post-Darwinian nightmare he is inhabiting while standing on the liminal environment of a beach.)[106] A further similarity to the Time Traveller is Prendick's misapprehension of his own circumstances for much of his narration, and consequent self-criticism of his ability as a narrator: 'My inexperience as a writer betrays me, and I wander from the thread of my story' (*Moreau*, ch. 16). *The Island of Doctor Moreau* is also a story prefaced by a sceptical frame narrative, as if its assertions too are not necessarily to be believed, produced by someone reportedly delusional and now, following

---

[104] MacKenzie and MacKenzie, *Life of H. G. Wells*, 128–30; Wagar, *World State*, 76–87.

[105] 'Thoughts on Cheapness and My Aunt Charlotte', *Certain Personal Matters* (London: Fisher Unwin, 1901), 7–11 (7).

[106] See *The Science of Life*, II, 867; Crossley, 'Taking it as a Story', 24.

Prendick's death, absent from the world of the frame. The frame narrator indicates that there is no physical evidence to support the story other than the topography of the island, and that his uncle had previously claimed to have lost his memory after being shipwrecked.[107]

This text's concern with late-Victorian aesthetics is less immediately clear than *The Time Machine*'s, but rather surprisingly, in the 1924 Preface to the Atlantic Edition, Wells claimed that the novel had been inspired by 'a scandalous trial about that time, the graceless and pitiful downfall of a man of genius', usually presumed to be Oscar Wilde.[108] Wells might condemn the aesthete for his irresponsible pursuit of pleasure, but as a champion of sexual freedom, he would not do so for sexual transgression. If Montgomery is found reprehensible by the narrative, it is not for the unnamed, perhaps homosexual transgression that has exiled him from Victorian London, but for his drunkenness and self-pity. (The presence of a queer threat in the text, however, may linger in Prendick's incurious reluctance to hear the rest of Montgomery's story, and repulsion from Montgomery's uncanny relationship with M'Ling.) This book's irresponsible aesthete is in fact the Victor Hugo-quoting scientist Moreau, 'well known in scientific circles for his extraordinary imagination' (*Moreau*, ch. 7), who describes the human vivisection that was the Spanish Inquisition as 'artistic torture' (*Moreau*, ch. 14).[109]

Like the Artilleryman, Chaffery (*Love and Mr. Lewisham*) and Masterman (*Kipps*), Moreau is employed by Wells to articulate a transgressive point of view that is not necessarily advocated by the text itself.[110] Moreau claims, like a decadent aesthete, that pain and pleasure are merely relative, rather than absolute, states of being. Having realized this, he then experiments towards a higher evolutionary state beyond them: 'Pain and pleasure—they are for us, only so long as we wriggle in the dust' (*Moreau*, ch. 14).[111] The pursuit of pleasure and freedom from pain by the Eloi's

---

[107] This Preface does not appear in editions of the novel published later in Wells's life: see Patrick Parrinder, 'Note on the Text', xxx–xxxiv.

[108] *Works*, II, ix. Yoonjoung Choi has convincingly suggested *The Wonderful Visit* is also a response to the trials: '*The Wonderful Visit* and the Wilde Trial', *Wellsian*, 31 (2008), 43–55.

[109] Cyndy Hendershot, *The Animal Within: Masculinity and the Gothic* (Ann Arbor: University of Michigan Press, 1998), 132–4. Even the Time Traveller's choice of furnishings carries some suggestion of a louche decadence: see the opening of chapter 3.

[110] Bernard Loing, *H. G. Wells à L'Oeuvre: Les Débuts d'un Écrivain (1894–1900)* (Paris: Didier Erudition, 1984), 336.

[111] See 'The Province of Pain', *Science and Art*, 8 (1894), 58–9, *Early Writings*, 194–9. Cf. also: 'He had been always enthralled by the methods of natural science, but the ordinary subject-matter of that science had seemed to him trivial and of no import. And so he had begun by vivisecting himself, as he had ended by vivisecting others. Human life—that appeared to him the one thing worth investigating. Compared to it there was nothing else of

ancestors leads the Eloi into an evolutionary dead end.[112] Moreau, however, imagines an organism which is evolved past either pain or pleasure, beyond good and evil, towards evolutionary perfection, ignoring Huxley's adjuration in 'Evolution and Ethics' (1893) that it is man's ethical separation from the cosmic process which distinguishes him from other animals.[113] Here, the aesthetic—Moreau's egoistic quest for perfection—corrupts the scientific—the disinterested quest for knowledge. Moreau turns animals into humans, rather than conducting another kind of experiment, because 'there is something in the human form that appeals to the artistic turn of mind more powerfully than any animal shape can' (*Moreau*, ch. 14); the Beast People are described as 'strange creations of Moreau's art' (*Moreau*, ch. 15).[114] ('Nature's secrets betray themselves more through the vexations of art than they do in their usual course', rules Francis Bacon in the *Novum Organum*).[115] Had Moreau maintained a path of purer research, ideally for Wells, state-supervised in the Baconian manner, Moreau's self-confessedly arbitrary and capricious choice to mould animal clay into the shape of a man might have been corrected, and his gift put to more constructive use.[116] Instead, however, Moreau is, like Griffin (in *The Invisible Man*), and even perhaps the Time Traveller, a

any value. It was true that as one watched life in its curious crucible of pain and pleasure, one could not wear over one's face a mask of glass, nor keep the sulphurous fumes from troubling the brain and making the imagination turbid with monstrous fancies and misshapen dreams. [. . .] And, yet, what a great reward one received! How wonderful the whole world became to one! To note the curious hard logic of passion, and the emotional coloured life of the intellect—to observe where they met, and where they separated, at what point they were in unison, and at what point they were at discord—there was a delight in that! What matter what the cost was? One could never pay too high a price for any sensation.' Oscar Wilde, *The Complete Works of Oscar Wilde*, 4 vols, III: *The Picture of Dorian Gray: The 1890 and 1891 Texts*, ed. Joseph Bristow (Oxford: Clarendon Press, 2006), 218. See Glendening, 'Track of the Sphinx', 154–5. Cf. also *The Research Magnificent*, *Works*, XIX, 31–2.

[112] Cf. Antonio Damasio, *Descartes' Error: Emotion, Reason and the Human Brain* (London: Papermac, 1996), 264.

[113] T. H. Huxley, *Evolution and Ethics*, in *The Major Prose of T. H. Huxley*, ed. Alan P. Barr (Athens: University of Georgia Press, 1997), 309–44. For an account that portrays Wells as seeking to claim mastery of the cosmic process, and thus in opposition to Huxley, see Leon Stover, 'H. G. Wells, T. H. Huxley and Darwinism', in *H. G. Wells: Reality and Beyond: A Collection of Critical Essays Prepared in Conjunction with the Exhibition and Symposium on H.G. Wells*, ed. Michael Mullin (Champaign: Champaign Public Library and Information Center, 1986), 43–59. Cf. John S. Partington, *Building Cosmopolis: The Political Thought of H. G. Wells* (Aldershot: Ashgate, 2003), 30–1, 49–51 and *passim*.

[114] Haynes, *H. G. Wells*, 31.

[115] Francis Bacon, Aphorism 98, *The Instauratio Magna Part II: Novum Organum and Associated Texts*, ed. and trans. Graham Rees with Maria Wakely, The Oxford Francis Bacon XI (Oxford: Clarendon Press, 2004), 157. This aphorism has been mistranslated as Bacon's recommending that nature should be 'tortured'.

[116] *New Worlds for Old*, 23.

dangerous narcissist who perverts scientific discovery towards technological gratification of his own selfish desires.[117] (None of these scientists, or
Cavor in *The First Men in the Moon*, chooses to benefit humanity in
disseminating their specialist knowledge by publishing their discoveries.)

This romance is an island narrative, a genre that characteristically
dramatizes two different social modes. The island is both an imperial
space outside society where the colonizer can do anything they wish
without fear of retribution from society, and a Robinsonade in which
society is portrayed in microcosm, bringing 'at once the notion of solitude
and a founding population'.[118] (Robinson Crusoe is explicitly alluded to
when Prendick constructs a raft which is too heavy for him to drag to the
shore.)[119] Moreau is a neglectful and abusive father towards his grotesque
offspring, a capricious Prospero who brings into being both the subservi-
ent Ariel M'Ling and the murderous Caliban of the Leopard Man.[120]
Crusoe's island becomes a civilization when he gives Friday clothes and
begins, like Prospero, to teach his uncivilized protégé English. The means
of interpellating the Beast Folk away from anarchy and into a parodic
version of human society are similarly clothing and speech.[121] The larynx
and the opposable thumb, which give humanity spoken and written
language, are the token of humanity's separateness from animals and are
also the elements of human physiology that Moreau finds most difficult to
graft successfully onto animal bodies.[122] The philologist Max Müller had
ruled that:

No animal thinks, and no animal speaks, except man. Language and thought
are inseparable. Words without thought are dead sounds; thoughts without

---

[117] On Griffin's irresponsibility, see Robert Sirabian, 'The Conception of Science in
Wells's *The Invisible Man*', *Papers on Language and Literature*, 37/4 (2001), 383–403.

[118] Bergonzi, *Early H. G. Wells*, 99–100; Gillian Beer, 'Island Bounds', in *Islands in
History and Representation*, ed. Rod Edmond and Vanessa Smith (London: Routledge,
2003), 32–42 (33); Elaine Showalter, 'The Apocalyptic Fables of H. G. Wells,' in *Fin de
Siècle/Fin du Globe*, ed. John Stokes (Basingstoke: Macmillan, 1992), 69–84.

[119] On this romance's allusions, see Sherborne, *H. G. Wells*, 101.

[120] For animal representation indicating a reversion, both to childhood and to an earlier
stage of evolutionary development, see Steve Baker, 'Of Maus and More: Narrative,
Pleasure and Talking Animals', *Picturing the Beast: Animals, Identity and Representation*
(Manchester: Manchester University Press, 1993), 120–61. On *The Tempest*, Darwinism
and colonialism, see Trevor R. Griffiths, '"This Island's Mine": Caliban and Colonialism',
Yearbook of English Studies, 13 (1983), 159–80. In deleted typescript pages of the novel,
Moreau brings a wife and child to the island (Illinois Collection, ID 44, 90–1).

[121] Christine Ferguson, 'The Law and the Larynx: R. L. Garner: H. G. Wells, and the
Dehumanization of Language', *Language, Science and Popular Fiction in the Victorian Fin-
de-Siècle: The Brutal Tongue* (Aldershot: Ashgate, 2006), 105–30.

[122] Darwin, *Descent of Man*, 106.

words are nothing. To think is to speak low; to speak is to think aloud. The word is the thought incarnate.[123]

When Prendick mistakenly believes the puma's initially inarticulate, signification-free screams to be those of a human, he flees from the compound into the jungle. As the puma's larynx is forcibly adapted, Moreau's experiment undergoes a category shift: Prendick can tolerate 'vivisection' of an inarticulate animal but not 'torture' of a sentient being.[124] Moreau adopts a rigidly Social Darwinist position towards the ethics of these practices in which the higher forms of human social activity allow the

> possibility of superseding old inherent instincts by new suggestions, grafted upon or replacing the inherited fixed ideas. Very much indeed of what we call moral education, he said, is such an artificial modification and perversion of instinct; pugnacity is trained into courageous self-sacrifice, and suppressed sexuality into religious emotion. And the great difference between man and monkey is in the larynx, he said, in the incapacity to frame delicately different sound-symbols by which thought could be sustained. In this I failed to agree with him, but with a certain incivility he declined to notice my objection. (*Moreau*, ch. 14)

For Moreau, the fact that mental or cultural constructions such as 'moral education' (ch. 14) might have a physiological or material basis means that such constructions might be altered by scientific know-how or even sheer exertion of will. Prendick's 'objection' is on the grounds that implanting the physical capacity to use language does not implant the mental capacity to use it dynamically, any more than teaching a gorilla the alphabet makes it capable of becoming Shakespeare.[125] 'If a lion could talk, we would not understand him,' claims Wittgenstein in the *Philosophical Investigations*.[126] The Monkey Man later irritates Prendick with his 'idea [...] that to gabble about names that meant nothing was the proper use of speech' (*Moreau*, ch. 21). Nonetheless, as Prendick is confronted with so

---

[123] Müller, *Lectures*, I, 439. See Sylvia Hardy, '*The Time Machine* and Victorian Mythology', in *Perennial Time Machine*, ed. Slusser et al., 76–96; McLean, *Early Fiction*, 46–50.

[124] For a thoughtful discussion of the semantic difference, and of the place of Huxley in the novel, see Mason Harris, 'Vivisection, the Culture of Science, and Intellectual Uncertainty in *The Island of Doctor Moreau*', *Gothic Studies*, 4/2 (2002), 100–15. On language, power, and torture, see Elaine Scarry, *The Body in Pain: The Making and Unmaking of the World* (New York: Oxford University Press, 1985), 3–59, and Kimberly Jackson's thoughtful 'Vivisected Language in H. G. Wells's *The Island of Doctor Moreau*', in *H. G. Wells's Fin-de Siècle*, ed. Partington, 27–40.

[125] McLean, *Early Fiction*, 46–51.

[126] Ludwig Wittgenstein, *Philosophical Investigations*, trans. G. E. M. Anscombe (Oxford: Blackwell, 1967), 223.

many meaningless linguistic utterances, his view of language in the abstract inevitably becomes denatured: 'Can you imagine language, once clear-cut and exact, softening and guttering, losing shape and import, becoming mere lumps of sound again?' (*Moreau*, ch. 21). As Gillian Beer comments on Charles Kingsley's *The Water Babies* (1864), 'the loss of language is the final phase of degeneration'; once he has stopped privileging the evolutionary acquisition of language, Prendick ceases to perceive the division between humanity and other animals as one that is epistemologically valid.[127] Following his terrifying encounter with the abject, wandering through (in Julia Kristeva's phrase) the 'fragile states where man strays on the territory of *animal*', Prendick experiences a terrifying Swiftian defamiliarization of modern urban civilization:[128]

> When I lived in London the horror was well-nigh insupportable. I could not get away from men: their voices came through windows; locked doors were flimsy safeguards. I would go out into the streets to fight with my delusion, and prowling women would mew after me; furtive craving men glance jealously at me; weary, pale workers go coughing by me with tired eyes and eager paces, like wounded deer dripping blood; old people, bent and dull, pass murmuring to themselves; and all unheeding a ragged tail of gibing children. Then I would turn aside into some chapel,—and even there, such was my disturbance, it seemed that the preacher gibbered Big Thinks even as the Ape-man had done; or into some library, and there the intent faces over the books seemed but patient creatures waiting for prey. Particularly nauseous were the blank, expressionless faces of people in trains and omnibuses; they seemed no more my fellow-creatures than dead bodies would be, so that I did not dare to travel unless I was assured of being alone. And even it seemed that I too was not a reasonable creature, but only an animal tormented with some strange disorder in its brain which sent it to wander alone, like a sheep stricken with gid. (*Moreau*, ch. 22)

While this text blurs the biological division between man and beast, however, social divisions of class are strongly reinforced. Prendick's status as an independently wealthy gentleman is marked in the very first chapter, and he notes of Montgomery 'the singularity of an educated man living on this unknown little island' (*Moreau*, ch. 4). Although the education of all

[127] Gillian Beer, *Darwin's Plots: Evolutionary Narrative in Darwin, George Eliot, and Nineteenth-Century Fiction* (London: Routledge, 1983), 139.
[128] Julia Kristeva, *Powers of Horror: An Essay on Abjection*, trans. Leon S. Roudiez (New York: Columbia University Press, 1982), 12. See Nick Redfern, 'Abjection and Evolution in *The Island of Doctor Moreau*', in *H. G. Wells's Fin-de Siècle*, ed. Partington, 17–25, and David Hinckley, 'Surgical Evolution, or, The Scalpel as Shortcut: The Doctor as Interface between Science Fiction and Horror', in *No Cure for the Future: Disease and Medicine in Science Fiction and Fantasy*, ed. Gary Westfahl and George Slusser (Westport, CT: Greenwood Press, 2002), 83–94.

three main characters is in the sciences rather than the humanities, the only books on the island apart from 'surgical works' are 'editions of the Latin and Greek classics' (*Moreau*, ch. 7); perhaps the Satyr-man is a remnant of a classical memory in Moreau's imagination. These fail to provide the same consolation that the Bible does for Robinson Crusoe, and 'a crib of Horace' (*Moreau*, ch. 8) is not sufficiently compelling to distract Prendick from the puma's screams. In Robert Louis Stevenson's island-story *The Ebb Tide* (1894), public school and Oxbridge serve as a class bond between the washed-up Herrick and the island's tyrant Attwater, separating them from the dissolute drunken captain Davis and the bestial Huish. (Wells deliberately alludes to *The Ebb Tide* in naming the captain of the *Ipecacuanha* John Davies.)[129] In perhaps another conscious echo of Stevenson, when Montgomery wishes to speak to Prendick without the Beast People understanding, he does so in hybrid dog-Latin, as if, since it is not language, what might really separate humanity from animals is a classical education. Prendick's objection to the Beast Men as a 'Comus rout' (*Moreau*, ch. 11), and Montgomery's of the Satyr as an 'Ollendorffian beggar' (*Moreau*, ch. 16) show knowledge of literature and linguistics respectively to be not a dynamic and improving practice, but the means of maintaining power, allusion only serving the purpose of maintaining a cultural elite.[130]

Language and knowledge here too fail, however, when confronted with a modern horror for which Latin provides the etymology, but does not have a word itself, as Moreau tries to speak over the heads of the Beast Folk: '*Hi non sunt homines; sunt animalia qui nos habemus—*vivisected' (*Moreau*, ch. 13). Even science does not offer a satisfactory means of understanding: Prendick notes that his own 'litter of scientific education' (*Moreau*, ch. 21) is no help in devising a plan to escape from the island, and on returning to civilization finds some refuge in astronomy, a science far removed from human concerns such as language and culture.[131]

---

[129] Stephen Derry, '*The Island of Doctor Moreau* and Stevenson's *The Ebb Tide*', *Notes and Queries*, 43 (1996), 437.

[130] Gilbert Murray claims in a disputatious footnote in the *Outline of History* that 'as the Head Master told me, "A good man was rather laughed at if he didn't know Shakespeare and Milton."' *Outline*, II, 663. Cf. 'The underways had developed a dialect of their own: above, too, had arisen a dialect, a code of thought, a language of "culture," which aimed by a sedulous search after fresh distinction to widen perpetually the space between itself and "vulgarity."' 'A Story of the Days to Come' (1899), *Short Stories*, 333–98 (374).

[131] Parrinder, *Shadows*, 24.

ARMY OF ONE: *THE INVISIBLE MAN*

The primacy of science, and biology in particular, over language and culture is insisted on in Wells's work through the topos of the body. Repeatedly in Wells's work the body is an encumbrance, or a limitation on higher intellectual aspirations.

> I need freedom of mind. I want peace for work. I am distressed by immediate circumstances. My thoughts and work are encumbered by claims and vexations and I cannot see any hope of release from them, any hope of a period of serene and beneficent activity, before I am overtaken by infirmity and death. [...]
>   I am putting even the pretence of other work aside in an attempt to deal with this situation. I am writing a report about it—to my self. [...]
>   There is nothing I think very exceptional in my situation as a mental worker. Entanglement is our common lot.[132]

Yet release is never achieved—the reining-in of the ideal and the abstract by the material is a condition of human existence. Robert P. Weeks has noticed a recurring pattern in Wells's fiction of a short burst of freedom, followed by a sudden arresting of movement, what Wells himself calls a 'fugitive impulse'; usually the body is to blame for imposing material limits on the imagination.[133] In 'The Story of the Late Mr. Elvesham' (1896), an ageing magician seems to cheat death by swapping his own body for a younger one, but he is hit by a carriage and dies all the same. Lewisham is distracted from intellectual pursuits by biological urges for food, sleep, and sex; Ann Veronica on two occasions crowns her formulation of a plan that will rescue her life by falling immediately asleep; Mr Polly's development is inhibited by his physical and 'mental indigestion'; after becoming a tramp he stops to admire the sunset, but then feels the need for 'coarser aesthetic satisfactions [...] "Provinder [...] Cold sirloin for choice. And nutbrown brew and wheaten bread."'[134]

Wells asserts in *The Science of Life* that, 'Saint and sinner, plutocrat and proletarian, judge and criminal must all observe a similar round. All men

---

[132] *Autobiography*, I, 15.

[133] Ibid., I, 21; Robert P. Weeks, 'Disentanglement as a Theme in H. G. Wells's Fiction', in *H. G. Wells: A Collection of Critical Essays*, ed. Bergonzi, 25–31; see also Reed, *Natural History of H. G. Wells*, 15–28, 152–5.

[134] Kenneth B. Newell, *Structure in Four Novels by H. G. Wells* (The Hague: Mouton, 1968), 85; *The History of Mr. Polly*, ed. Simon J. James (Harmondsworth: Penguin, 2005), 189.

must eat. All the rest of their activities are secondary to this daily necessity.'[135] According to Darwin, also a notorious dyspeptic, 'that the state of the body by affecting the brain, has great influence on the moral tendencies is known to most of those who have suffered from chronic derangements of the digestion or liver'.[136] Hunger in particular is a recurrent reminder of embodiment in Wells: texts from *Doctor Moreau* to *Lewisham* to *Mr. Polly* to *William Clissold* to the *Autobiography* warn of the unreliability of judgements made when the brain is distracted by the rest of the body: 'one may argue that a conviction of reality which is so finely poised that it totters at a light excess or defect of oxygen or suchlike factor in the blood cannot be a very soundly established one'.[137]

Griffin dreams of a bodiless existence as pure mental abstraction, but the plot of *The Invisible Man* dismantles such narcissistic and Nietzschean delusions by refuting them thus on his own body. The would-be superman proves instead to be Faust.[138] Griffin's megalomaniacal plans of world domination are compromised by his simple needs to eat, sleep, and protect himself from the British climate; the appearance of his blood is a reminder of his body's fissibility.[139] Griffin is still subject both to power and to the laws of physical science, in particular to time (this text pays detailed, if not always consistent, attention to clocks and to telling the time). Griffin's invisibility is compromised shortly after mealtimes as unmetabolized food in his stomach is still visible; thus he has to disguise his invisible body as a visible one in order to survive.

The sergeant who attempts to arrest Griffin argues that since the warrant includes the word 'body', he is still subject to law even while invisible. Griffin is surprised at how circumscribed his freedom of action is by the crowds of the city—but the experience of feeling oneself socially unrecognized and physically oppressed in London is hardly unusual for a central character in Victorian fiction, even for an invisible man.

"The more I thought it over, Kemp, the more I realised what a helpless absurdity an Invisible Man was—in a cold and dirty climate and a crowded

---

[135] *The Science of Life*, I, 26. On Wells and food, see 'The Edible Predator', Kemp, *H. G. Wells and the Culminating Ape*, 7–72.

[136] Darwin, *Descent of Man*, 148. On indigestion, see *The Science of Life*, I, 118; 'Drawn from Life?: Famous Characters in Modern Fiction and How They Were Conceived: H. G. Wells and *Mr. Polly*', *Strand*, 76 (1928), 595–6; Wells, Foreword to Brian Ború Dunne, *Cured! The 70 Adventures of a Dyspeptic* (Philadelphia: Wonston, 1937), 9. Cf. *Correspondence*, I, 99.

[137] *The World of William Clissold; A Novel from a New Angle* (London: Ernest Benn, 1926), 29.

[138] Robert Philmus, *Into the Unknown: The Evolution of Science Fiction from Francis Godwin to H. G. Wells* (Berkeley: University of California Press, 1970), 100.

[139] See Laura Otis, *Membranes: Metaphors of Invasion in Nineteenth-Century Literature, Science, and Politics* (Baltimore: Johns Hopkins University Press, 1999).

civilized city. Before I made this mad experiment I had dreamt of a thousand advantages. That afternoon it seemed all disappointment. I went over the heads of the things a man reckons desirable. No doubt invisibility made it possible to get them, but it made it impossible to enjoy them when they are got." (*Invisible Man*, ch. 23)

'"An invisible man is a man of power"' (*Invisible Man*, ch. 9) he warns Marvel, but also complains, '"what is the good of pride of place when you cannot appear there?"' (*Invisible Man*, ch. 23). Griffin errs in supposing that since his body evades scrutiny by society, he therefore becomes an autonomous subject. As long as Griffin has money, he manages to be independent from society, remaining unseen by not leaving his rented room. When Griffin begins to rob the villages outside Iping, onlookers seem to see money floating in mid-air (a strikingly Marxist image of capital's independent agency).[140] Lacking money, Griffin needs to go out again, not into the anonymity of the city, or the natural world that is so indifferent to his comfort, but the 'knowable community' of a country village, where he cannot do without the legible social body that is provided by clothing.[141]

In *The Wheels of Chance*, published in the same year as *The Invisible Man*, as well as in *Love and Mr. Lewisham* and *Kipps*, Wells's narrator pays great attention to the signification produced by clothing, and to how this process of signification can be altered by money (see next chapter). In *The Invisible Man*, without the signifiers of social being produced by clothing, Griffin's body only exists as a set of needs without the means of fulfilling them. He mistakenly believes that he is able to escape the reality of his body by making it impervious to public scrutiny. Slavoj Žižek has playfully suggested that 'vampires are invisible in the mirror [. . .] because they have read Lacan and, consequently, know how to behave', thus avoiding the painful separation of the psyche into ego and id.[142] Griffin undergoes a reverse of Lacan's 'mirror stage' when he contemplates his own reflection in a looking glass and disappears from view, as if the invisibility of his body will liberate him from psychic crisis.[143] (In a book of only forty-eight thousand words, the word 'glass' occurs over sixty times.) No longer

---

[140] Paul A. Cantor, '*The Invisible Man* and the Invisible Hand: H. G. Wells's Critique of Capitalism', *American Scholar*, 68/3 (1999), 89–102.

[141] Raymond Williams, *The Country and the City* (London: Hogarth Press, 1993), 165–81; McConnell, *Science Fiction*, 114–15.

[142] Slavoj Žižek, *Enjoy your Symptom! Jacques Lacan in Hollywood and Out*, rev. edn (New York: Routledge, 2001), 126.

[143] Jacques Lacan, 'The Mirror Stage as Formative as the Function of the *I* as Revealed in Psychoanalytic Experience', in *Écrits: A Selection*, trans. Alan Sheridan (London: Routledge, 2001), 1–8.

subject to the gaze of others, Griffin loses the restraint of first his superego, and then his ego, becoming only id, a being, according to Kemp, of 'pure selfishness' (*Invisible Man*, ch. 25) who 'has cut himself off from his kind' (*Invisible Man*, ch. 25) and from 'the common conventions of humanity' (*Invisible Man*, ch. 23).[144] The tropes of psychoanalysis are indeed more prominent in this than other Wells texts: Griffin's first theft results in his father's death, and a dream subsequently torments him with Oedipal guilt.[145] After the stranger's first mysterious appearance in Iping, Mrs Hall dreams of the *corps morcelé* of a disembodied head. Griffin echoes a crime committed by late Victorian fiction's most prominent allegory of the unconscious, Mr Hyde, when he too murders a saintly looking stranger and splinters his (phallic) walking stick in two.[146] Lacking an ego, Griffin is thus unrepressed and so prone to limitless acquisitiveness and to anger. He is also free from shame or self-censorship, when talking to himself or when making a confession to Kemp that makes no effort to expiate or justify his crimes. 'Being transparent, of course, he couldn't avoid telling the truth', rules the narrator Clayton of the subject of Wells's short story 'The Inexperienced Ghost' (1902): the same is true of this invisible man.[147] When remembering his journey, Griffin even seems to observe himself from outside: 'I remember myself as a gaunt black figure, going along the slippery, shiny pavement, and the strange sense of detachment I felt from the squalid respectability, the sordid commercialism of the place' (*Invisible Man*, ch. 20).

Griffin has not escaped the reality of his body, only its visible signifiers: after becoming invisible, his first destination is the department store Omnium, which promises the gratification of every consuming desire.[148] In such a spectacle of potential consumption, however, even an invisible man is subject to scrutiny, and the unsuccessful experiment in the

---

[144] Williams, *Country and the City*, 54.

[145] Kathryn Hume, 'Eat or Be Eaten: H. G. Wells's *The Time Machine*', *Philological Quarterly*, 69/2 (1990), 233–51 (243). On Wells and dreams, see Smith, *Desperately Mortal*, 34–5; for an acute psychoanalytic reading of the scientific romances, see Kirby Farrell, 'Traumatic Prophecy: H. G. Wells at the End of Time', *Post-Traumatic Culture: Injury and Interpretation in the Nineties* (Baltimore: Johns Hopkins University Press, 1998), 105–38.

[146] Bergonzi, *Early H. G. Wells*, 20; McLean, *Early Fiction*, 84. In the typescript of *The Island of Doctor Moreau*, Prendick tells Mrs Moreau, who is hungry for talk of new books and plays, about *Dr Jekyll and Mr Hyde* while her son kills flies (Illinois Collection, ID-45). A letter to J. B. Pinker, Wells's agent, of 16 April 1896 suggests that the *Invisible Man* was conceived as a horror story on the model of *Jekyll and Hyde* (Illinois Collection).

[147] *Short Stories*, 467–76 (471). On the uncanny effect of voice without presence, see throughout Connor, *Dumbstruck*.

[148] On lines of sight and consumerist desire in the department store, see Rachel Bowlby, *Just Looking: Consumer Culture in Dreiser, Gissing and Zola* (London: Methuen, 1985).

department store is followed by Griffin's robbery of a theatrical costumiers, as if, since identity cannot be physically produced, it might at least be temporarily staged. Ultimately, however, as in the endings of so many Victorian narratives from *Great Expectations* to *Lady Audley's Secret* to many Sherlock Holmes cases, the narrative's ending stages the stripping away of a masqueraded identity. The reincorporation of Griffin's body is not technically necessary, but thematically appropriate. Subject again to vision, Griffin's body is shown as subject to knowledge, and to power:

> And so, slowly, beginning at his hands and feet and creeping along his limbs to the vital centres of his body, that strange change continued. It was like the slow spreading of a poison. First came the little white nerves, a hazy grey sketch of a limb, then the glassy bones and intricate arteries, then the flesh and skin, first a faint fogginess and then growing rapidly dense and opaque. Presently they could see his crushed chest and his shoulders, and the dim outline of his drawn and battered features.
>
> When at last the crowd made way for Kemp to stand erect, there lay, naked and pitiful on the ground, the bruised and broken body of a young man about thirty. His hair and beard were white—not grey with age but white with the whiteness of albinism, and his eyes were like garnets. His hands were clenched, his eyes wide open, and his expression was one of anger and dismay. (*Invisible Man*, ch. 28)

This is not, however, the final image of the novel. Wells's scientific romances often close with an image of unintelligibility: Weena's flower in *The Time Machine*, unclassifiable within any known 'natural order' (*Time Machine*, ch. 12), Prendick's unprovable confession in an unverifiable posthumous manuscript, science's bafflement by the remains of the Martians, Cavor's barely intelligible broadcasts from the moon.[149] Griffin's notebooks, illegible to Marvel, survive him, 'weather-worn and tinged with an algal green—for once they sojourned in a ditch and some of the pages have been washed blank by dirty water' (*Invisible Man*, Epilogue). This text's narrator suggests that the events of the plot have, like historical time in Lyell and Darwin's book of nature, partially erased the 'true' secret of invisibility. Like the Time Traveller's audience and Carlyle's academician, the readers of this text within a text lack the correct education, classical or scientific, to read it correctly:

"I'm—dear me! It's all cypher, Bunting."

"There are no diagrams?" asked Mr. Bunting. "No illustrations throwing light—"

---

[149] See also *All Aboard for Ararat* (London: Secker & Warburg, 1940), 99.

"See for yourself," said Mr. Cuss. "Some of it's mathematical and some of it's Russian or some such language (to judge by the letters), and some of it's Greek. Now the Greek I thought *you*—"

"Of course," said Mr. Bunting, taking out and wiping his spectacle and feeling suddenly very uncomfortable—for he had no Greek left in his mind worth talking about; "yes—the Greek, of course, may furnish a clue." (*Invisible Man*, ch. 11)

The Invisible Man also manifests itself as a partial document, Griffin's invisibility allowing Wells again to test the limits of the language available for describing the fantastic. The coach driver Hall's 'vocabulary [is] altogether too limited to express his impressions' (*Invisible Man*, ch. 3): so is that of the story's narrator, whose account is in places again deliberately partial: it is 'impossible to give a consecutive account of affairs in Iping' (*Invisible Man*, ch. 12). The narrator imagines 'a curious listener' (*Invisible Man*, ch. 1) trying and failing to observe Griffin; rather than trying to focalize the narration more closely around someone who can't be seen, the narrative withholds knowledge of what is actually occurring. The narration cannot be omniscient, for in parts of the plot there is nothing to see. As with the biology of *The Time Machine* and of *The Island of Doctor Moreau* (although not the temporal physics of the former), the text's scientific explanation for its fantastic manifestations is suspended rather than provided straightaway, experience again a priori to the language available to describe it. This romance's other characters of the novel unsurprisingly fail to grasp the reality of what they are experiencing: as in *The Wonderful Visit*, even the professional discourses of the lawyer, the doctor, and the scientist only succeed in grasping a fragment of the truth.[150] The structuralist critic Tsvetan Todorov has argued that critics must 'disengage language from its illusory transparence, learn to perceive it, and at the same time study its techniques of disappearing—like Wells's invisible man swallowing his chemical formula—before our eyes'.[151] Such is the sequence of Wells's narrative evasions; *The Invisible Man*, and the other scientific romances, can never be fully seen through.

---

[150] Choi, '*Wonderful Visit*', 46.
[151] Tsvetan Todorov, 'An Introduction to Verisimilitude', *The Poetics of Prose*, trans. Richard Howard (Oxford: Blackwell, 1977), 80–8 (81).

3

The Uses of Literacy

Reading and Realism in Wells's Novels

> I have heard affirmed (surely in jest) [. . .] by not unphilanthropic persons, that it were a real increase of human happiness, could all young men from the age of nineteen be covered under barrels, or rendered otherwise invisible; and there left to follow their lawful studies and callings, till they emerged, sadder and wiser, at the age of twenty-five. (Thomas Carlyle, *Sartor Resartus*)[1]

Wells's imaginings of both fantastic and utopian futures engage with the forces that shape identity and civilization in the present: education, class, money, gender, literacy. Writing realist fiction, Wells attempts to show that the identities created by such forces are not irreversible but contingent, subject to history: that if the nature of these operant forces can be altered, so might the kind of subjectivities that they produce. Characters in Wells's earlier realist and comic texts (in the genres that Northrop Frye collocated as the 'low mimetic') are all seeking to obey the biological imperative to develop, for their identities to be something more than they are at present.[2] The genre which the heroes are unfortunate enough to inhabit, however, forbids either fantastic or utopian routes for further progression. Wells's realist fiction's mimesis of failure constitutes the interrogation of a problem, the proposed solution to which is found elsewhere, in his political writing. *Mankind in the Making*, a utopian text that seeks in real life to redress the inequalities dramatized in the novels, makes an eloquent plea on behalf of the kind of frustrated individualities dramatized by the novels:

> These poor little souls are born, amidst tears and suffering they gain such love as they may, they learn to feel and suffer, they struggle and cry for food,

---

[1] Carlyle, *Sartor Resartus*, 97.
[2] Northrop Frye, *Anatomy of Criticism: Four Essays* (Princeton, NJ: Princeton University Press, 1971), 151–5.

for air, for the right to develop; and our civilization at present has neither the courage to kill them outright quickly, cleanly, and painlessly, nor the heart and courage and ability to give them what they need. [...] They fight their pitiful little battle for life against the cruellest odds; and they are beaten. (*Mankind in the Making*, ch. 3)

Franco Moretti has condemned the English *Bildungsroman* for the stress it lays upon conformity to a social ideal, for rewarding not singularity but obedience.[3] Wells inverts the genre's emphasis. Instead of the hero's wayward desires being corrected by a more morally clear-sighted world, the insufficient world is instead blamed for not fulfilling the more laudable of those desires.[4]

FIN-DE-CYCLE: *THE WHEELS OF CHANCE*

In his Preface to the 1925 Atlantic Edition of *The Wheels of Chance*, Wells describes the book as one of a 'series of close studies in personality', adding Lewisham, Kipps, Mr Polly, and Ann Veronica as further examples of 'personalities thwarted by the defects of our contemporary civilisation'; in the *Autobiography*, they are described as 'caricature-individualities'.[5] The protagonists are less frequently representative types than singular individuals, distinguished by an imaginative longing for something higher, those on whom the success of future civilization ought to depend. '"Yet I'm not such muck that I might not have been better—with teaching"' complains Hoopdriver. '"If I'd been exercised properly, if I'd been fed reasonable, if I hadn't been shoved out of a silly school into a silly shop"' (*The Wheels of Chance*, ch. 26, ch. 27).[6] The *Autobiography* hopes that 'in the course of a few decades [such characters] may become incomprehensible' to readers who inhabit a civilization that is now organized in a better and fairer way.[7]

The narrators of Wells's realist novels right up to *You Can't Be Too Careful* (1942) frequently emphasize the youth of the protagonists: both narrator and implied reader have achieved the maturity and education not yet achieved by the central character.[8] The Atlantic Preface to *The Wheels*

---

[3] Franco Moretti, *The Way of the World: The* Bildungsroman *in European Culture* (London: Verso, 1987), 207–11.

[4] Wells wrote to his agent J. B. Pinker that *Kipps* would be 'the complete study of a life in relation to English social conditions full of humour and subtle observations'. Letter to Pinker of 24 November 1903 (Illinois Collection).

[5] *The Wheels of Chance: A Holiday Adventure*, *Works*, VII, ix; *Autobiography*, 499.

[6] *The Wheels of Chance: A Holiday Adventure* (London: Dent, 1896), 171, 111.

[7] *Autobiography*, II, 499.

[8] Parrinder, *H. G. Wells*, 54.

of Chance adds that, 'it is a very "young" book; indeed, in some respects it is puerile, but the character of Hoopdriver saves it from being altogether insignificant'.[9] *Love and Mr. Lewisham* is subtitled *The Story of a Very Young Couple* ('The Story of an Adolescence' in the manuscript).[10] At the beginning of *Love and Mr. Lewisham*, the hero is barely distinguishable physically from the boys whom he teaches; by the end, 'the enormous seriousness of adolescence was coming to an end; the days of his growing were numbered' (*Lewisham*, ch. 30). In Wells's hands, the *Bildungsroman* genre is informed by a very specific programme about exactly what kind of 'education' is appropriate for its protagonist. Late nineteenth-century literary realism often chooses to dramatize the forming of character by environment, and Wells frequently shows the childhood and early education of his protagonists in detail.[11] *The History of Mr. Polly*, for instance, moves analeptically from the impending financial insolvency that even the hero's inadequate schooling cannot quite prevent him from foreseeing—'the absence of book-keeping and a total inability to distinguish between capital and interest could not blind him for ever to the fact that the little shop in the High Street was not paying'—back to an idyllic childhood state 'when two people had thought Mr. Polly the most wonderful thing in the world', thence to a detailed description of his poor education (*Polly*, ch. 1, ch. 2).[12] Poor education fails to satisfy intellect or imagination, so Polly becomes an autodidact:

> He began to read stories voraciously, and books of travel, provided they were also adventurous. He got these chiefly from the local institute, and he also "took in," irregularly but thoroughly, one of those inspiring weeklies that dull people used to call "penny dreadfuls," admirable weeklies crammed with imagination that the cheap boys' "comics" of to-day have replaced. At fourteen, when he emerged from the valley of the shadow of education, there survived something, indeed it survived still, obscured and thwarted, at five and thirty, that pointed [...] to the idea that there was interest and happiness in the world. Deep in the being of Mr. Polly, deep in that darkness, like a creature which has been beaten about the head and left for dead but still lives, crawled a persuasion that over and above the things that are jolly and "bits of all right," there was beauty, there was delight. (*Polly*, ch. 2)

---

[9] *The Wheels of Chance, Works*, VII, ix.

[10] Illinois LL-1b-102.

[11] See Simon J. James, 'Realism and the Fiction of Modern Life: From Meredith to Forster', in *The Oxford History of the Novel*, vol. IV: *The Reinvention of the British Novel, 1880–1940*, ed. Patrick Parrinder and Andrzej Gasiorek, 87–102.

[12] A deleted passage in the manuscript reads: 'A mind can be hurt just as much as it can be helped in a school. If minds were invincible to schools there would be no need to send them there' (Illinois Collection, HP-43).

While Polly does, unusually, achieve an ultimately happy ending, his taste for reading proves to have been a wrong turn on the road towards the Potwell Inn, if anything a distraction from the satisfaction of his bucolic desires. The contrast here between Polly's and the narrator's more Arnoldian vocabularies exposes the yawning gulf between culture's mission and its actual achievement by the Edwardian era.[13]

Often in Wells's realist fiction, the author's antagonism towards a notion of disinterested high culture that Wells sees as backward-looking and harmful is expressed in a satire of the practice of reading itself, in particular the reading of fiction. Hoopdriver and Jessie in *The Wheels of Chance*, Adeline Glendower in *The Sea Lady*, Muriel in *The Wealth of Mr. Waddy* (an early version of *Kipps*), and Lady Laxton in *Bealby* (1915) are afflicted by delusory, *Bovaryste* expectations acquired from reading the wrong kinds of stories.[14] Like Mr Polly, Hoopdriver has juvenile taste in reading matter and fantasizes about the 'gallant rescue of generalised beauty in distress from truculent insult or ravening dog' (*Polly*, ch. 10); as in the later novel, the fantasy is temporarily indulged but ultimately satirized, and he ends up using imaginary dogs only to escape from embarrassing social situations. Jessie Milton's misguided plan for imaginative self-determination is inspired by a naïve reading of novels by George Egerton, Eliza Lynn Linton, Olive Schreiner, and her own stepmother. The narrator imagines her as a *tabula rasa* defaced by cheap popular fiction, her 'motives [. . .] bookish, written by a haphazard syndicate of authors, novelists, biographers, on her white inexperience' (*Wheels of Chance*, ch. 16); the narrator's ironic orthography mocks Jessie's stereotyped desire '"to write Books and alter things [. . .] to lead a Free Life and Own myself"' (ch. 18). In the world of Wells's realist fiction, such fictions must not be confused with 'real life'. Hoopdriver's rescue of Jessie takes place in an imagined pastiche of the 'world of Romance and Knight-errantry' (*Wheels of Chance*, ch. 22), derived from 'Doctor Conan Doyle, Victor Hugo, and Alexander Dumas' (*Wheels of Chance*, ch. 17), Walter Besant, Mrs Braddon, Rider Haggard, Marie Corelli, and Ouida.[15]

[13] In the typescript of *The Wealth of Mr. Waddy*, Kipps is more explicit in outlining to Ethel his desire for education: '"I don't mean not about pictures and great authors and artis, and Walter Crane and Ruskin and 'Omer and all that. What makes people think their selves superior to other people, and nothin' else, Ann. I mean learning to think without gettin' muddley like I do when I try and think"' (Illinois Collection, WW-30).

[14] Cf. *Anticipations*, 106.

[15] The language of medieval romance is often used by Wells to characterize erotic attachments: the TS of *Love and Mr. Lewisham* includes a deleted passage which describes Lewisham's devotion to Ethel as 'Knight Errantry of the purest description' (Illinois Collection, LL-397).

(Wells often uses images from cod-medieval romance when describing a lofty over-elevation of the erotic.)[16] The rascally seducer Bechamel attempts, like Manning in *Ann Veronica* (1909), to seduce with talk of 'art and literature' (*Wheels of Chance*, ch. 24).

Although books even by high-cultural authors such as Emerson and the historian J. R. Motley also fail to provide a means of making experience intelligible, Wells's main target in *The Wheels of Chance* is the stereotyping and cheap appeal of popular fiction. As noted previously, Wells usually sees romance as an innately conservative genre. The imaginations of the mass reading public only turn to romance out of dissatisfaction with the real world; romance cheaply amuses, sapping the desire to make the real world better instead.[17]

> The apprentice is nearer the long, long thoughts of boyhood, and his imagination rides *cap-à-pie* through the chambers of his brain, seeking some knightly quest in honour of that Fair Lady, the last but one of the girl apprentices to the dress-making upstairs. He inclines rather to street fighting against revolutionaries—because then she could see him from the window. (*Wheels of Chance*, ch. 2)

Wells's romance writing, on the other hand, seeks to inspire its reader to fight alongside, rather than against, revolutionaries.

Not having been properly educated by the right kind of reading matter, the text's characters are persistently misled by sexual desire and by the misleading clichés of romance. Wells's fondness for the metaphor of knowledge as light is given literal substance in *The Wheels of Chance* in the opposition between deceptive, romantic moonlight and the revealing light of day.

> There is a magic quality in moonshine; it touches all that is sweet and beautiful, and the rest of the night is hidden. [...] The firm substantial daylight things become ghostly and elusive. [...]
>
> Nowhere was the moon shining quite so brightly as in Mr. Hoopdriver's skull. (*Wheels of Chance*, ch. 24)

Romantic moonlight produces 'moonshine', the blurring of things as they really are ('appearance without substance; something unsubstantial or unreal; esp. foolish or fanciful talk, ideas, plans, etc.' (*OED* 2a)—the sense in which Wells uses the word in subtitling *The Sea Lady*). In the light of more accurate self-knowledge, such pseudo-lyrical delusions are revealed for what they really are. ' "Beastly cheap, after all, this suit

[16] *The Wheels of Chance* (London: Dent, 1896).

[17] For an influential case against popular culture along such lines, see Theodor W. Adorno and Max Horkheimer, 'The Culture Industry: Enlightenment as Mass Deception', in *Dialectic of Enlightenment*, trans. John Cumming (London: Verso, 1997), 120–67.

does look, in the sunshine"' (*Wheels of Chance*, ch. 27) muses Hoopdriver
when his romantic fantasy of a new suit making him look an aristocrat is
finally deflated.

Hoopdriver's guidebook informs him that Guildford is the setting for
Martin Tupper's historical romance *Stephan Langton* (1858), in which the
low-born hero saves a maiden from villainous noblemen. The narrator of
this text claims the authority of fact for showing familiar and unexciting
Surrey as home to stirring historical incidents, even 'romantic biography':

> I will concentrate my pictured fancies in a framework of real scenery round
> characters of strict historic fame. [. . .] I will set before your patience rather
> reality than romance, drawing both landscapes and persons from the truth.
> [. . .] It may be possible [. . .] to make classic ground of certain sweet retired
> spots set among the fairest hill and vale county in South England [. . .] to
> invest familiar Surrey scenes [. . .] with their due historic interest; [. . .] to
> connect for your better entertainment our evident modern scenes (changed
> belike in such accidental features as culture brings about, yet substantially the
> same as to geography) with antique but actual incidents.[18]

In Wells's text, the mapping of romance on to the landscape is not
underwritten by history, but instead ironized by the humdrum nature of
reality.[19] Hoopdriver fantasizes about 'pedalling Ezekiel's Wheels across
the Weald of Surrey, jolting over the hills and smashing villages in his
course' (*Wheels of Chance*, ch. 12), but he would need Martian technology
actually to do so.[20] In contrast to Tupper's assertion that romance might
have occurred in the same place as contemporary life, here reality keeps
intruding into fantasy through reminders of the limits imposed on the
romantic imagination: by the body, by class, and by money, or rather
its lack.

The Wheels of Chance's generic dissonance is generated by the variations
in its tone, especially that of the archly self-conscious narrator, who
repeatedly deflates the central characters' aspirations to be respectively
the all-conquering hero of a romance and the independent heroine of a
New Woman novel.[21] The narrator's vision is limited, and he is alternately outside and inside the plot, occasionally present as a character, like a
Thackeray narrator. He is overt that he is relating a story—pleading that
'these things take so long in the telling' (*Wheels of Chance*, ch. 4)—and
repeatedly calls attention to Hoopdriver's misreading of his own plot.

---

[18] Martin Tupper, *Stephan Langton*, 2 vols (London: Hurst and Blacket, [1858]), I, 2–6.
[19] On topography and imaginary destruction, see MacKenzie and MacKenzie, *Life of
H. G. Wells*, 28.
[20] Cf. *Autobiography*, 101.
[21] Reed, *Natural History of H. G. Wells*, 211.

You must not think that there was any telling of these stories of this life-long series by Mr. Hoopdriver. He never dreamt that they were known to a soul. If it were not for the trouble, I would, I think, go back and rewrite this section from the beginning, expunging the statements that Hoopdriver was a poet and a romancer, and saying instead that he was a playwright and acted his own plays. He was not only the sole performer, but the entire audience, and the entertainment kept him almost continuously happy. Yet even that playwright comparison scarcely expresses all the facts of the case. After all, very many of his dreams never got acted at all, possibly indeed, most of them, the dreams of a solitary walk for instance, or of a tramcar ride, the dreams dreamt behind the counter while trade was slack and mechanical foldings and rollings occupied his muscles. (*Wheels of Chance*, ch. 10)

Romance traditionally privileges the singularity of its protagonist: this narrator ironically contrasts his hero's external appearance of ordinariness with his internal imaginary heroism:

Like I know not how many of those who do the fetching and carrying of life [...] his real life was absolutely uninteresting, and if he had faced it as realistically as such people do in Mr. Gissing's novels, he would probably have come by way of drink to suicide in the course of a year. But that was just what he had the natural wisdom not to do. On the contrary, he was always decorating his existence with imaginative tags, hopes, and poses, deliberate and yet quite effectual self-deceptions; his experiences were mere material for a romantic superstructure. [...] His entire life, you must understand, was not a continuous romance, but a series of short stories. (*Wheels of Chance*, ch. 10)[22]

If Hoopdriver were the hero of a naturalist novel (a school of which, somewhat unfairly, Gissing is the representative), his identity would be determined entirely by his circumstances. Once those circumstances had been observed he would be entirely predictable, and would thus fail to surprise the reader. However, if the real world might limit Hoopdriver, he can at least privately escape its determinations within his imagination. Although Wells may disapprove of late-Victorian romance in its most formulaic expressions, and even though the protagonist's imaginative liberty may be curtailed by poverty both financial and educational, that Hoopdriver might possess such an imagination at all, and its playful mental exploration of romance freedoms, demonstrates a distinct individuality beyond his apparent ordinariness.

---

[22] Cf. also Wells's much later essay 'The Illusion of Personality', *Nature*, 1 April 1944, *H. G. Wells in 'Nature', 1893–1946: A Reception Reader*, ed. John S. Partington (Frankfurt: Lang, 2008), 139–47.

The Wheels of Chance both employs and mocks the certainties of the late nineteenth-century literary naturalist, certainties that claim their epistemological certainty from the methods of scientific enquiry.[23] The opening apes realism's presentation of outward surfaces ('nothing can be further from the author's ambition than a wanton realism', the narrator later avers, ch. 7) and the codes that may be read from them:

> If you (presuming you are of the sex that does such things)—if you had gone into the Drapery Emporium—[...] you might have been served by the central figure of this story that is now beginning. [...] Under which happier circumstances you might—if of an observing turn of mind and not too much of a housewife to be inhuman—have given the central figure of this story less cursory attention.

The narrator indicates how nondescript Hoopdriver's appearance and speech seem to be, but then claims how misleading such conclusions might be:

> But real literature, as distinguished from anecdote, does not concern itself with superficial appearances alone. Literature is revelation. Modern literature is indecorous revelation. It is the duty of the earnest author to tell you what you would not have seen. (*Wheels of Chance*, ch. 1)

The opening pretends to dramatize a process of scientific induction: because Hoopdriver is perceived as a shop assistant, he is expected to behave in a certain way. Such inductive certainty is limited by observation and experience, however, and Wells's implied reader, here assumed to be female and of the leisured shopping class, has paid insufficient attention beyond the limits of the counter for any such inductive judgement to be reliable. Karl Popper demonstrated in 1934 the weakness of the inductive method: 'no matter how many instances of white swans we have observed, this does not justify the conclusion that *all* swans are white'.[24] While Hoopdriver may be perceived as unremarkable, this does not preclude him in the future from doing, or at least dreaming of doing, remarkable things.

The opening chapter alludes to late-Victorian realism's outstanding exponent of this technique of inductive observation, Sherlock Holmes. Holmes's 'method' depends on all individual members of a certain category behaving in an identical way.[25] Recent critical tradition has tended to

---

[23] See, for instance, Emile Zola's much-quoted 'The Experimental Novel' (1880), collected in *Documents of Modern Literary Realism*, ed. George J. Becker (Princeton: Princeton University Press, 1963), 162–96.

[24] Karl Popper, *The Logic of Scientific Discovery* (London: Hutchinson, 1959), 27. Cf. Sidgwick, *Use of Words*, 44.

[25] Rosemary Jann, 'Sherlock Holmes Codes the Social Body', *English Literature in Transition 1880–1920*, 57 (1990), 685–708.

read Holmes as a force for social order and thus, like romance in Wells's estimation, ultimately a maintainer of the status quo.[26] Hoopdriver's presentation as an identifiable 'type' is thus ironic. In 'The Novel of Types' (1896), Wells argues that typology in fiction should still have the capacity to accommodate individuality:

> The peculiar characteristic of Turgenev's genius is the extraordinary way in which he can make his characters typical, while at the same time retaining their individuality. [...] Turgenev people are not avatars of theories nor tendencies. They are living, breathing individuals living under the full stress of this social force or that.[27]

Mrs Milton's aestheticist suitors are mocked for their reversal of this dictum:

> "A novel deals with typical cases."
> "And life is not typical." (*Wheels of Chance*, ch. 31)

'"If I were a Sherlock Holmes,"' says Jessie later, '"I suppose I could have told you were a Colonial from little things like that"' (*Wheels of Chance*, ch. 34): Hoopdriver, of course, is nothing of the kind. The rascally seducer Bechamel suggests to Jessie that 'men are really more alike than you think' (*Wheels of Chance*, ch. 21), but the text encourages resistance to the notion that Hoopdriver's romantic aspirations are essentially the same as Bechamel's more carnal 'Palaeolithic' ones. Wells's early journalism lays an obsessive emphasis on individuality, even down to, in the title of one essay, 'The Possible Individuality of Atoms'.[28] The status quo can be resisted by showing that the linguistic and epistemological codes by which inductive judgements are made are arbitrary, and inaccurate because they rely on generalizations. Indeed, the whole plot depends on Jessie's ignorant misreading of Hoopdriver's clothing, language, culture, and class:

> His English was uncertain, but not such as books informed her distinguished the lower classes. His manners seemed to her good on the whole, but a trifle over-respectful and out of fashion. He called her "Madam" once. He seemed a person of means and leisure, but he knew nothing of recent concerts, theatres, or books. How did he spend his time? (*Wheels of Chance*, ch. 29)

---

[26] See Catherine Belsey, *Critical Practice* (London: Methuen, 1980), 109–17.

[27] 'The Novel of Types', *Saturday Review*, 81 (1896), 23–4, *Literary Criticism*, 67–70 (67–8).

[28] See Wells's 1894 letter to A. Davies advocating 'individualism in ethics, socialism in economy', *Correspondence*, I, 213; also 'The So-Called Science of Sociology', *Independent Review*, 6 (1905), 21–37, in *An Englishman Looks at the World*, 192–206 (195–6); *Autobiography*, I, 223–7.

In order to generate the plot, Hoopdriver has to behave against the expectations of the opening; to escape being moulded by his economic role, he must go on holiday.[29] (The book was subtitled *A Holiday Adventure* in its first British publication and *A Holiday Idyll* in the United States). Crucial to this liminal change of conditions that is his holiday is Hoopdriver's opportunity to change his appearance, particularly his clothes.[30]

Wells himself had been apprenticed as a draper when a boy, and his narrative eye always carefully discriminates in matters of clothing and cloth, an ability shared by his draper-hero.[31]

> Mr Hoopdriver, very uncomfortable, and studying an easy bearing, looked again at the breakfast things, and then idly lifted the corner of the tablecloth on the ends of his fingers, and regarded it. "Fifteen three," he thought privately. (*Wheels of Chance*, ch. 34)

In his history of the late-Victorian period, R. C. K. Ensor notes that, as mass-produced clothes became cheaper, the working class began to abandon clothing distinctive to an individual and recognizable occupation.[32] Codes for reading appearance thus started to become less reliable; the barmaid even prophesies that Rational Dress, the cycling outfit for women, will even make it too difficult (as with the Eloi) to distinguish between the sexes.[33] Hoopdriver's cycling fashion of a brown chequered suit allows confusion between his read identity and Bechamel's; Bechamel is angry at this bounder's imitation of bourgeois fashion:

---

[29] See Wells's anonymous 'The Holiday of a Draper's Assistant: Life in a Margin', *Pall Mall Gazette*, 5 June 1894.

[30] I owe to Yoonjoung Choi's 'Real Romance Came Out of Dreamland' the insight into the importance to Wells of the carnivalesque, an inverting of hierarchies that often involves the exchange of clothes between classes. See also *The Work, Wealth and Happiness of Mankind*, 196.

[31] For Wells's narrative persona pretending to deny this, see 'The Shopman', *Certain Personal Matters*, 80–4. Wells's Fabian pamphlet *This Misery of Boots* extrapolates the inequality of the entire social system from observing the boots of the poor: 'The clothes people wear are no better than their boots; and the houses they live in far worse. And think of the shoddy garments of ideas and misconceptions and partial statements into which their poor minds have been jammed by way of education! Think of the way *that* pinches and chafes them! If one expanded the miseries of these things ... Think, for example, of the results of poor, bad, unwise food, of badly-managed eyes and ears and teeth! All these miseries are preventable miseries, which it lies in the power of men to cure.' *This Misery of Boots: Reprinted with Alterations from the Independent Review* (London: Fabian Society, 1907), 12–14.

[32] R. C. K. Ensor, *England 1870–1914* (Oxford: Clarendon Press, 1936), 168.

[33] See James McGurn, *On Your Bicycle: An Illustrated History of Cycling* (London: John Murray, 1987), 100–7 on cycling and women's fashions.

"Greasy proletarian," said the other man in brown, feeling a prophetic dislike. "Got a suit of brown, the very picture of this. One would think his sole aim in life had been to caricature me." (*Wheels of Chance*, ch. 7)

The romance-plot thus depends on the democratizing effects both of new styles of clothing alongside another class-levelling, cheaply mass-produced technological innovation, the safety bicycle.[34] 1896, the year of the text's publication, marked the height of the cycling craze.[35] The narrator initially plays on Hoopdriver being caught in a machine (as an economic metaphor, indeed he is); but the 'shocking' or at least surprising fact of Hoopdriver's appearance in the first chapter is the state of his legs, for the 'machine' in which he has been caught is a bicycle.[36] When Wells's health permitted in the 1890s, he was himself a very enthusiastic cyclist; the narrator of *The War of the Worlds* spends a summer learning to cycle while writing 'a series of papers discussing the probable developments of moral ideas as civilisation progressed' (*War of the Worlds*, bk 1, ch. 1). Because of its expansion of the possibilities of travel for sexual selection, the invention of the bicycle is, according to geneticist Steve Jones, 'the most important event in recent human evolution'.[37] The bicycle is democratic, progressive technology available to all classes; as well as granting additional freedom of movement and of dress to women such as Jessie, it also blurs class divisions (unlike segregated rail travel).[38] The priggish central character of Wells's story 'A Perfect Gentleman on Wheels' (1897) is insulted to be spoken to as an equal by a capable cycling 'bounder'.[39] George's tricycling Uncle from *Select Conversations with an Uncle* (who makes a brief reappearance in *The Wheels of Chance*, ch. 14, which suggests that the narrators of both books are the same character) is insulted by working-class cyclists

---

[34] The bicycle manufacturer Sid Pornick in *Kipps* advertises the 'Best machine at a democratic price' (*Kipps: The Story of a Simple Soul*, ed. Simon J. James (London: Penguin, 2005), 140). 'In 1890, twenty-seven factories produced about 40,000 bicycles. Six years later 250 factories were producing 1,200,000 machines' (McGurn, *On Your Bicycle*, 98). In 1944, Wells wrote to the BBC, who were considering adapting *The Wheels of Chance*, that 'in the old days a bicycle was romance—now it's hard and driving necessity'. *Correspondence*, IV, 493.

[35] McGurn, *On Your Bicycle*, 113.

[36] Cf. 'Dimly he perceived [. . .] how the great machine of retail trade had caught its life into his wheels, a vast, irresistible force which he had neither strength of will nor knowledge to escape'. *Kipps*, 50.

[37] Steve Jones, *The Language of the Genes: Biology, History and the Evolutionary Future* (London: HarperCollins, 1994), 237.

[38] McGurn, *On Your Bicycle*, 90–3.

[39] 'A Perfect Gentleman on Wheels', *The Humours of Cycling: Stories and Pictures*, ed. Jerome K. Jerome et al. (London: Bowden, 1897), 5–14. See also Wells's 'Specimen Day [From a Holiday Itinerary]', *Science Schools Journal*, 33 (1891), 17–20.

asking him the price of his machine.[40] (Hoopdriver correctly guesses the value of Jessie's.) The cheapness of the bicycle did allow the more affluent of the working and lower middle classes greater freedom of movement; for Wells this translates into corresponding freedom of thought. Riding a bicycle, like reading a Wellsian romance, should be a liberating imaginative activity like dreaming. 'The bicycle in its early phases has a peculiar influence upon the imagination,' Wells claims in 'A Perfect Gentleman On Wheels'.[41] The nature of learning to ride requires the correct exercise of the imaginative and romantic as well as physical capacities: 'To ride a bicycle properly is very like a love affair; chiefly it is a matter of faith' (*Wheels of Chance*, ch. 4). While cycling allows the imagination some romantic freedom, however, realism again periodically intrudes, especially in the undermining presence of the body: 'talk of your *joie de vivre*! Albeit with a certain cramping sensation about the knees and calves slowly forcing itself upon his attention' (*Wheels of Chance*, ch. 4). The deformation of the body by material, especially economic, circumstances is a recurrent trope in Wells. In this text the body repeatedly lets the self down: through hunger and thirst, clumsiness, untidiness, blushing, and wobbling when trying to ride a bicycle. Hoopdriver cannot continue his masquerade of presenting the physical codes of a gentleman indefinitely because of the deforming effect on his body of the economic 'machine' in which the book's opening sees him trapped. Meeting Jessie, Hoopdriver's 'business training made him prone to bow and step aside' (*Wheels of Chance*, ch. 5); later he bows 'over his saddle as if it was a counter' (*Wheels of Chance*, ch. 8). (George Bernard Shaw accused Wells of the same kind of revealing posture when speaking in public.)[42] Jessie claims to be 'blessed or afflicted with a trick of observation', and eventually notices the draper's habits of 'bowing as you do and rubbing your hands, and looking expectant' (*Wheels of Chance*, ch. 34), and of keeping pins in his lapel, a habit that Hoopdriver had hoped to escape when on holiday. Even Hoopdriver's language is deformed, since the narrator chooses to render his speech as phonetic cockney rather than in correct orthography.[43] Eventually, Hoopdriver confesses to Jessie, 'Ay'm a deraper' (*Wheels of Chance*, ch. 35—he is also, of course, a de-raper in the sense

---

[40] 'On a Tricycle', *Select Conversations with an Uncle with Two Hitherto Unreprinted Conversations*, ed. David C. Smith and Patrick Parrinder (London: University of North London Press, 1992), 54–7.

[41] 'Perfect Gentleman', 8.

[42] *Bernard Shaw and H. G. Wells*, 66.

[43] See P. J. Keating, 'The Phonetic Representation of Cockney', *The Representation of the Working Classes in Victorian Fiction* (London: Routledge & Kegan Paul, 1971), 246–68.

that he saves Jessie from rape). The romantic imagination can take the man out the draper's, it seems, but not the draper out of the man.

Reality also asserts itself through reminders of money: Hoopdriver's wobbling bicycle imaginatively at first leaves 'a track like one of Beardsley's feathers' (*Wheels of Chance*, ch. 5), but the track of Jessie's is 'milled like a shilling' (*Wheels of Chance*, ch. 20). Monetary metaphors serve as a reminder that the hero and heroine's romantic holiday adventures are realistically underwritten by money, and are thus finite. Jessie's chastity is assailed by Bechamel as '"If saving it is—this parsimony"' (*Wheels of Chance*, ch. 21); when abandoned by Jessie, he feels 'sold' (*Wheels of Chance*, ch. 23). The escapade in the moonlight leaves Hoopdriver with 'profit and loss; profit, one sister with bicycle complete, wot offers?—cheap for tooth and 'air brush, vests, night-shirt, stockings, and sundries' (*Wheels of Chance*, ch. 27). Finally, the exhaustion of Hoopdriver's five-pound note and Jessie's £2 7s. ends their picaresque: 'Hoopdriver, indeed, was quite spent, and only a feeling of shame prolonged the liquidation of his bankrupt physique' (*Wheels of Chance*, ch. 37).

Without money, the carnivalesque holiday, and the narrative, must end. Hoopdriver returns to un-narratable work, and Jessie to her domestic imprisonment now at the hands of Widgery as well as Mrs Milton. For a comic romance, the conclusion is realistically pessimistic. Jessie will lend Hoopdriver books, but the reader has already been told how little leisure for reading the life of a draper affords, and reminded of the gulf separating books from real life. '"Anyhow, if I'm not to see her—she's going to lend me books," he thinks, and gets such comfort as he can. And then again: "Books! What's books?"' (*Wheels of Chance*, ch. 41).[44]

That Wells later thought the ending too pessimistic, for Jessie at least, is shown by his revisions of the ending for the American edition of *The Wheels of Chance* (the 1925 Atlantic Edition, volume seven of his collected *Works*, retains most, if not all, of these alterations).[45] Jessie feels that her prospects are too limited by her not being a man; for all of his interlude of masculine chivalry, Hoopdriver also feels that he is not enough of a man to realize his and Jessie's hopes for his future. He accurately diagnoses his lack of education as an incurable state, since the hours required by his job will forever prevent him from making up the gap. While Jessie's education is patchier, her level of education, in spite of her gender, might allow her to

---

[44] Cf. '"One book's very like another—after all, what is it?"' wonders Kipps. "Something to read and done with [sic]. It's not a thing that matters like print dresses or serviettes where you either like 'em or don't, and people judge you by. They take what you give 'em in books and lib'ries, and glad to be told what to"' (*Kipps*, 429).

[45] *The Wheels of Chance: A Bicycling Idyll* (New York: Macmillan, 1896).

escape the certainties of the realist ending. The Macmillan version of the text prepared for the American market, even suggests the possibility of a possible future Woolfian independence: saying goodbye to Hoopdriver, a scene elided in the earlier version:

> "I want a room of my own, what books I need to read, to be free to go out by myself alone, Teaching—"
> "Anything," said Mrs Milton. "Anything in reason." (Macmillan, ch. 39)[46]

The *Wheels of Chance*'s narrator does, as in many of Wells's early pieces, make a claim for the value of lowly types such as Hoopdriver:

> But if you see how a mere counter-jumper, a cad on castors, and a fool to boot, may come to feel the little insufficiencies of life, and if he has to any extent won your sympathies, my end is attained. (*Wheels of Chance*, ch. 41)

The author's choice of an unromantic, unhappy ending deprives his readers of the comfort of believing that the underlings who serve them in shops all live contented lives. This form of ending forces the reader to confront the economic and class inequalities of such a relationship. Hoopdriver is himself a reader, albeit one with less time for reading than the text's own implied reader, and the narrator hopes that Hoopdriver's disillusionment over the course of the narrative might turn his imagination away from romantic fantasy towards more concrete political goals:

> To-morrow, the early rising, the dusting, and drudgery, begin again—but with a difference, with wonderful memories and still more wonderful desires and ambitions replacing those discrepant dreams. (*Wheels of Chance*, ch. 41)

UNIVERSITY OF LIFE: *LOVE AND MR. LEWISHAM*

Although Wells distanced himself from the comparison, *Love and Mr. Lewisham*, his first and perhaps only attempt at the classic realist novel, clearly shows the influence of Wells's friends the realist novelists George Gissing and Arnold Bennett.[47] Its theme of a young man frustrated in high aspirations is common in many novels of the 1890s such as Gissing's

---

[46] In Wells's unproduced dramatic version of the story, *Hoopdriver's Holiday*, ed. Michael Timko (Lafayette: English Literature in Transition, 1964), the absence of the narrator reduces the farcical tone and emphasizes political and sociological aspects. Jessie successfully escapes from her stepmother to a liberal-minded aunt, Mrs Latham, and Hoopdriver is allowed a soliloquy to protest against social conditions.

[47] *Arnold Bennett and H. G. Wells*, 45, 48; Sherborne, *H. G. Wells*, 142.

Born in Exile (1892), Hardy's *Jude the Obscure* (1895), and Bennett's *A Man from the North* (1898).[48]

Highly prolific as Wells was early in his career, no other book was revised as frequently or extensively during its composition as this novel.[49] Its predominant theme is the difficulty of achievement, a theme mirrored in the author's protracted experience of finishing it.[50] As Wells feels the difficulty of writing to an extent that he had never before experienced, *Love and Mr. Lewisham* itself dramatizes difficulty in reading and writing. It begins by showing the hero neglecting physical comforts such as food and sleep for the sake of reading. In an early article for the *University Correspondent*, Wells wrote sympathetically of those seeking to rise by means of education:

> The educational ideal of an ambitious illiterate man does not stop short of omniscience. He toils incessantly and breathlessly at his growing heap of information. He gallantly strains his mind to comprehend an illimitable chaos. Either he strains it to the pitch of injury, or he learns in time the meaning of infinity, and devotes himself thoughtfully to some possible portion of the world of human learning.
>
> There is something splendid and Titanic about these ambitious and self-taught men. They work in the dark and under a tremendous disadvantage; they often have to content themselves with few and insufficient books, second-hand books, and old editions; they begin subjects, haphazard at the most difficult points, and yet withal they will often emerge at last with ideas cleverer, sounder, and stronger than many a student who has had all the advantages—and relaxations—of a University. There is, I believe, a great future before these pilgrims from the proletariat to wisdom.[51]

As so often in Wells, the body reasserts itself against more recondite aspirations. '"I'd rather have a good sensible actin' stummik than a full

---

[48] Wells responded very enthusiastically as a reviewer to *Jude the Obscure*, and may well have been thinking of it while writing his first 'serious' novel: 'For the first time in English literature the almost intolerable difficulties that beset an ambitious man of the working class—the snares, the obstacles, the countless rejections and humiliations by which our society eludes the services of these volunteers—receive adequate treatment. [. . .] The man of the lower class who aspires to knowledge can only escape frustration by ruthlessly suppressing affections and passions; it is a choice of one tragedy or another. [. . .] This is the voice of the educated proletarian, speaking more distinctly than it has ever spoken before in English literature. The man is, indeed, at once an individual and a type.' 'Jude the Obscure', *Saturday Review*, 81 (1896), 153–4, *Literary Criticism*, 79–82 (81–2). See also Ingvald Raknem, *H. G. Wells and his Critics* (Oslo: Universitetsforlaget; London: Allen & Unwin), 303–4.

[49] Loing, *H. G. Wells à L'Oeuvre*, 229–36.

[50] The Atlantic Preface states that this novel 'was written with greater care than any of the author's earlier books. It was consciously a work of art' (*Works*, VII, ix).

[51] 'What is Cram?', *University Correspondent*, 18 March 1893, 10.

head," said Mrs. Monday, "any day." "I'm different, you see," snapped
Mr. Lewisham' (*Lewisham*, ch. 4). Wells's realism articulates a mimesis of
the same material limits that his utopian writing seeks to dismantle, limits
often reflected in *Love and Mr. Lewisham* by language which marks
boundaries. The window, which for James marks the detachment of the
artist from the world, is for Wells a nexus between the controlled interior
of work, duty, responsibility, idealism, and reading, and the uncontrolla-
ble exterior of Nature, sexual drive, and play.[52] Lewisham arranges his
study in an attempt to achieve an entirely controlled environment, like
Moreau's island, in which his intellectual researches will be undisrupted
by material interruptions. Since his room has a window that can be looked
through, however, and since the environment outside is blossoming into
springtime, Lewisham is distracted from his text by the kind of evolutionary imperatives to mate that are hinted at, but which he fails to recognize
as such, in the passage of Horace he is translating: 'The beauty of Glycera
sets me on fire.'[53] As in *Jude the Obscure*, the academic aspirations of the
male hero are threatened by instinctive sexual urges: 'love can find
entrance not only into an open heart, but also into a heart well fortified,
if watch be not well kept', warns Francis Bacon in the novel's epigraph.
The pull of reproductive imperatives repeatedly brushes culture aside: the
bookish Miss Heydinger would theoretically be a better match for producing intelligent offspring, but Lewisham selects the more conventional-
ly physically attractive Ethel, and with her he will produce consequently
strong, healthy and, in their turn, sexually attractive children. Miss Heydinger is closely associated with Lewisham's 'Career' of education and
political action, but she fails her exams and, after learning of her sexual
rejection by Lewisham, is cruelly eliminated from the narrative.

Lewisham is initially attracted by Ethel's having seen Carlyle's house,
but this tenuous association with literary culture contributes nothing to
the success of their subsequent marriage. Instead, the young couple argue
over Ethel's juvenile taste for cheap novelettes, and about Lewisham's
fruitless attempt to write one. Ethel's career as a typist stalls because of her
poor level of literacy (in an early manuscript version she considers giving
up typing to go on the stage).[54] The Lewishams are defrauded of five
pounds by the dastardly novelist Lucas Holderness; and the poet Edwin

---

[52] John Huntington, *The Logic of Fantasy: H. G. Wells and Science Fiction* (New York:
Columbia University Press, 1982), 71–3.

[53] A deleted passage in the typescript reads, 'An outlying, possibly an unexplored region
of his mental structure had suddenly usurped control of him, and urit me was forgotten.
The cause of the footfall was a girl', Illinois Collection, LL-343.

[54] The narrator notes Ethel has been misled by 'research into fiction' (Illinois Collection,
LL-163, 230).

Peak Baines (playfully named after two Gissing protagonists), makes sexual advances towards Ethel. Even the simplest kinds of writing fail to have a positive effect on their courtship: Ethel writes the lines that her cousin should produce for this punishment; her letters to Lewisham have a blank where his first name should be, as she has forgotten it.

In spite of its short length, *Love and Mr. Lewisham* is Wells's most allusive work. As ironic commentary on the hero's progress, the narrative is interleaved with commonplace book entries from Bacon, Thomas à Kempis, Carlyle, Emerson, Confucius, Spencer, Goethe, Shakespeare, hymns, and the Bible. The novel not only gives very careful attention to what characters are reading, but also to their interpretations of texts.[55] Lewisham is converted to Socialism by reading Henry George's *Progress and Poverty* (1879) and Morris's *Commonweal* (1885–94), more practical and instrumental choices of reading matter than poetry or fiction. Lewisham's failure to apply the lesson of Horace's *Odes* is only the first example of the misinterpretation of texts from the residuum of high culture. Lewisham makes notes on Tennyson's *The Princess*, another story of sexuality competing with academic achievement, but fails to make the connection. He is moved by Robert Browning's 'The Statue and the Bust', but Miss Heydinger's allusion to 'Sludge, the "Medium"' only shows how little effect Browning's satire has had in reality, since fraudulent mediums such as Chaffery continue to flourish. Miss Heydinger is impermeable herself to the 'implicit meanings' (*Lewisham*, ch. 16) of the paintings she has chosen to decorate her study. The veneering of culture in Lagune's study does not allow him to see things as they really are, but serves to encourage his self-delusion. (In the earliest surviving manuscript version, Lagune dies overnight while reading, 'in the midst of his lonely futilities'.)[56] Dunkerley's reading of poetry makes him '"Shelley-witted"' (*Lewisham*, ch. 18); Parkin's foolish advocacy of Ruskin's *Sesame and Lilies* provokes an irreparable argument with Lewisham. Characters frequently visit the South Kensington museum, but its relics provide only a backdrop for scenes of failed self-fulfilment, not a fresh mode of understanding. Instead, the text looks to more modern mass modes of cheap reproduction: the stylographic pen, typewriter, oleograph, jellygraph. (Interestingly, however, music is excepted in this novel and elsewhere from Wells's critique of artistic culture, acting beneficially on Lewisham's emotions.)[57]

---

[55] On the importance of this self-reflexive trope, see Ruth Robbins, *Pater to Forster, 1873–1924* (Basingstoke: Palgrave Macmillan, 2003), 39.

[56] Illinois Collection, LL-87; Loing, *H. G. Wells à L'Oeuvre*, 238.

[57] *Exasperations* contains a disquisition on Wells's views of painting and music's places within high culture.

One scene in the Museum takes place in front of Raphael's cartoon 'The Sacrifice at Lystra' (wrongly given in the novel as 'The Sacrifice of Lystra'), which depicts the scene in which St Paul's healing of a lame beggar provokes the pagan Lystrians into mistakenly hailing him a god. The crowd are presented with a spectacle which they interpret using the wrong, archaic set of beliefs. The novel itself dramatizes another conflict between different epistemologies: Chaffery's (fraudulent) spiritualism, and Lewisham's science. The division between scientific positivism and the metaphysical was less certain in the 1890s, when the difference between the two was less clear: Arthur Conan Doyle, for instance, could claim both to be a man of science and a believer in spiritualism.[58] According to Gowan Dawson, 'Occult practices like mesmerism and spiritualism [. . .] appeared to many in Victorian Britain as entirely logical extensions of the concern with disclosing otherwise unseen forces and energies, often during spectacular public demonstrations, that characterised many of the physical sciences at this time.'[59] In this novel, spiritualism stands in for a false means of understanding which mistakes appearances for reality, or presents wish-fulfilment, like the Lystrians', for the truth. Chaffery claims to have pierced the veil of the perceptual world and that his mind is able to perceive 'noumena', abusing both philosophical idealism and evolutionary theory to justify actions that are in truth motivated only by selfishness:

> "Let the world have no illusions for you, no surprises. Nature is full of cruel catastrophes, man is a physically degenerate ape, every appetite, every instinct, needs the curb; salvation is not in the nature of things, but whatever salvation there may be is in the nature of man; face all these painful things."
> (*Lewisham*, ch. 28)

Chaffery declares himself a disciple of Bishop Berkeley, but twists Berkeley's meaning to claim that 'all consciousness is *essentially* hallucination' (*Lewisham*, ch. 23). The sophist cites Ibsen, Shaw, and, most preposterously, New Woman fiction to justify his selfish desertion of Ethel's mother.

Even when sincere, characters find themselves unable to express themselves truthfully. Miss Heydinger 'would have given three-quarters of the years she had still to live, to have had eyes and features that could have

---

[58] Martin Booth, *The Doctor, the Detective and Arthur Conan Doyle: A Biography of Arthur Conan Doyle* (London: Hodder & Stoughton, 1997), 309–20. For Wells's views, see 'Pecularities of Psychical Research', *Nature*, 6 December 1894, in *H. G. Wells in 'Nature'*, 47–57.

[59] Gowan Dawson, 'Introduction: Science and Victorian Poetry', *Victorian Poetry*, 41/1 (2003), 1–10 (3). Chaffery mentions stage magician John Nevil Maskelyne, whose *Modern Spiritualism: A Short Account of its Rise and Progress* (1876) exposes the tricks used by fraudulent mediums.

expressed her' (*Lewisham*, ch. 10); Ethel complains that, '"The things I say . . . aren't the things I feel"' (*Lewisham*, ch. 32). '"Only people who are well off can be—complex,"' Lewisham later admits to her (*Lewisham*, ch. 32). Truth, in this novel, is reliably found neither in outward appearances nor in language; indeed it is frequently difficult to determine the value of truth at all. The maxim 'Magna est veritas et praevalebit', pinned to the wall next to Lewisham's fatefully situated window claims that 'truth is great and will prevail', but the novel's reality is suspended between the truth that civilization is an artificial sham, and the no less pressing truth of Lewisham's dwindling finances. Chaffery's Carlylean exposure of clothing as a deceitful covering of essential facts and of money does not alter in the slightest the harsh reality of the fact that Lewisham is too poor to dress well enough to secure a position in a high-paying school. Even such an insistently materialist novelist as Wells acknowledges that, at the present time, life cannot wholly be lived by principles of abstract scientific truth:

> In the abstract world of reasoning science there is no green, no colour at all, but certain lengths of vibration; no hardness, but a certain reaction of molecules; no cold and no pain, but certain molecular consequences in the nerves that reach the misinterpreting mind. In the abstract world of reasoning science, moreover, there is a rigid and inevitable sequence of cause and effect; every act of man could be foretold to its uttermost detail, if only we knew him and all his circumstances fully; in the abstract world of reasoned science all things exist now potentially down to the last moment of infinite time. But the human will does not exist in the abstract world of reasoned science, in the world of atoms and vibrations, that rigidly predestinate scheme of things in space and time. The human will exists in this world of men and women, in this world where the grass is green and desire beckons and the choice is often so wide and clear between the sense of what is desirable and what is more widely and remotely right. (*Anticipations*, ch. 9)

Bacon's claim that 'Knowledge is Power' is another of Lewisham's youthful maxims, but the power of money and class is greater still, as Lewisham discovers when receiving a 'commercial education' (*Lewisham*, ch. 25) in how low his real market value as a teacher actually is.[60] Whether civilization is a lie or not, Lewisham must nonetheless obey its dictates or he and his family will starve.

The story's most prominent imaginative, even utopian, text is of course the 'Schema' which the deluded young Lewisham believes will plot the narrative of his life. In the final chapter, the hero looks at the piece of paper 'as if it was the writing of another man, and indeed it was the writing

---

[60] See also the short story 'A Slip Under the Microscope' (1896), *Short Stories*, 250–64.

of another man' (*Lewisham*, ch. 32). Lewisham is eventually reconciled to the limits of his fate by recognizing an evolutionary truth beyond the merely linguistic and rational. 'He knew love now for what it was, knew it for something more ancient and more imperative than reason' (*Lewisham*, ch. 27). The *Daily Chronicle* noted in its review of *Love and Mr. Lewisham*:

> For one moment we are positively harrowed because we feel that poverty having entered the door Love is really about to fly out of the window, as he undoubtedly would have flown had Mr. Gissing had anything to do with it. But he doesn't. He never gets further than the window-ledge. He remains, though he is the only good thing that does remain.[61]

Love is eventually contained within the novel's interior space, however, and the novel's two titular antagonists are reconciled. Wells would complain in *Mankind in the Making* that 'at present it is a shameful and embittering fact that a gifted man from the poorer strata of society must too often buy his personal development at the cost of his posterity' (*Mankind in the Making*, ch. 2). This utopian text both opens and closes with the figure of the child; *Love and Mr. Lewisham* also begins and ends with a child, but the second child is a different individual: not Mr Lewisham, but Master Lewisham, his son.[62] (In earlier manuscript versions, this ending is followed by an epilogue in which Lewisham's child, here a daughter, appears.)[63] Lewisham recognizes that the 'Future' is not a document, the Schema, but a more material kind of (re)production that really does belong to, indeed own, the future:[64]

> "Come to think, it is all the Child. The future is the Child. The Future. What are we—any of us—but servants or traitors to that? . . .
> "Natural Selection—it follows . . . this way is happiness . . . must be. There can be no other."
> He sighed. "To last a lifetime, that is.
> "And yet—it is almost as if Life had played me a trick—promised so much—given so little! . . .
> "No! One must not look at it in that way! That will not do! That will *not* do.
> "Career! In itself it is a career—the most important career in the world. Father! Why should I want more?

[61] *Critical Heritage*, ed. Parrinder, 81.

[62] *Mankind in the Making*, 69. In the review quoted earlier, Wells praises the development of Gissing's realism in *The Whirlpool* as 'a return to the essential, to honourable struggle as the epic factor in life, to children as the matter of morality and the sanction of the securities of civilization' (*George Gissing and H. G. Wells*, 258); see also Kemp, *H. G. Wells and the Culminating Ape*, 73–4.

[63] Illinois Collection, LL-191, 292–305.

[64] Cf. *Mind at the End of its Tether* (London: Heinemann, 1945), 28.

"And...Ethel! [...] No wonder she was restless. Unfulfilled...What had she to do? She was drudge, she was toy...

"Yes. This is life. This alone is life! For this we were made and born. All these other things—all other things—they are only a sort of play...

"Play!"

His eyes came back to the Schema. His hands shifted to the opposite corner and he hesitated. The vision of that arranged Career, that ordered sequence of work and successes, distinctions and yet further distinctions, rose brightly from the symbol. Then he compressed his lips and tore the yellow sheet in half, tearing very deliberately. He doubled the halves and tore again, doubled again very carefully and neatly until the Schema was torn into numberless little pieces. With it he seemed to be tearing his past self. [...]

"It is the end of adolescence," he said; "the end of empty dreams..."
(*Lewisham*, ch. 32)

The student of science chooses to look to the future—his child—rather than to the past—Latin grammar and Shakespeare's *Henry VIII*. This novel, and others by Wells, contains repeated images of torn, crumpled, or mutilated paper: the destruction of the Schema proves not Lewisham's failure, but his maturity.

DON'T!: *KIPPS*

In *Kipps*, the next of his 'little tragedies of [...] clipped and limited little lives' (*Kipps*, bk 3, ch. 2, 5), Wells makes still more explicit his critique of written language, and of high culture in particular, as a paradigm of understanding and as a means of educating. The conduct manual *Manners and Rules of Polite Society*, for example, functions throughout as an ironic intertext, in which Kipps's real bodily behaviour is mocked by the book's imagined paradigm of social interaction. The aesthetic litter of Coote's study also reveals that its association with the inequalities of the class system has put an end to culture's successful execution of its social mission, and even to science's potential to educate:[65]

---

[65] 'Leisure in the narrower sense, as distinct from exploit and from any ostensibly productive employment of effort on objects which are of no intrinsic use, does not commonly leave a material product. The criteria of a past performance of leisure therefore commonly take the form of "immaterial" goods. Such immaterial evidences of past leisure are quasi-scholarly or quasi-artistic accomplishments and a knowledge of processes and incidents which do not conduce directly to the furtherance of human life. So, for instance, in our time there is the knowledge of the dead languages and the occult sciences; of correct spelling; of syntax and prosody; of the various forms of domestic music and other household art; of the latest properties of dress, furniture, and equipage.' Thorstein Veblen, *Theory of the Leisure Class* (New York: Macmillan, 1912), 44–5. See also 380, on the leisure class's hostility to the new science.

An array of things he had been led to believe indicative of culture and refinement—an autotype of Rossetti's *Annunciation*, an autotype of Watts's *Minotaur*, a Swiss carved pipe with many joints and a photograph of Amiens Cathedral (these two the spoils of travel), a phrenological bust, and some broken fossils from the Warren. A rotating bookshelf carrying the *Encyclopaedia Britannica* (tenth edition), [. . .] a number or so of the *Bookman* [. . .]. A table under the window bore a little microscope, some dust in a saucer, some grimy glass slips, and broken cover glasses, for Coote had "gone in for" biology a little. The longer side of the room was given over to bookshelves [. . .], and with an array of books—no worse an array of books than you find in any public library; an almost haphazard accumulation of obsolete classics, contemporary successes, the Hundred Best Books (including Samuel Warren's *Ten Thousand a Year*), old school-books, directories, the *Times* atlas, Ruskin in bulk, Tennyson complete in one volume, Longfellow, Charles Kingsley, Smiles, a guide-book or so, several medical pamphlets, odd magazine numbers, and much indescribable rubbish—in fact, a compendium of the contemporary British mind. (*Kipps*, bk 2, ch. 2, 1)[66]

For Pierre Bourdieu, the petit bourgeois' 'disparate, often devalued information which is to legitimate knowledge as his stamp collection is

---

[66] The manuscript of *Kipps* shows Wells experimenting with different versions of Coote's canon: in different versions, Coote in fact prefers Marie Corelli and Hall Caine to Meredith, James, and Hardy, and his editions of Turgenev are partly uncut. A cancelled passage shows the depth of Wells's frustration with Victorian literary culture's failure to achieve what it might have done:

The praises of books and reading are in Coote's mouth, and the praise of the unparalleled roll of England's literary greatness, but you & I, dear Reader, stand there also, silent & unseen, in Coote's room, as he talks before his shelves, & you and I dear Reader, think. We look at these books, and there we have the literature of the Nineteenth Century in brief, poets, novels, essays, science, sentiment & cant, the thought stuff out of which Coote has grown. We regard these shelves, & the familiar names upon the backs recall pictures & photographs, booms & revelations, hair tossing back from brows, & great hearts almost scandalously bare & public, & we think of the enthusiasms and excitements, the tens of thousands of writers, reporters, paragraphs and preachers, the Eminent Critics, the Distinguished litterateurs, the Personal Friends, the rag tag and bobtail of the Republic of Letters, who made it, who are in a swelling multitude now hang upon the beginning of the yet vaster accumulation this century will leave, & for a moment the voice of Coote fades into nothingness.

The shadow of the judgement of the future lies upon the library, and it seems to us a . . .

The literature of the Nineteenth Century recedes in quality, the whole preceding literature of the world since letters began, & what is there in it . . .

There have been literatures, we reflect, that have mothered great peoples. (Illinois Collection, 781–2)

to an art collection, is a miniature culture'.[67] This novel shows that poor social organization has associated high artistic culture so closely with class privilege that now culture can never fulfil its regenerative Victorian role.

The only text that can adequately represent the nature of Kipps's existence is *Kipps* itself. As in *The Wheels of Chance*, the tone of this novel belittles and distances the protagonist, but pleads in mitigation for his weakness the fact of his having been determined by material circumstances; the novel then in turn directly condemns those circumstances. After Lewisham, Wells's heroes find different means to escape from their determination by the certainties of literary realism: as Kenneth Newell points out, the plot of *Kipps* is too governed by chance for this to be a truly naturalist novel.[68] Such homiletic passages as the following are key to Wells's notion of realism, that artistic representation should offer resistance to the status quo, not complicity within it:

> As I think of them lying unhappily there in the darkness, [...] like some great, clumsy, griffin thing, like the Crystal Palace labyrinthodon, like Coote, like the leaden goddess of the Dunciad, [...] like all that is darkening and heavy and obstructive in life. It is matter and darkness, it is the anti-soul, it is the ruling power of this land, Stupidity. My Kippses live in its shadow. Shalford and his apprenticeship system, the ideas of Coote, the ideas of the old Kippses, all the ideas that have made Kipps what he is—all these are a part of its shadow. But for that monster they might not be groping among false ideas to hurt one another so sorely; but for that, the glowing promise of childhood and youth might have had a happier fruition; thought might have awakened in them to meet the thought of the world, the quickening sunshine of literature pierced to the substance of their souls; their lives might not have been divorced, as now they are divorced, from the apprehension of beauty that we favoured ones are given—the vision of the Grail that makes life fine for ever. I have laughed, and I laugh at these two people; and I have sought to make you laugh . . .
> But I see through the darkness of the souls of my Kippses as they are, as little pink strips quivering, living stuff, as things like the bodies of little, ill-nourished, ailing, ignorant children—children who feel pain, who are naughty and muddled and suffer, and do not understand why. And the claw of the Beast rests upon them! (*Kipps*, bk 3, ch. 2, 5)

As a child, Kipps experiences education and socialization largely as interdiction: his upbringing, both at home and at Shalford's shop, is intended

---

[67] Pierre Bourdieu, *Distinction: A Social Judgement of the Critique of Taste*, trans. Richard Nice (New York: Routledge 1992), 329.
[68] Newell, *Structure in Four Novels*, 70–1.

not to encourage self-expression, but to repress noise.[69] Nonetheless, like Hoopdriver, the young Kipps possesses both strong desires and the imagination to enlarge their scope. The narrative implies that in an alternative utopian world, such romantic imaginings might have been channelled in his being allowed to go to sea, that if he had been born German he would have been better educated.[70] Instead, Kipps is 'packed like a boy with tastes in some other direction—not ascertained' (*Kipps*, bk 1, ch. 2, 2) as the institutions of family and class restrict him to becoming a draper. Kipps's schoolteacher is untrained, and it is in Shalford's interest to keep apprentices under-educated. Shalford, who laments inaccurately that Kipps's education has contained too much '"lit'ry stuff"' (*Kipps*, bk 1, ch. 2, 1), neglects his pastoral responsibilities as well as his educational ones. The employer's duty to educate is 'a mere rhetorical flourish' (*Kipps*, bk 1, ch. 2, 2); Kipps is given a blotting pad and inkpot that he will never use. Like Hoopdriver, Kipps is moulded into physical postures and linguistic clichés to fit into Shalford's cherished 'system' (a system that, the narrator confirms, in fact wastes both Shalford's own money as well as the human potential imprisoned within it); the instruction '"to shape the lad a bit"' (*Kipps*, bk 1, 1, 5) an uneasy reminder of the Selenite embryos of *The First Men in the Moon*.

The adolescent Kipps's inability to read and write adequately bar him permanently from full adult development: after leaving Shalford's, he cannot even spell well enough to apply for a new job. The only route he is able to perceive through the 'bogs of ignorance' (*Kipps*, bk 1, ch. 3, 1) that surround him, is towards a class in woodcarving. (At one stage, despite having written nothing more than window tickets, he improbably fantasizes about being a writer, a 'mute inglorious Dickens' (*Kipps*, bk 1, ch. 3, 4).) Hoopdriver too had experimented with woodcarving and extension lectures as a means of extending his limited horizons. Kipps misidentifies sham artistic culture as an effective means of self-improvement: but he is not to blame for his mistake, since the hierarchies of the Edwardian class system have encouraged the connection.[71]

[69] In the typescript, his aunt advises Kipps '"Don't you say nothing about anything and then you won't be sorry"' (Illinois Collection, KS-2011). William Naismith, *A Young Draper's Guide to Success* (London: Gardner, 1901), 124–6 contains a list of thirty 'don'ts' for aspirant drapers. Wells's own 'Advice to Grocers' Assistants', *Grocers' Assistant*, February 1900, 154, concludes facetiously, 'Above all let him avoid dancing classes, Sunday-schools, the society of condescending persons of a superior class, the banjo, fiction, and the feminine sex.'

[70] In a passage deleted from the novel, a dying Masterman, nursed by Kipps, wonders, '"Suppose you and I, Kipps, were what we might have been! Eh?"' Harris Wilson, 'The Death of Masterman: A Repressed Episode in H. G. Wells's *Kipps*', *PMLA*, 86 (1971), 63–9 (66).

[71] Bourdieu, *Distinction*, 250–1.

Coote became, not only the exponent of 'Vagner or Vargner,' the man whose sister had painted a picture to be exhibited at the Royal Academy, the type of the hidden thing called culture, but a delegate, as it were, or at least an intermediary from that great world 'up there', where there were men-servants, where there were titles, where people dressed for dinner, drank wine at meals, wine costing very often as much as three and sixpence the bottle, and followed through a maze of etiquette, the most stupendous practices. (*Kipps*, bk 2, ch. 1, 2)

Thorstein Veblen suggests in *The Theory of the Leisure Class* (1899) that:

It is noticeable that the humanities which have so reluctantly yielded ground to the sciences are pretty uniformly adapted to shape the character of the student in accordance with a traditional self-centred scheme of consumption; a scheme of contemplation and enjoyment of the true, the beautiful, and the good, according to a conventional standard of propriety and excellence, the salient feature of which is leisure. [...] The enjoyment and the bent derived from habitual contemplation of the life, ideals, speculations, and methods of consuming time and goods, in vogue among the leisure class of classical antiquity, for instance, is felt to be 'higher', 'nobler', 'worthier', than what results in these respects from a like familiarity with the everyday life and the knowledge and aspirations of commonplace humanity in a modern community.[72]

Kipps exposes the gap between culture as its ideal of liberating, expressive activity and its reality as a set of codified practices for maintaining class difference. Kipps attempts to follow a Home Educator, and to read Shakespeare, Bacon, and Herrick, but, as a consequence of his poor education finds that:

the 'English Literature', with which Mr. Woodrow had equipped him, had vanished down some crack in his mind. He had no doubt it was very splendid stuff, but he couldn't quite make out what it was all about. There was an occult meaning, he knew, in literature, and he had forgotten it. (*Kipps*, bk 1, ch. 3, 1)[73]

Coote proposes that Kipps should take 'Extension Literature', as if, by some kind of cultural alchemy, lectures on the Elizabethan dramatists will

---

[72] Veblen, *Theory of the Leisure Class*, 390–1.
[73] Even after inheriting money, Kipps still hasn't learnt. '"When I get that study [...] I shall do a bit of reading I've long wanted to do. I shall make a nabit of going in there and reading something an hour every day. There's Shakespeare and a lot of things a man like me ought to read. Besides, we got to 'ave *somewhere* to put the Encyclopaedia. I've always thought a was about what I've wanted all along. You can't 'elp reading if you got a study. If you 'aven't, there's nothing for it, so far's *I* can see, but trashy novels"' (*Kipps*, 223).

both compensate for years of inadequate schooling and relieve Kipps's anxiety about dress and deportment. He proposes to educate Kipps into the class into which money has lifted him, but the course that Coote proposes is not the self-enculturation of the successful autodidact, but unfocused and self-indulgent dilettantism. There is no more systematic practice in the books on display in Chester Coote's study than in the random selection of books bought by Kipps's uneducated uncle at a saleroom.[74]

His wish 'to be, if not a "gentleman", at least mistakably like one' (*Kipps*, bk 1, ch. 2, 5) does not, then, liberate Kipps from the restrictions placed on a draper's apprentice by the class system, but merely places him underneath a different set of interdictions, manners here not a mode of social relation but 'the voucher of the life of leisure'.[75] After beginning the woodcarving class, Kipps had bought the penny manuals 'What to Avoid' and 'Common Errors in Speaking'; Coote gives Kipps a conduct manual entitled *Don't*. Helen, in turn, also 'forms' Kipps, correcting his dress and pronunciation: her culture too is only a matter of surface, not development, as she models her appearance on a Rossetti picture and dabbles pointlessly in writing. (In his notes for the uncompleted draft of *Kipps*, *The Wealth of Mr. Waddy*, the narrator affirms diegetically that 'putting it crudely, she is an over-educated aesthetic prig'.)[76]

From being an anxious retailer of bourgeois clothing, Kipps becomes now an anxious consumer of it, enduring a nightmare of 'wearing innumerable suits of clothes, and, through some terrible accident, wearing them all wrong' (*Kipps*, bk 1, ch. 6, 5).[77] Helen reproves Kipps for his choice of dress by telling him that, '"It makes you look like a shop"' (*Kipps*, bk 2, ch. 3, 6). His money does not liberate, but reifies him. Like so many Victorian protagonists who come into their inheritances prematurely, before having demonstrated the moral qualities to make the best use of them—Pip, or Richard Mutimer in Gissing's *Demos*, or Tittlebat

---

[74] Sherborne, *H. G. Wells*, 166, suggests that Coote is a portrait of Henry James. A passage in Wells's 1944 article 'Hard Facts About Art Treasures' protests: 'To claim the artistic temperament was like taking out a licence for licence, and as the prestige of artistry spread throughout our world an immense cloud of artistic pretenders came into being, necessitating schools, colleges, Latin quarters [sic] Bohemias, galleries, demanding and receiving the patronage of wealthy men of fame and public authorities, and amounting altogether to a collateral accumulation of intolerable rubbish at which no unsophisticated human being would look, or listen, for more than a moment, were it not for the highly organised efforts of those to whom entrust our education to thrust it upon our reluctant eyes and ears.'

[75] Veblen, *Theory of the Leisure Class*, 49; cf. Bourdieu, *Distinction*, 70.

[76] *The Wealth of Mr. Waddy: A Novel*, ed. Harris Wilson (Carbondale: Southern Illinois University Press, 1969), 149.

[77] Cf. *The Passionate Friends*, 30.

Tittlemouse in Samuel Warren's *Ten Thousand a Year* (one of the books in Coote's study)—Kipps discovers that without the knowledge of how to use it best, the power of money is curtailed.[78] In his essay 'The Power of Money', Karl Marx suggests that in bourgeois society money is the mediator between the imagination and the real world, bringing to money's possessor that which is desired by the imagination.[79] For Jean Baudrillard, the consumption of cultural artefacts constitutes for the petit bourgeois an attempt to construct through bricolage some kind of meaningful existence out of an existence privatized by capital.[80] In *Kipps*, however, even money cannot reverse the stunting effects of poor education and the class system on the imagination itself. Once Kipps's childish desires for two breakfasts a day (a consequence of adolescent starvation) and for a banjo are fulfilled, the only thing that Kipps can desire is to be other than himself.

Wells's protagonists are often obliged by their poverty and class to court in public. An anxiety common to many of Wells's protagonists is the fear of being watched, especially while eating, under 'the Argus eyes of the social system' (*Kipps*, bk 3, ch. 1, 1).[81] Kipps's anxieties over clothing and food reach a Dickensian climax in the set piece of his disastrous dinner in the Royal Grand Hotel. The narrator describes him as experiencing 'what psychologists call a conversion' (*Kipps*, bk 2, ch. 7, 6). The psychologist Wells is referring to is William James, to whom Wells always refers admiringly.[82] In *The Varieties of Religious Experience* (1902), James describes a conversion as 'the process, gradual or sudden, by which a self hitherto divided, and consciously wrong inferior and unhappy, becomes unified and consciously right superior and happy', adding that 'conversion is in its essence an adolescent phenomenon'.[83] Through unhappiness

---

[78] 'Having a million does not in itself make one able to live like a millionaire.' Bourdieu, *Distinction*, 374.

[79] 'The Power of Money', in *Economic and Philosophical Manuscripts of 1844*, 5th edn (Moscow: Progress, 1977), 127–32.

[80] Jean Baudrillard, *The Consumer Society: Myths and Structures*, trans. George Ritzer (London: Sage, 1998); see also *For A Critique of the Political Economy of the Sign*, trans. Charles Levin (St Louis, MO: Telos Press, 1981).

[81] *The Work, Wealth and Happiness of Mankind*, 174; Kemp, *H. G. Wells and the Culminating Ape*, 66–7, Haynes, *H. G. Wells*, 17–19; Michael Pinsky, *Future Present: Ethics and/as Science Fiction* (London: Associated University Presses, 2003), 65–9.

[82] *Anticipations*, 206; *First and Last Things*, 71n.; *Mankind in the Making*, 223; see also *Henry James and H. G. Wells*, 79; *Socialism and The Great State* (New York: Harper, 1922), 39.

[83] William James, *The Varieties of Religious Experience: Being the Gifford Lectures on Natural Religion Delivered at Edinburgh in 1901–1902* (New York: Longman, 1902), 189, 196. Wells later paraphrased James thus: 'it describes an initial state of distress with the aimlessness and cruelties of life, and particularly with the futility of the individual life, a state of helpless self-disgust, of inability to form any satisfactory plan of living' (*God the Invisible King* (London: Cassell, 1917), 25).

Kipps comes to maturity, and resolves the division in his self, by growing out of artistic culture:

> The novel lay at home on the chiffonier; it was one about society and politics—there is no need whatever to give the title or the author—written with a heavy-handed thoroughness that overrode any possibility of resistance on the part of Kipps's mind. It had crushed all his poor edifice of ideals, his dreams of a sensible, unassuming, existence, of snugness, of not caring what people said, all the rest of it, to dust; it had reinstated, squarely and strongly again, the only proper conception of English social life. There was a character in the book who trifled with Art, who was addicted to reading French novels, who dressed in a loose, careless, way, who was a sorrow to his dignified, silvery haired, politic-religious mother [...]. He treated a "nice" girl to whom they had got him engaged, badly; he married beneath him—some low thing or other.
>
> Kipps could not escape the application of the case. (*Kipps*, bk 3, ch. 2, 2)

Kipps's engagement with reading and writing reaches its nadir in the Anagram Tea's chastening apocalypse of letters. With heavy irony, though, Kipps's salvation is ultimately attained through a genre of writing—although Chitterlow claims that, '"plays aren't literature"' (bk 1, ch. 3, 3). Indeed, Wells tends to classify theatre as popular entertainment, rather than high literary culture: theatre is at least a dynamic popular entertainment rather than an ossified cultural relic. (The novel's peculiar diversion into the Associated Bookseller's Trading Union shows Wells preoccupied with the practical details of the methods of distribution and exchange for literature.)[84] Kipps begins life in a shop that sells 'books to read and to give away' (1, 1); the narrator ultimately withholds confirmation of whether 'it is Kipps that keeps the bookshop or the bookshop that keeps him' (bk 3, ch. 3, 7).[85]

Although Sid's friend Masterman prophesies a forthcoming social apocalypse, the ending of the novel is left unresolved. Like Lewisham, Kipps is brought to maturity by fatherhood. Having learned the lesson of biology's primacy over culture, Kipps is awakened to the nature of reality by a scientific, rather than artistic book:

> Turning over the pages of the *Physiology* again, he came upon a striking plate, in which a youth of agreeable profile displayed his interior in an unstinted

[84] In a novel as late as 1928, the eponymous hero of *Mr. Blettsworthy on Rampole Island* loses money in a bookselling business.

[85] One version of the ending in the typescript reads 'It may be Kipps will sell this book and sell it clean out of his shop, before ever it occurs to him to open a copy and find himself therein' (Illinois Collection).

manner to the startled eye. It was a new view of humanity altogether for Kipps, and it arrested his mind. "Chubes," he whispered. "Chubes!"

This anatomised figure made him forget for a space that he was "Practically a gentleman" altogether. (*Kipps*, bk 2, ch. 1, 4)

In a pattern repeated throughout Wells's work, science provides a conclusion where art fails to do so.

THE ROMANCE OF COMMERCE: *TONO-BUNGAY*

Tono-Bungay is often taken by critics as the high point of this brilliant but over-productive author's fictional output.[86] Many critical studies of Wells even terminate with the polemical *Ann Veronica*, published in the same year, or 1910's escapist fantasy *The History of Mr. Polly*, adjudging the novels that Wells wrote over the following thirty-five years less worthy of attention. (John Batchelor's 'Introductory Critical Study' is a notable exception). Wells declared in his 1934 autobiography:

> I shall never come as near to a deliberate attempt upon the Novel as I did in *Tono-Bungay*. [...] It was an indisputable Novel, but it was extensive rather than intensive. [...] It was planned as a social panorama in the vein of Balzac.[87]

Tono-Bungay questions its own validity as a work of art, and yet at the same time is Wells's finest piece of work.

It would be another six years before Wells and James's dispute, but already in *Tono-Bungay* one can see Wells irritably turning against James's valorization of the aesthetic for its own sake. Here the *Bildung* narrative of moral development is both evaded and parodied: narrative closure does not demonstrate society's eventual accommodation of the protagonist: rather, the result is of deliberate social *dis*commodation, splintering the material frame of the realist narrative. The struggle for moral conduct is rendered moot by society's decay and George's rejection of norms that might limit his freedom of action.[88] Art, here, entirely fails to 'make life', and Victorian literary culture is assailed in both the content and form of the novel.

---

[86] John Batchelor, *H. G. Wells* (Cambridge: Cambridge University Press, 1985), 94; Parrinder, *H. G. Wells*, 86; Warren W. Wagar, *H. G. Wells: Traversing Time* (Middletown, CT: Wesleyan University Press, 2004), 128–34.

[87] *Autobiography*, II, 503.

[88] Hammond, *Modern Novel*, 204.

For instance, the country house is no longer the deserved reward of nineteenth-century fiction, but becomes the conspicuous symbol of the evil of existing social conditions, the 'Bladesover theory that dominates our minds'.[89] Bladesover was based on Up Park, the country house where Wells grew up, according to Kirby Farrell, itself 'a museum of early-nineteenth-century culture'.[90] Rural and urban topography are no longer, as in much Victorian fiction, morally antithetical, but equally the by-products of absurd economic and social conditions. The country retreat that traditionally rewards the fortunate, singular protagonist of Victorian fiction is the first place from which George escapes. Nor will there be a Romantic union with nature, since the landscape has been disfigured by advertising hoardings and suburban jerry-building. The London topography that has been employed by so many Victorian novelists to educate their protagonists about the moneyed nature of the world and the material limits to desire is finally escaped as George leaves the Thames on the lethal battleship *X-2*.[91] Finally, the social conditions, particularly class, that have shaped such narratives will be transformed by the forthcoming apocalypse of which *X-2* is a part, Wells perceiving the looming international crisis that will lead to the Great War (see the final chapter). History and art are in states of flux as Wells writes this 'Condition of England' novel; 1914 will accelerate the force of change in both.

Wells wrote in the Preface to the Atlantic Edition of the novel:

> It was to give a view of the contemporary social and political system in Great Britain, an old and degenerating system, tried and strained by new inventions and new ideas and invaded by a growing multitude of mere adventurers.[92]

The Balzacian description of the history of Lady Grove pastiches the classic realist novel's genealogy of its own setting. Although *Tono-Bungay* is a first-person autobiographical narrative, the novel surprisingly omits the birth and early childhood of the hero. The temptations of (family) romance are resisted, and even strenuously assailed as they never would have been in Balzac. The hero's missing father and the erotic charge between George and his aunt are included not to lead the plot anywhere, but because they contingently occur.[93] This sense of reality's inherent

---

[89] *Tono-Bungay*, 95.
[90] Farrell, *Post-Traumatic Culture*, 113–14; *Autobiography*, 136.
[91] Lucille Herbert, '*Tono-Bungay*: Tradition and Experiment', in *H. G. Wells: A Collection of Critical Essays*, ed. Bergonzi, 140–56.
[92] *Tono-Bungay*, 3.
[93] In a deleted passage in the typescript, George tells her '"If you weren't my aunt I believe I should fall in love with you this minute"' (Illinois Collection, TO 1320).

waywardness also leads the narrator frequently to violate the chronology of his story: 'the objective story is made up of little things that are difficult to set in a proper order', George says of his relationship with Beatrice (*Tono-Bungay*, bk 3, ch. 3, 7).[94] Avoidance of expiatory narrative has previously been a trait of Wells's fiction: in the confessed ignorance of the narrators of *The Food of the Gods* and *The Sea Lady*, Prendick's refusal to hear the story of Montgomery's past in *The Island of Doctor Moreau*, or the indecipherable texts that end *The Invisible Man* and *The First Men in the Moon*. This trait becomes more prominent still in *Tono-Bungay*. George rejects providential ordering in his novel, asserting to his cousins that 'you might do just as you liked [. . .] if you were cad enough' (*Tono-Bungay*, bk 1, ch. 2, 1). Even the admission of once having murdered a man merits only a small part of George's effort to tell his own story.[95]

Rather than focusing a coherent moral gloss on the novel's plot, Wells's representation of reality instead expands, demonstrating an aesthetic more extensive and inclusive than 'economical', and thus, by its nature, wasteful. 'I have called this novel *Tono-Bungay*, but I had better have called it *Waste*,' notes George ruefully towards the end of the novel (*Tono-Bungay*, bk 4, ch. 3, 1). *Tono-Bungay*'s commitment to the inclusion of unmanageable contingent realities accounts for both the scope of its content (including the characteristic recycling of numerous autobiographical elements from Wells's own life) and also the internal structural disorder of its form.[96] 'Mess is *Tono-Bungay*'s structural principle,' writes Peter Kemp. 'The book is given shape by a regular motif of irregularity.'[97] *Tono-Bungay*'s formal wastefulness, its rhetorical over-production, mimetically reproduces the wasteful over-production and inflation of the consumer economy that is its subject.[98] Its dissolution of both the moral certainties and the formal limits of the Victorian novel articulates the dissolution of Victorian faith in social progress. The novel's language is characterized throughout by flux, change, dissolution, and decay, as if, similar to the scientific romances, none of its assertions is to be wholly believed; or, to paraphrase James, the 'fluidity' of all the narrator's self-revelations is so 'terrible' that he cannot help but incriminate himself, as he wilfully

---

[94] *Autobiography*, II, 639; J. R. Hammond, 'The Timescale of *Tono-Bungay*: A Problem in Literary Detection', *Wellsian*, 14 (1991), 1–8.

[95] See the account of George's indifference in the post-colonial reading of Suzanne Keen, *Victorian Renovations of the Novel: Narrative Annexes and the Boundaries of Representation* (Cambridge: Cambridge University Press, 1998), 167–77.

[96] William Kupinse, 'Wasted Value: The Serial Logic of H. G. Wells's *Tono-Bungay*', *Novel* 33/1 (1999), 51–72. Wells wrote, and then deleted, a preface denying that *Tono-Bungay* is an autobiographical novel (Illinois Collection, TO 3–4).

[97] Kemp, *H. G. Wells and the Culminating Ape*, 131.

[98] Baudrillard, *Consumer Society*, 42–3.

declares his own unreliability.[99] George declares himself 'a lax, undisciplined story-teller' (*Tono-Bungay*, bk 1, ch. 1, 2) and is too bored and disordered to make his story more comprehensive by including, for instance, the official reports on Mordet Island or on his uncle's bankruptcy. (An earlier manuscript draft presents the narrative, like Prendick's, in a posthumous frame after George's death in an aeroplane accident.)[100] The first-person novel characteristically masquerades as an authentic narrative—a diary, an autobiography, a suicide note—but George Ponderevo repeatedly calls his story a 'novel', violating the expectation of realism's claim to verisimilitude.

James's praise for Wells's previous novels had been effusive but mixed; in the opening to *Tono-Bungay*, one almost receives the impression of a rather hurt Wells, aware of his own technical shortcomings as a writer, defending himself from yet another Jamesian harangue:[101]

> I warn you this book is going to be something of an agglomeration [...] as this is my first novel and almost certainly my last, I want to get in too all sorts of things that struck me, things that amused me and impressions I got—even though they don't minister directly to my narrative at all. [...] My ideas of a novel all through are comprehensive rather than austere. [...]
>
> I'll own that here, with the pen already started, I realise what a fermenting mass of things learned and emotions experienced and theories formed I've got to deal with, and how, in a sense, hopeless my book must be from the outset [...] I've found the restraints and rules of the art (as I made them out) impossible for me. [...] And it isn't a constructed tale I have to tell but unmanageable realities. (*Tono-Bungay*, bk 1, ch. 1, 1)

For Wells, experience is too multifarious either for the progressive moral certainties of Victorian fiction or the aesthetic certainties of the Jamesian novel. The epistemological faith needed for such formal rigour requires an ultimately stable place in society, and, unlike David Copperfield or Henry James, George Ponderevo is not a man who feels at home in the society in which he lives. Instead, George narrates from a 'cross-wise' point of view a 'miscellaneous tasting of life' (*Tono-Bungay*, bk 1, ch. 1, 1), an anti-Victorian attempt at a *Bildung* that will allow him to be singular enough to control his own narrative, self-authored and free from moral restraints.

[99] Booth, *The Doctor, the Detective and Arthur Conan Doyle*, 174–5; J. R. Hammond, 'The Narrative Voice in *Tono-Bungay*', *Wellsian*, 12 (1989), 16–21; Jeffrey Sommers, 'Wells's *Tono-Bungay*: The Novel Within the Novel', *Studies in the Novel*, 17/1 (1985), 69–79; Preface to *The Ambassadors*, James, *Prefaces*, 1304–21 (1316). For James's strictures on the first-person *The New Machiavelli*, see *Henry James and H. G. Wells*, 128–9.

[100] 'In this book George Ponderevo who was killed at Ditchling in November 1906 through the collapse of a flying machine, tells the story of his life' (Illinois Collection, TO-1).

[101] Lodge, '*Tono-Bungay* and the Condition of England', 117.

This novel replaces the *Bildungsroman* as its narrative model with the art of the advertisement. Commodities such as Tono-Bungay are advertised, like virtuous conduct in the traditional *Bildungsroman*, as a remedy that will cure ills and ensure happiness. Such a narrative threatens to elide morality from narrative entirely, however, for at its ending gratification is separated from the consumer not by correct conduct, but by the act of purchase—as Pasi Falk notes, in order to be effective an advertisement should always have a happy ending.[102] Advertising is the negative image of Wells's ideal of didactic art, in which the effect of beauty to inspire, move, and change the mind is used to cause harm to the body. The sharing of the book's name with that of the patent medicine at its heart shows fiction to be just as much a commodity as Moggs's Domestic Soap. George speaks of 'those Moggs' Soap Advertisements, that wrought a revolution in that department of literature' (*Tono-Bungay*, bk 3, ch. 1, 2); (Graves in *Mr. Blettsworthy on Rampole Island* (1928) is a writer who is the first 'to enter literature by way of writing advertisements'—*Mr. Blettsworthy*, ch. 4, 14).[103] Like patent medicine, art is a worthless nostrum that promises relief from the demands of reality, but which does no material good; writing is (as in Derrida's account of Plato) 'passed off as a helpful remedy whereas it is in truth harmful'.[104] Literature and advertising are tellingly collocated on the cover of the literary magazine that Edward purchases, *The Sacred Grove*:

> "THE SACRED GROVE"
> *A Weekly Magazine of Art, Philosophy, Science and Belles Lettres*
> HAVE YOU A NASTY TASTE IN YOUR MOUTH?
> IT IS LIVER
> YOU NEED ONE TWENTY-THREE PILL
> (JUST ONE).
> NOT A DRUG BUT A LIVE AMERICAN REMEDY.

CONTENTS
A Hitherto Unpublished Letter from Walter Pater.
Charlotte Brontë's Maternal Great Aunt.
A New Catholic History of England.
The Genius of Shakespeare.

---

[102] Ellen Gruber Garvey, *The Adman in the Parlor: Magazines and the Gendering of Consumer Culture, 1880s to 1910* (New York: Oxford University Press, 1996), 106 and *passim*; Pasi Falk, *The Consuming Body* (London: Sage, 1994), 179; L. A. Loeb, *Consuming Angels: Advertising and Victorian Women* (Oxford University Press, Oxford, 1994), 13, 102, 120; Judith Flanders, *Consuming Passions: Leisure and Pleasure in Victorian Britain* (London: Harper Perennial, 2007), 133; Baudrillard, *Consumer Society*, 127.

[103] *Mr. Blettsworthy on Rampole Island*, 277.

[104] Jacques Derrida, 'Plato's Pharmacy', in *Dissemination*, trans. and ed. Barbara Johnson (Chicago: University of Chicago Press, 1981), 62–171 (103).

Correspondence:—The Mendelian Hypothesis; The Split Infinitive; "Commence," or "Begin"; Claverhouse; Socialism and the Individual; The Dignity of Letters.

Folk-lore Gossip.

The Stage; the Paradox of Acting.

Travel, Biography, Verse, Fiction etc.

THE BEST PILL IN THE WORLD FOR AN

IRREGULAR LIVER. (*Tono-Bungay*, bk 3, ch. 1, 5)[105]

George then suggests, like Wells's utopian writing, that medical and literary criticism are too important to be left to private enterprise.

As discussed in the first chapter, the greater visibility after 1870 of literature as a commodity had produced an anxiety that the aesthetic capital of literature would be devalued. 'Culture is a paradoxical commodity,' Theodor Adorno later warned. 'So completely is [culture] subject to the law of exchange that it is no longer exchanged; it is so blindly consumed in use that it can no longer be used. Therefore it amalgamates with advertising.'[106] Advertisement co-opts and conquers the aesthetic; literature and visual art become copy-writing and illustration, as the talents of George, his uncle, and Ewart are prostituted by the specious manufacturing of signs, including money, that is the Tono-Bungay enterprise.[107] George dallies briefly with Fabian socialism, but while recognizing that the consumer economics in which his birthright has been fraudulently invested is founded on a civilized lie, he accommodates himself to the lie, since it profits him personally. (Indeed, as it is the

---

[105] John Gross, in *The Rise and Fall of the Man of Letters*, describes this pastiche as 'scarcely a caricature of the real thing' (214); see also McDonald, *British Literary Culture*, 89. Cf.:

> On the façade to the right a huge intensely bright disc of weird colour span incessantly, and letters of fire that came and went spelt out –
> "DOES THIS MAKE YOU GIDDY?"
> Then, a pause, followed by
> "TAKE A PURKINJE'S DIGESTIVE PILL."
> A vast and desolating braying began. "If you love Swagger literature, put your telephone on to Bruggles, the Greatest Author of all Time. The Greatest Thinker of all Time. Teaches you Morals up to your scalp! The very image of Socrates, except the back of his head, which is like Shakespeare. He has six toes, dresses in red, and never cleans his teeth. Hear HIM!" 'A Story of the Days to Come', 367.

[106] Theodor Adorno and Max Horkheimer, 'The Culture Industry: Enlightenment as Mass Deception', *Dialectic of Enlightenment*, 120–67 (161). For a more historicized account of the nineteenth-century culture industry, see Andreas Huyssen, 'Adorno in Reverse: From Hollywood to Richard Wagner', in *After the Great Divide: Modernism, Mass Culture, Postmodernism* (Bloomington: Indiana University Press, 1986), 16–43.

[107] *First and Last Things*, 119.

success of Tono-Bungay that lifts the horizons of Wells's autobiographical hero, it was literature that enriched the author himself.)[108]

Adorno and Horkheimer add that 'the triumph of advertising in the culture industry is that consumers feel compelled to buy and use its products even though they see through them'.[109] In the economy of *Tono-Bungay*, the label entirely supersedes the product—one may as well label recycled rubbish like cinder-biscuits. As in Dickens's *Our Mutual Friend* (1862–3), rubbish is transmuted into money; both novels remind of money's dangerous power to distort or falsify signification.[110] Carlyle had feared in *Past and Present* that monetary representation would take precedence over the now-receding truth, the spectacle victorious over the reality: 'The symbol shall be held sacred, defended everywhere with tipstaves, ropes and gibbets; the thing signified shall be composedly cast to the dogs.'[111] At a loss to define what Tono-Bungay actually *is*, his uncle replies to George, 'It's the secret of vigour. Didn't you read that label?' (*Tono-Bungay*, bk 3, ch. 1, 2). Tono-Bungay is a fake medicine with no beneficial effect, an apparent panacea that is in fact slightly harmful to the kidneys. A British Medical Association pamphlet of 1909 records ingredients in supposed remedies such as salt, sugar (one 100% sugar), aniseed, liquorice, honey, turmeric, powdered rhubarb, flour, butter-fat, lard, soap, chalk, talcum-powder, ammonia, water, sulphur, ash, dye, tar, lead, hemlock, atropine, caffeine, alcohol, morphine and chloroform.[112] The labelling of Tono-Bungay's ingredients as a panacea represents the detachment for ever of the signified from an accurate signifier.

The universal power of false commercial signification is reinforced by the novel's topography, especially 1880s London:

> But this London was vast! it was endless! it seemed the whole world had changed into packed frontages and hoardings and street spaces. (*Tono-Bungay*, bk 1, ch. 3, 5)

---

[108] See H. G. Wells, 'Mr. Wells Explains Himself', *T. P.'s Magazine* (December 1911), author's TS, Illinois Collection; David Lodge, 'Assessing H. G. Wells', *The Novelist at the Crossroads: And Other Essays on Fiction and Criticism* (Ithaca: Cornell University Press, 1971), 205–20 (217–19).

[109] Adorno and Horkheimer, 'The Culture Industry', 167. Cf. *The Work, Wealth and Happiness of Mankind*, 223.

[110] *Christina Alberta's Father* reuses the image: 'to work cinder heaps for residual gold' (Toronto: Macmillan, 1925), 13.

[111] Thomas Carlyle, *Past and Present*, ed. Chris R. Vanden Bossche, Joel J. Brattin, and D. J. Trela (Berkeley: University of California Press, 2005), 193.

[112] See *Secret Remedies: What They Cost and What they Contain, Based on Analysis Made for the British Medical Association* (London: British Medical Association, 1909); also E. S. Turner, *The Shocking History of Advertising*, rev. edn, Penguin, Harmondsworth, 1952), 159. Wells refers to the pamphlet in *An Englishman Looks at the World* (86).

And then my eye caught the advertisements on the south side of "Sorber's food," of "Cracknell's Ferric Wine," very bright and prosperous signs, illuminated at night, and I realised how astonishingly they looked at home there, how evidently part they were in the whole thing. (*Tono-Bungay*, bk 2. ch. 2, 5)[113]

Advertisements are for Wells an inescapable component of urban topography, not merely a symbol for the modern economy, but synecdoche, indissolubly a part of 'a capitalistic system gigantic and invisible' (*Tono-Bungay*, bk 2, ch. 1, 3).[114]

Advertising's power is immanent, irresistible, its power of misleading so strong that it even affects its consumers' experience of their own bodies. Tono-Bungay is a false compensation for bodily deficiency, called into existence not by a need but by the creation of an unfulfillable desire, the desire for wholly perfect health. Patent medicine is thus the perfect model for modern consumption: advertising creates the illusion of an internal lack, a deficit, that only the product can fill.[115]

Commerce possesses such invincible creative power because its products seek to repair an imaginary deficiency in the body; and the image of the reified body is an insistent presence in the novel.[116] Its most visible body is Edward's: his Napoleonic ambitions are continually undermined

---

[113] Compare Pip's arrival in London: '"while dry rot and wet rot and all the silent rots that rot in neglected roof and cellar [. . .] addressed themselves faintly to my sense of smell, and moaned, "Try Barnard's Mixture"'. Charles Dickens, *Great Expectations*, ed. Margaret Cardwell (Oxford: Clarendon, 1993), 168.

[114] Cf.: 'Roper's meadows are now quite frankly a slum; back doors and sculleries gape towards the railway, their yards are hung with tattered washing unashamed; and there seem to be more boards by the railway every time I pass, advertising pills and pickles, tonics and condiments, and suchlike solicitudes of a people with no natural health nor appetite left in them', *The New Machiavelli*, 42. Patent medicines and advertising were clearly obsessions for Wells: see *Literary Criticism*, ed. Parrinder and Philmus, 94; *Anticipations*, 55, 145–6n.; *Mankind in the Making*, 219, 262; *The Food of the Gods*, *Works*, V, 59–66, in which Caterham, the Prime Minister, is addicted to drugs; *The Wealth of Mr. Waddy*, 107, 139, 171, 204–5; *In the Days of the Comet*, *Works*, X, 163; *The Future in America* (London: Chapman and Hall, 1906), 222; *New Worlds for Old*, 119; *The War in the Air: And Particularly How Mr Bert Smallways Faired While It Lasted*, ed. Patrick Parrinder (London: Penguin, 2005), 63; *First and Last Things*, 118; *Marriage*, 490; *The Dream*, 352; *The World of William Clissold*, 187; *Meanwhile: The Picture of a Lady* (New York: George-Doran, 1927), 303; *The Open Conspiracy*, 109; *Science of Life*, I, 766; *The Shape of Things to Come: The Ultimate Revolution* (London: Hutchinson, 1936), 181; *Babes in the Darkling Wood*, 242; *Science and the World-Mind*, 19; *You Can't Be Too Careful: A Sample of Life* (London: Secker & Warburg, 1941), 37.

[115] Falk, *Consuming Body*, 162–8.

[116] Cf. Baudrillard, *Consumer Society*, 129. In a passage cut from the *English Review* proofs, George frets, 'I was "commercialized" in spite of myself. We're all commercialized and debased, each in our measure, by the universal system that produces us. We must have money, that is the gist of it . . . ' (Illinois Collection, TO-1989).

by the narrator's mockery of his speech impediment, malevolent clothing, fidgeting, and foolishly conspicuous affair, obvious 'like a placard on a hoarding' (*Tono-Bungay*, bk 3, ch. 2, 9). Aunt Susan, privy to the fraud of Tono-Bungay, would like to take the body of the impostor and 'put an old label onto *him* round the middle like his bottles are' (*Tono-Bungay*, bk. 1. ch. 3, 2). Edward's body subsequently undergoes the same 'stupendous inflation' (*Tono-Bungay*, bk 3. ch 2, 7) as his financial empire, George feeling on his first visit to the Schäfers' Hotel 'a magic change in our relative proportions' (*Tono-Bungay*, bk 2, ch. 2, 1). Edward undergoes an accelerated, parodic form of social mobility that will end either in a peerage or a disaster, and, like Kipps, indulges in limitless bodily consumption, buying greater quantities of an item than he could ever possibly need. Consumerism's obsession with novelty is heavily emphasized in the new products cited in the novel: the Marconigram, electric light, telephone, motorcycle, and even branded Garibaldi biscuits.[117] Consumer economics trivializes technology, which should be the enabler of utopia, into mere novelty.

The narrative that George projects for himself tries to evade the encumbrance of his body. He first resolves to escape his class identity when Beatrice, like Estella in *Great Expectations*, taunts him with his 'dirty hands' and 'the fray to his collar' (*Tono-Bungay*, bk 1, ch. 1, 7). One's body can no more be fully escaped, however, than class or economics, and George's body makes its presence felt regardless through intoxication, injury, and sexual desire. Not only is Edward Ponderevo's financial empire founded on a drug, but most of the book's dialogue (between its male characters at least) takes place, like that of much *fin-de-siècle* fiction, through an alcoholic haze and a fug of tobacco smoke.[118] George suffers from sea-sickness, radiation sickness, and injuries sustained in aircraft crashes. The most prominent of these bodily reminders is sexual desire, which compels George to enter the marriage market. His relationship with Marion begins when George provides her with money for a bus fare. The offer from Edward of morally indefensible money allows the purchase of Marion, 'the careless proprietor of a physical property that had turned my head like strong wine' (*Tono-Bungay*, bk 2, ch. 1, 4). George's brief admission of carnal desire compromises his attempted self-definition: he must barter his socialist politics for the new clothes and the fraudulently derived income desired by his fiancée Marion.

---

[117] See throughout W. Hamish Fraser, *The Coming of the Mass Market, 1850–1914* (London: Macmillan, 1981).

[118] Newell, *Structure in Four Novels*, 77–8; Chan, *Economy of the Short Story*, 34; Veblen, *Theory of the Leisure Class*, 108.

Wells's model of the consumer subject, is, as commonly, gendered as specifically female. The narrator of Wells's 1895 collection of newspaper dialogues *Select Conversations with an Uncle* is also called George. He too has a consuming uncle, who pathologizes advertisement and shopping as a female condition:

> "Do you know, George, I sometimes fancy that [tradesmen] have hypnotised womankind into the belief that all these uncomfortable things are absolutely necessary to a valid marriage—just as they have persuaded the landlady class that no house is complete without a big mirror over the fireplace and a bulgy sideboard. There is a very strong flavour of mesmeric suggestion about a woman's attitude towards these matters, considered in the light of her customary common sense. Do you know, George, I really believe there is a secret society of tradesmen, a kind of priesthood, who get hold of our womankind and muddle them up with all these fancies. It's a sort of white magic. Have you ever been in a draper's shop, George?"
> "Never," I said. "I always wait outside—among the dogs."
> "Have you ever read a ladies' newspaper?"
> "I didn't know," said I, "that there was any part to read. It's all advertisements; all the articles are advertisements, all the paragraphs, the stories, the answers to correspondents—everything."[119]

George notes that Marion's own choice of clothing displays her body better than most girls of her class. To possess her body, however, he must surrender to her taste for conspicuous consumption, and, in a sensation common in Wells's short stories, he must become reified, feminized, alienated from his own body, even textualized:

> What was all this fuss for? The mere indecent advertisement that I had been passionately in love with Marion! [. . .] I knew too well I didn't look myself. I looked like a special coloured supplement to *Men's Wear*, or *The Tailor and Cutter*, Full Dress For Ceremonial Occasions. [. . .] I felt lost—in a strange body, and when I glanced down myself for reassurance, the straight white abdomen, the alien legs confirmed that impression. (*Tono-Bungay*, bk 2, ch. 4, 4)[120]

When this sense of dislocation between consciousness and body recurs at his aunt's imitation-aristocratic garden-party, George flees from public gaze, hiding in the house and tearing off his uncomfortable new collar.

---

[119] *Select Conversations*, 66.

[120] On the 'alienated body', see Bourdieu, *Distinction*, 207. Later, Beatrice ponders, '"We're shadows. We've got out of our positions, out of our bodies—and together. That's the good thing of it—together. But that's why the world can't see us and why we hardly see the world"' (*Tono-Bungay*, 317). Cf.: '"Nature has set about this business in a CHEAP sort of way. She is like some pushful advertising tradesman. She isn't frank with us; she just humbugs us into what she wants with us."' *The Secret Places of the Heart, Works*, XXV, 366.

The collar of his marriage is later torn off as well. The gratification George expects from marriage proves as illusory as that offered by the adverts for Tono-Bungay, and as physically unsatisfactory as the purchased gratification of his honeymoon. Offered the more responsive body of the 'magnificently eupeptic' (possessing good digestion—*Tono-Bungay*, bk 2. ch. 4, 11) Effie on better terms, the 'bargain' with Marion is broken.

George's ideal mate is the woman who initially encouraged him to escape from his class, the Hon. Beatrice Normandy, who also seeks to escape from her own doomed, aristocratic class. She has achieved this, however, by surrendering her body to the market, as the kept woman of the 65-year-old rake Lord Carnaby. Trying to impress her too, George becomes implicated in the same kind of 'economy of substance' (*Tono-Bungay*, bk 3, ch. 3, 5) for the sake of spectacular display as Tono-Bungay in order 'to advertise my return to Beatrice' (*Tono-Bungay*, bk 4, ch. 1, 2). The intrusive reality of Tono-Bungay's eventual failure forces a final accounting, however, and their marriage cannot take place either unless George's money funds it. After George and Beatrice part for the last time, one of the last words he hears her say is possibly 'chloral' (*Tono-Bungay*, bk 4, ch. 2, 3); she too, like Effie's poet-lover and the rest of the body-politic, has become addicted to the consolation of narcotics.

The novel's final book fully exposes the nature of Tono-Bungay's 'rascal enterprise and rubbish-selling' (*Tono-Bungay*, bk 2. ch. 4, 5).[121] Participation in the economy of signs and misleading appearances requires a kind of artistic suspension of disbelief:

> It was all a monstrous payment for courageous fiction, a gratuity in return for the one reality of human life—illusion. [. . .] Yet it seems to me at times that all this present commercial civilisation is no more than my poor uncle's career writ large, a swelling, thinning bubble of assurances; that its arithmetic is just as unsound, its dividends as ill-advised, its ultimate aim as vague and forgotten; that it all drifts on perhaps to some tremendous parallel to his individual disaster. . . (*Tono-Bungay*, bk 3, ch. 1, 3)[122]

The success of the Ponderevos' business, 'the giving of nothing coated in advertisements for money' (*Tono-Bungay*, bk 3, ch. 1, 3) has parodically proven money's merely imaginary status. With the imaginary promises of paper money Edward Ponderevo briefly funds an empire.[123] Edward

---

[121] Cf.: 'The selling of rubbish for money, exemplified by the great patent medicine fortunes and the fortunes achieved by the debasement of journalism' (*New Worlds for Old*, 95).

[122] See *Mankind in the Making*, 256.

[123] In 1887, Thomas J. Barratt of Pear's Soap debased 250,000 French small coins by stamping 'Pears' on them—Turner, *Shocking History*, 115, 76. The Sleeper's immense fortune is also derived in part from advertising (*When the Sleeper Wakes*, 91).

Ponderevo has not been producing anything tangible, but 'mint[ing] faith' (*Tono-Bungay*, bk 3, ch. 1, 3); when supplies of that faith run low, his financial empire collapses. Tono-Bungay's deception can thus hardly be a crime, for it merely embodies capitalism in its present form. The deficit can only be supplied by ingesting/investing additional capital, in the criminal act of taking quap from Mordet Island.

The structural validity of this episode has been much discussed, but George admits it would 'make a book by itself' (*Tono-Bungay*, bk 3, ch. 4, 3). A thematic, rather than structural, link attaches the quap episode to this disordered novel. Quap is a waste material, radioactive and in the process of decaying. The body of Edward Ponderevo's empire is ailing, and George hopes that it can be healed, on the model of the newly developing cancer treatment of radiation therapy, by ingesting the poisonous African quap. Edward Said has contested that for imperial powers '(following the general principles of free trade) outlying territories are available for use, at will, at the novelist's discretion, usually for relatively simple purposes such as immigration [*sic*.], fortune or exile'.[124] (In the 1890s, the term 'imperialism' first began to be generally employed in this sense.)[125]

Wells often uses ships as metaphors for society.[126] A boat was also the subject of an artistic disagreement between Wells and Conrad:

> But it was all against Conrad's over-sensitized receptivity that a boat could ever be just a boat. He wanted to see it with a definite vividness of its own. But I wanted to see it and to see it only in relation to something else—a story, a thesis.[127]

If a whole book were to be made of the quap episode, as George suggests, with the boat as a macrocosm of society, it would surely be best written by Conrad. (The captain and Pollack are spiteful portraits of Conrad and Ford Madox Ford, in whose *English Review Tono-Bungay* originally appeared, the cause of a subsequent rift between Ford and Wells.)[128] Quap

---

[124] Edward Said, *Culture and Imperialism* (London: Chatto & Windus, 1993), 88.

[125] Eric Hobsbawm, *Industry and Empire: 1750 to the Present Day* (Harmondsworth: Penguin, 1969), 60, 74; on the novel as a proto-modernist account of imperialism, see Benita Parry, '*Tono-Bungay*: The Failed Electrification of the Empire of Light', in *Postcolonial Studies: A Materialist Critique* (London: Routledge, 2004), 148–61.

[126] *A Modern Utopia*, 7, 32; *The Future in America*, 31; see also Linda Dryden, 'H. G. Wells and Joseph Conrad: A Literary Friendship', *Wellsian*, 28 (2005), 1–13; Born, *Birth of Liberal Guilt*, 156–8; and Nicholas Delbanco, *Group Portrait: Joseph Conrad, Stephen Crane, Ford Madox Ford, Henry James and H. G. Wells* (London: Faber, 1982), 178–9.

[127] *Autobiography*, II, 619.

[128] See Martin Ray, 'Conrad, Wells, and *The Secret Agent*: Paying Old Debts and Settling Old Scores', *Modern Language Review*, 81/3 (1986), 560–73; Wells, letter to the *Daily Mail*, *Correspondence*, II, 285.

is volatile and radioactive, like (supposedly) the real-life patent medicine Pesqui's Uranium Wine.[129] When the crew become ill from the quap, George runs out of quinine and has nothing to treat them with but another patent medicine: unsurprisingly, it has no beneficial effect. 'Mordet' has an obvious suggestion of 'mort', death; the word 'quap' may owe something to 'Cowap', a patent medicine-selling Midhurst quack chemist under whom Wells studied as a boy, and possibly onomatopoeia for the sound of something sinking. It is also close to the slang 'crap', which in nineteenth-century slang could variously mean waste, excrement, and also money, and the dice gambling game 'craps'.[130] The society on board the brig is both literally and metaphorically radioactive: its component parts are highly disordered, subject to 'the ultimate eating away and dry-rotting and dispersal of all our world' (*Tono-Bungay*, bk 3. ch, 4, 5); for lack of technological advancement (it is wooden rather than a metal steamer like *X-2*), the bottom literally drops out of it. Edward's desired panacea ends on the ocean bed, of as little benefit as the silver in Conrad's 1904 novel *Nostromo*.

The imaginary freedom granted by wealth controls and destroys Edward.[131] As his empire collapses, so his physique deflates. Edward pays now for the gratification he has previously enjoyed, and the market in turn consumes him, no longer 'afloat' but sinking like quap, the pill-dealer addicted to drugs, the eager consumer unable to eat, the advertising genius whose ruin is proclaimed on every placard, the would-be newspaper proprietor denounced by the press as a forger. The relationship between publishers and patent medicine manufacturers was long-established in the nineteenth century: one original partner in Tono-Bungay, along with a chemist and 'some pirate printers' (*Tono-Bungay*, bk 2, ch. 2, 1) was a newspaper proprietor.[132] Newspapers would, of course, be a major carrier of adverts for Tono-Bungay. By 1903, half the branches of Boots the Chemist contained libraries; in 1904 Boots bought up the front page of the *Daily Mail* for eight consecutive days. Edward Ponderevo unsuccessfully attempts to buy up the *Lancet* and *British Medical Journal*, as if trying to purchase the control of scientific truth: historically, the latter was

---

[129] *Secret Remedies*, 76.
[130] *Autobiography*, I, p. 138; Eric Partridge, *A Dictionary of Slang and Unconventional English*, 2 vols (London: Routledge & Kegan Paul, 1967–70), I, 189; J. McDonald, *A Dictionary of Obscenity, Taboo and Euphemism* (Sphere, London, 1988), 32. For the symbolic correspondences between money and excrement, see Sigmund Freud, 'Character and Anal Erotism', *The Standard Edition of the Complete Psychological Works of Sigmund Freud*, 24 vols, trans. James Strachey (London: Hogarth Press, 1953–74), IX, 169–75.
[131] Linda R. Anderson, 'Self and Society in H. G. Wells's *Tono-Bungay*', *Modern Fiction Studies*, 26/2 (1980), 199–212.
[132] Vincent, *Literacy and Popular Culture*, 166–7.

willing to accept adverts for patent medicines.[133] The word 'tabloid' was coined from 'tablet' and 'alkaloid' in 1884 and successfully defended in a patent action in 1903 by the drug manufacturer Wellcome. In 1901, the *Westminster Review* used the word as an adjective for a particular kind of newspaper journalism, epitomized by the *Daily Mail*'s Lord Northcliffe (another model for Edward), presumably because it is easy to swallow.[134] Space in newspapers is nonetheless available for purchase by unscrupulous advertisers such as Edward Ponderevo.[135] The capacity of newspaper readers to swallow anything that the powerful have paid for makes Wells fret in *First and Last Things* (and elsewhere):

> Since the common man is, as Gustave le Bon has pointed out, a gregarious animal, collectively rather like a sheep, emotional, hasty and shallow, the practical outcome of political democracy in all large communities under modern conditions is to put power into the hands of rich newspaper proprietors, advertising producers and the energetic wealthy generally who are best able to flood the collective mind freely with the suggestions on which it acts.[136]

George attempts, like Prendick, to escape from the disorder of the world of the novel into the objective truth of science, 'the one reality I have found in this strange disorder of experience' (*Tono-Bungay*, bk 3, ch. 3, 1). During this period he turns his back on commercial 'rascality', and gives up alcohol and tobacco. However, even this higher reality requires funding. When building the Lord Roberts Alpha, named after the imperial hero, George enjoys 'sustained research [...] not hampered by want of money', and 'the same lavish spirit of expenditure that was running away with my uncle' (*Tono-Bungay*, bk 3, ch. 3, 1). When his research can no longer be subsidized by Tono-Bungay, George must inevitably turn to a different kind of commerce. Since the terrifyingly destructive *X-2* is not 'intended for the Empire, or indeed for the hands of any European power' (*Tono-Bungay*, bk 4. ch. 3, 4), but will be sold to another, higher bidder, the end result of George's engineering researches is not a universal benefit to humanity, but another harmful consumer product. Tono-Bungay 'invaded' England, marked with flags on a map; '"the romance of modern

---

[133] Ibid., 169.

[134] 'A compressed or concentrated version of something, in later use esp. with implication of a sensationalist, populist, or reductive approach resembling that of tabloid journalism', *OED* 2; 'A newspaper having pages half the size of those of the average broadsheet, usually characterized as popular in style and dominated by sensational stories' (*OED* 3). It is used in this sense in *The Food of the Gods*, 257.

[135] Wells is still complaining about 'patent medicines, whose advertisements subsidised and so controlled and perverted press criticism' in *Exasperations* (Illinois Collection, 29).

[136] *First and Last Things*, 192. Cf. *The Sea Lady*, 307.

commerce"' says Edward. '"Conquest. Province by province. Like so-gers."' 'I put as much zeal into this Tono-Bungay as any young lieutenant who suddenly finds himself in command of a ship,' agrees George (*Tono-Bungay*, bk 2, ch. 3, 1). War is usually depicted in Wells as provoked by arms dealers and newspaper proprietors for their own financial benefit, 'the elimination of violent competition'; to paraphrase Clausewitz, war is the continuation of capitalism by other means.[137] In *The New Machiavelli*, *Tono-Bungay*'s 'political companion', Remington remembers Harcourt's imposition of death duties in 1894 as like 'a socialist dawn' (*The New Machiavelli*, bk 1, ch 4, 4).[138] Inheritance tax was imposed ostensibly to pay for rearming the navy, in a programme that led in 1906 to the launching of the *Dreadnought*, a battleship considered so powerful as to force the world's other powers to re-arm or let their navies become obsolete.[139] Wells refers in his later article 'The Great State' to dread-noughts as 'politically necessary but socially useless': his pre-First World War writing is consistent in his opposition to the arms race, or as Wells himself termed it, 'armament competition'.[140] When Edward smashes, like Kipps and the real-life chemist-turned-fraudster Whitaker Wright and the ruined financier Albert Grant before him, he leaves behind a half-finished country house.[141] George begins his life on a doomed country estate, and ends his novel on a powerful battleship, escaping the London topography that has dominated his, and previous, narratives of self-develop-ment (passing on the way two tugboats incongruously named *Caxton* and *Shakespeare*). Such freedom will only be temporary should, as Wells later correctly predicted, Europe and even the world be transformed by a war that is as much the consequence of lunatic consumer economics as Tono-Bungay itself.

---

[137] *First and Last Things*, 171; also *Correspondence*, I, 258; *The Shape of Things to Come*, 46, 72. For economic anxiety about Germany, see *Mankind in the Making*, 249; for advertising and imperialism, see Turner, *Shocking History*, 104; Loeb, *Consuming Angels*, 79–85; Thomas Richards, *The Imperial Archive: Knowledge and the Fantasy of Empire* (London: Verso, 1993), 119–67.

[138] Letter to Frederick Macmillan, *Correspondence*, II, 289; compare *Mankind in the Making*, 283.

[139] See *New Worlds for Old*, 50.

[140] 'The Past and the Great State', 38; 'The Common Sense of Warfare', *An Englishman Looks at the World*, 132–47. See also *Socialism and the Great State*, 38 and the section on Sir Basil Zaharoff in *The Work, Wealth and Happiness of Mankind*, 612–19.

[141] Geoffrey West, *H. G. Wells: A Sketch for a Portrait* (London: Gerald Howe, 1930), 180; Raknem, *H. G. Wells and his Critics*, 255–61; *Mankind in the Making*, 251; Dianne Sachko Macleod, *Art and the Victorian Middle Class* (Cambridge: Cambridge University Press, 1996), 224–5. The typescript of the novel has a single stray line in which Edward exclaims, '"That chap Whitaker Wright, he'd got his stuff ready. I haven't."' (Illinois Collection, TO-2013)

If, as David Lodge has influentially suggested, *Tono-Bungay* is a twentieth-century 'Condition of England' novel, the condition is terminal.
(When accused later in life of a Panglossian scientific optimism, Wells
retorted in a letter to the *British Weekly* that his work shows, 'the clearest
insistence on the insecurity of progress and the possibility of human
degeneration'.[142]) The distorted economic growths of Edward's empire
and body have not been healthy ones: the novel contains numerous images
of unhealthy physical growth, particularly cancer.[143] Analysing the pro-
verbial 'great wen' of London, George's prognosis is gloomy:

> All these aspects have suggested [...] some tumourous growth-process.
> [...] To this day I ask myself will these masses ever become structural,
> will they indeed shape into anything new whatever, or is that cancerous
> image their true and ultimate diagnosis? (*Tono-Bungay*, bk 2, ch. 1, 1)

John Allett uses the initials of Tono-Bungay—'T. B.'—to read the novel's
portrayal of the body-politic as tubercular, and Maria Theresa Chialant
persuasively traces the novel's disease metaphors.[144] There is, however, a
further ambiguity in Wells's use of metaphors of 'consumption'. Such a
topos may have come to Wells from Carlyle, who mocked apparent
political panaceas as a 'Morison's Pill', after the mid-nineteenth century's
most successful manufacturer of patent medicines.[145] Tono-Bungay has
sold so well to Britain's 'consumers' (a word which entered economic
theory for the first time in the 1890s) because society is sick, perhaps
incurably.[146]

George's new, unspecified freedom at the end of the book is also Wells's
escape from 'the restrictions of form'.[147] This novel reiterates Wells's
critique of high culture as a social palliative. Edward buys the decaying

[142] Letter of 26 June 1936, *Correspondence*, IV, 227. On *Tono-Bungay* as a decadent
novel, see J. H. Buckley *The Triumph of Time: A Study of the Victorian Concepts of Time,
History, Progress and Decadence* (Cambridge, MA: Belknap Press; London: Oxford Univer-
sity Press, 1967), 86–8.
[143] Lodge, 'Condition of England', 116.
[144] *Autobiography*, I, 298–304; John Allett, '*Tono-Bungay*: The Metaphor of Disease',
Wellsian, 10 (1987), 2–10; Maria Theresa Chialant, 'Disease as a Dickensian Metaphor in
Tono-Bungay', in Patrick Parrinder and Christopher Rolfe, eds, *H.G. Wells under Revision:
Proceedings of the International H.G. Wells Symposium, London. July 1986* (Selinsgrove:
Susquehanna University Press; London: Associated University Presses, 1990), 97–107. The
opening of *The History of Mr. Polly* describes the hero's internal body politic as in a state of
civil war (*Polly*, 9).
[145] *OED* 2; *Past and Present*, 26. Even Carlyle failed to escape this kind of commodification: in the 1920s, Hazeline Rose Frost skin cream was advertised with the slogan from
Carlyle, 'The strong thing is the just thing'. See Ken Arnold and Tilly Tansey, *Pills
and Profits: The Selling of Medicines since 1870* ([London]: Wellcome Trust, 1994), 52.
[146] See Baudrillard, *Consumer Society*, 167.
[147] *Henry James and H. G. Wells*, 139.

country house Lady Grove after reading a Kipling poem; as for Kipps, the detritus of Victorian art and letters that it contains are a brake on, rather than a spur to, possible development. Edward's bohemian mistress lives 'at the intellectual level of palmistry and genteel fiction' (*Tono-Bungay*, bk 3, ch. 3, 3). The novels read by Marion and George's aunt bring her only a set of unrealistic expectations; the quap 'came in as a fairy-tale and became real', advertised by the romantic Gordon-Nasmyth, who has an 'artistic temperament' (*Tono-Bungay*, bk 3, ch. 4, 3). Ewart has the artist's privilege of speaking the truth about the nature of the novel's transactions, yet his truth-telling alters nothing. He exposes the delusive nature of Tono-Bungay's ability to heal, but Ewart shares with James a practical 'detachment [...] from the moral condemnation and responsibilities that played so fine a part in his talk' (*Tono-Bungay*, bk 2, ch. 1, 3), and makes no effective difference to the sales of the product, or the plot of the novel. So much for culture's role of 'unacknowledged legislation': Ewart's cultural solutions, 'pure art', or the 'City of Women', vanish like the Holy Grail of the chalice he is paid, and fails, to produce for George's uncle.[148]

Anticipations had complained that:

> the factory-syren voice of the modern "boomster" touches whole sections of the reading public no more than fog-horns going down Channel. One would as soon think of Skinner's Soap for one's library as So-and-so's Hundred Thousand Copy Success. Instead of "everyone" talking of the Great New Book, quite considerable numbers are shamelessly admitting they don't read that sort of thing. One gets used to literary booms just as one gets used to motor cars, they are no longer marvellous, universally significant things, but merely something that goes by with much unnecessary noise and leaves a faint offence in the air. (*Anticipations*, ch. 4)

There can be no such thing as a tenable autonomous art in the economy of production represented here. In *Tono-Bungay*, high culture becomes advertising and ends in apocalypse. Edward's 'romantic exchange of commodities and property' (*Tono-Bungay*, bk 2, ch. 2, 2) reduces property, commodities, and romance alike to a mere circulation of unreliable signs.[149] *Tono-Bungay* had appeared in the year of 'the People's Budget and the Lords' veto of it; the Minority Report; suffragette hunger strikes;

---

[148] In 1886, John Everett Millais's painting *Bubbles* was purchased for £22,000 by Pears Soap to use as a poster, causing a controversy that was still being discussed in *The Times* 13 years later; Charles Lever bought William Powell Frith's *The New Dress*, and added the slogan 'So Clean' to use the image to promote Sunlight Soap. Mike Dempsey, ed., *Bubbles: Early Advertising Art from A. & F. Pears Ltd* (London: Fontana, 1978), 4; Macleod, *Art*, 341–4.

[149] Baudrillard, *Consumer Society*, 65 and throughout.

[and] the panic over German naval superiority'.[150] For Wells, both Liberal politics' strange death and James's claims for the functional autonomy of Art were no more than fiddling while Rome was already alight.

ONE VERSION OF PASTORAL: *THE HISTORY OF MR. POLLY*

If *Tono-Bungay* is Wells's last 'deliberate' attempt upon the novel proper, *The History of Mr. Polly* is a flippant one. The hero commits arson and deserts his wife, and is rewarded with a romantic, pastoral, even utopian ending. However, as in *The Wheels of Chance*, the text's parodic deployment of romantic motifs ironizes both 'real life' for its distance from the imaginary but appealing solutions offered by romance, and romance for the insufficiency of those solutions.

Polly's process of maturing takes him in the reverse direction from most nineteenth-century *Bildungsromanen* protagonists, away from marriage and a snugly fitting social role. This novel is uncharacteristically positive towards romance, but the romance that Polly ultimately finds is that of lived experience, rather than the kind found in books. (Thirteen years after reviewing it, Wells takes a further swipe in this novel at Le Gallienne's *The Golden Girl*, describing it as a 'very detrimental book'—*Polly*, ch. 5, 1.) For obvious reasons, in most novels enthusiasm for reading is usually portrayed as a positive character trait. Polly's enthusiasm for reading is never correctly channelled, however, and hinders—rather than assists—his development. (Perhaps one reason for George Ponderevo's relative success compared to the other protagonists is that he grows up with few books to read.) Poor schooling means that Polly loves reading, but hates writing, and thus he will only, like the Sea People, be a passive consumer, and never a producer of texts. 'Words attracted him, and under happier conditions he might have used them well' (*Polly*, ch. 2, 5): Polly's mangling of language is another symptom of his maimed education and of frustrated creativity.

Polly's reading is not directed towards the improvement of either himself or the world (nor is Rusper's equally fruitless reading of economics), but is an escape from everyday tedium; as objects, his books are a physical obstacle in Miriam's unsuccessful struggle to keep the house tidy. The narrator praises Polly's enthusiasm and attempts towards discrimination, but ironizes, even deprecates, his choice of reading matter:

---

[150] Samuel Hynes, *The Edwardian Turn of Mind* (Princeton: Princeton University Press, 1968), 86.

He still read books when he had a chance, books that told of glorious places abroad and glorious times, that wrung a rich humour from life and contained the delight of words freshly and expressively grouped. But alas! there are not many such books, and for the newspapers and the cheap fiction that abounded more and more in the world Mr. Polly had little taste. [...] Great land of sublimated things, thou World of Books, happy asylum, refreshment and refuge from the world of everyday! (*Polly*, ch. 7, 1)

Like Hoopdriver, Polly fantasizes in the clichés of romance. 'Drinking at the poisoned fountains of English literature, fountains so unsuited to the needs of a decent clerk or shopman' (*Polly*, ch. 5,4) leads him, in the chapter entitled 'Romance', first into the disastrous flirtation with the schoolgirl Christabel (her name an allusion to Coleridge), and then into an over-hasty marriage to his cousin. Polly's father is said by his local practitioner to have died of 'imagination' (*Polly*, ch. 3, 1), rather than appendicitis; the poor choices that Polly makes when influenced by fiction demonstrate that he shares such dangerous inherited characteristics. Once he becomes ferryman at the Potwell Inn (latterly 'Omlets', after Polly's ignorant orthography proves to be not a disadvantage, but a quaint selling point), Polly invents words less frequently.[151] Since reality now fulfils his desires, he no longer needs to sublimate his wishes into pointless creativity. '"You didn't seem to mean anything you said,"' complains Miriam (*Polly*, ch. 6, 2), surprised that Polly has proposed to her: his unfocused linguistic over-production has actually inhibited effective communication.

Parsons is the closest that the novel has to an artist, with his Bohemian dress, and declamatory enthusiasm for Shakespeare, Milton, Rabelais, and Carlyle. 'Like many a fellow-artist', however, he falls 'prey to theories' (*Polly*, ch. 2, 1), and seeks to embellish his social role as a window dresser with artistic flourishes. Parsons's consequent sacking shows that taste for culture is more likely to lead to unemployment and failure than to sweetness and light.[152]

After the flirtation with Christabel, Polly suffers fifteen years of non-narratable marriage and labour in the real world. It thus takes a form of the end of the world to rescue him. The narrator shares his hero's arsonist tendencies towards art and architecture: 'a large number of houses deserve to be burnt, most modern furniture, an overwhelming majority of pictures and books' (*Polly*, ch. 10, 1). As in the *War of the Worlds* and *The War in the Air*, since catastrophe necessitates reconstruction, sometimes catastrophe is to be actively desired:

---

[151] Haynes, *H. G. Wells*, 193.
[152] Kevin Swafford, 'Aesthetics, Narrative, and the Critique of Respectability in *The History of Mr. Polly*', *H. G. Wells's Fin-de-Siècle*, ed. Partington, 70–81.

When a man has once broken through the paper walls of everyday circum-
stance, those unsubstantial walls that hold so many of us securely prisoned
from the cradle to the grave, he has made a discovery. If the world does not
please you *you can change it*. Determine to alter it at any price, and you can
change it altogether. You may change it to something sinister and angry, to
something appalling, but it may be you will change it to something brighter,
something more agreeable, and at the worst something much more interesting. (*Polly*, ch. 9, 1)

Like all of Wells's realist fictions, *Mr. Polly* pays close attention to
clothing. In this text especially, clothing does not 'fit': the Pollys' argument at the beginning of the novel is over a hat, clothes make Polly
uncomfortable at his wedding and his father's funeral, his unprofitable
stock in trade includes clothes. Lewisham is confined to his washable
collar; Ponderevo tears off his collar; to escape the 'collar' of his job, Polly
sets fire to all the clothing he owns.[153] Having decided at the last minute
not to die because he realizes he hasn't yet lived, Polly is reborn in the
fire.[154] 'Life was already in their imagination rising like a Phoenix from the
flames' (*Polly*, ch. 8, 5), rules the narrator on the inhabitants of Fish-
bourne. (Wells himself used the title *Phoenix* for a book in 1942; in *Sartor
Resartus*, Carlyle imagines Society as a phoenix, needing to be burnt before
it can be reborn.)[155] Reversing Crusoe's gift to Friday, Polly de-civilizes
himself through surrendering his trousers. Polly himself makes the comparison between his unclothed state after the fire and a new-born baby:
'"Funny not to have a pair of breeches of one's own... Like being born
again. Naked came I into the world...."' (*Polly*, ch. 8, 5).

Reborn, Polly can thus begin his 'education' over again, enjoying
landscape free from romantic corruption of its meanings before vanquish-
ing Jim and settling down miscellaneous, rather than repetitive, labour as
an odd-job man. The difference for Wells between realism and romance is
escape: *The History of Mr. Polly* is Wells's last liminal irresponsibility
before growing into the titanic global Wells of his post-Great War writing.
Appearing finally to Miriam, Polly explains away his presence by claiming
to be a 'Visitant from Another World' (*Polly*, ch. 10, 2): *Mr. Polly*'s ending
is insubstantial, ghostly, evanescent. As Polly melts away, Wells's attention
turns to more pressingly real and solid matters.

---

[153] 'Collar' is slang for 'work'—*The Concise New Partridge Dictionary of Slang and
Unconventional English*, ed. Tom Dalzell (New York: Routledge, 2008), 154.
[154] Christopher Rolfe, '"A Blaze and New Beginnings": The Ironic Use of Myth in *The
History of Mr. Polly*', *Wellsian*, 4 (1981), 24–35.
[155] Carlyle, *Sartor Resartus*, 171–5.

4

The Idea of a Planned World

H. G. Wells's Utopias

Wells prophesies, very inaccurately, in the opening of *A Modern Utopia* that the following book will be the last in the utopian/political/sociological series of which *Anticipations* (1901) had been the first. Since '*Anticipations* did not achieve its end,' Wells wrote in the first edition, it is now necessary to bring the next book in the series into being: thus (literary) utopias must repeatedly be written until (actual) Utopia is achieved.[1] In the realist novels, Wells rewrites narratives that are often different versions of his own past in order to resolve in imagination wrongs done to him, and others like him. The rewritings of his utopian visions also constitute a kind of forward revision, as if by periodic repetition of the same process of literary creation, reality might each time be improved.[2] *A Modern Utopia* closes with the corresponding prophecy:

> There will be many Utopias. Each generation will have its new version of Utopia, a little more certain and complete and real, with its problems lying closer and closer to the problems of the Thing in Being. Until at last from dreams Utopias will have come to be working drawings, and the whole world will be shaping the final World State, the fair and great and fruitful World State, that will only not be a Utopia because it will be this world. (*A Modern Utopia*, ch. 11, 5)

According to Marxist theorist Ernst Bloch, all art is in essence utopian, since it provides an image of the world as it might be if it were improved.[3] Art aims at *Vorschein*—'anticipatory illumination' of a world better than

---

[1] 'Note to the Reader', *A Modern Utopia* (London: Chapman and Hall, 1905), v–xii (v).
[2] A. L. Morton complains that this is the weakness of Wells's utopian writing in *The English Utopia* (London: Lawrence & Wishart, 1953), 183–94.
[3] Ernst Bloch, 'The Artistic Illusion as the Visible Anticipatory Illumination', in *The Utopian Function of Art: Selected Essays*, trans. Jack Zipes and Frank Mecklenburg (Cambridge, MA: MIT Press, 1988), 141–55.

the real; and the route it takes is *Uberchuss*—the 'overshot' that takes it beyond the boundaries of the real (as Wells has it, 'we live not in the truth but in the promise of the truth').[4] Such a vision for Bloch must remain fragmentary, dialectical, partially unfinished: the work of art does not satisfy in its autarkical self-completion, but as becoming. Wells leaves his literary utopias unfinished because the utopias they describe will be unfinished, in a perpetual process of coming into being. A perfect work of art for Wells risks obsolescence if its perfection leads to its over-revered isolation from the outside world; a perfect society too risks extinction if its perfection means that it will fail to evolve.[5] If Wells leaves his utopias deliberately incomplete, they will not ossify along with other artistic relics: indeed, this is part of the reason why Wells will keep revising his utopian visions, as the Open Conspiracy is continually remade: 'in a modern Utopia there will, indeed, be no perfection; in Utopia there must also be friction, conflicts, and waste, but the waste will be enormously less than in our world' (*A Modern Utopia*, ch. 1, 9).

A Modern Utopia, for example, claims the liberty of the literary, as opposed to sociological, text in disagreeing with itself: this utopia is dialogized by the Voice's disagreement not only with the botanist and with the blond *poseur*, but also with himself, when debating, for instance, whether a Utopia should eliminate or retain beer, or pets.[6] Jameson characterizes such a strategy in utopian writing thus:

> Wish-fulfillments are after all by definition never real fulfillments of desire; and must presumably always be marked by the hollowness or absence or failure at the heart of their most dearly fantasized visions [. . .]. Even the process of wish-fulfillment includes a kind of reality principle of its own, intent on not making things too easy for itself, accumulating the objections and the reality problems that stand in its way so as the more triumphantly and 'realistically' to overcome them. [. . .] What in literature or art remains an irreconcilable existence of so many absolutes [. . .] becomes in the Utopian tradition a Bakhtinian dialogue or argument between positions

---

[4] *Mankind in the Making*, 355. Cf. 'The external world impresses me as being, as a practical fact, common to me and many other creatures similar to myself; the internal, I find similar but not identical with theirs. It is *mine*. It seems to me at times no more than something cut off from that external world and put into a sort of pit or cave, much as all the inner mystery of my body, those living, writhing, warm and thrilling organs are isolated, hidden from all eyes and interference so long as I remain alive. And I myself, the essential me, am the light and watcher in the mouth of the cave' (*First and Last Things*, 55). Cf. Plato, *The Republic*, trans. Desmond Lee, 2nd edn (Harmondsworth: Penguin), bk 6.

[5] See John S. Partington, '*The Time Machine* and *A Modern Utopia*: The Static and Kinetic Utopias of the Early H. G. Wells', *Utopian Studies*, 13/1 (2002), 57–68.

[6] Parrinder, *H. G. Wells*, 91.

which claim the status of the absolute but are willing to descend into the field of struggle of representability and desire in order to win their case and convert their readership.[7]

Wells's utopias are not only in dialogue with each other, but also with previous literary utopias: Plato, in particular, is a constant point of reference, especially throughout the highly meta-textual *A Modern Utopia*.[8] In order for his text to have the effect on 'things to come' that Wells desires, he must make reference to 'things accomplished' as well.[9] Utopia is to the future as myth is to the past, but at the same time, as Jameson has argued, in utopian writing, 'the individual text carries with it a whole tradition, reconstructed and modified with each new addition'.[10] The utopias which Wells consciously imitates or to which he pays homage—the *Republic*, More's *Utopia*—are themselves part of the cultural residuum, and retain value for Wells only as long as they continue to address the historical present.[11] Even Plato's *Republic*, the utopia with the strongest influence on Wells, is described in *A Modern Utopia* as a 'museum of specific ideals' (*A Modern Utopia*, ch. 1, 5). What Wells calls 'the literature of foresight' is evaluated using the canon of hindsight.[12]

Wells's utopias must also adapt over time and improve upon their ancestors if they are to survive, since Wells's notion of the ideal society is, of course, evolutionary. *Mankind in the Making*, for example, frequently uses evolutionary terminology. In *First and Last Things*, evolutionary understanding means that, since the notion of species is mutable, there are no essential categories of being.[13] *A Modern Utopia* addresses its literary ancestors in post-Darwinian terms:

> The Utopia of a modern dreamer must needs differ in one fundamental aspect from the Nowheres and Utopias men planned before Darwin quick-

[7] Jameson, *Archaeologies*, 83.

[8] 'If anyone is to be called the Father of the Modern State it is Plato', *The Shape of Things to Come*, 107; also *Autobiography*, I, 178–9. In his article, 'The Ten Most Important Books in the World', Wells declared: 'If I were asked to name any specific books that everyone should read I doubt if I should name any but the Gospels and Plato's "Republic." [. . .] Plato's "Republic" I name because it releases the mind from all sorts of traditional and conventional views about human institutions', *John O'London's Weekly*, 26 May 1923, 210. On Wells's creations as self-aware meta-utopias, see Parrinder, *Shadows*, 97–100; Wagar, *World State*, 227.

[9] *Discovery of the Future*, 23.

[10] Jameson, *Archaeologies*, 2.

[11] Ibid., 143. *A Modern Utopia* names 'the Republic and Laws of Plato, and More's Utopia, Howells' implicit Altruria, and Bellamy's future Boston, Comte's great Western Republic, Hertzka's Freeland, Cabet's Icaria, and Campanella's City of the Sun', as well as Butler's Erewhon, and Lord Erskine's Armata' (10–13).

[12] *The World Set Free*, 171.

[13] Cf. *A Modern Utopia*, 19–21; McLean, *Early Fiction*, 158.

ened the thought of the world. Those were all perfect and static States, a balance of happiness won for ever against the forces of unrest and disorder that inhere in things. One beheld a healthy and simple generation enjoying the fruits of the earth in an atmosphere of virtue and happiness, to be followed by other virtuous, happy, and entirely similar generations, until the Gods grew weary. Change and development were dammed back by invincible dams for ever. But the Modern Utopia must be not static but kinetic, must shape not as a permanent state but as a hopeful stage, leading to a long ascent of stages. Nowadays we do not resist and overcome the great stream of things, but rather float upon it. We build now not citadels, but ships of state. [. . .] That is the first, most generalised difference between a Utopia based upon modern conceptions and all the Utopias that were written in the former time. (*A Modern Utopia*, 1, 1)

Wells's vision of utopia, like Darwin's of Nature, is holistic: Wells is imagining not an enclave, but a universe.[14] Evolutionary theory teaches Wells that his utopia cannot remain static, or it will become extinct.[15] In order for Darwin's prophecy of 'a secure future of great length' to come true, the ideal society must continually seek to adapt, to improve, and, particularly, for Wells, to encourage specialization. Utopia must not only imply a better future, but also embed the possibility of a further future still better than that.

Point of view in the genre of literary utopia is formally divided 'between expression and creation', between description and advocacy.[16] 'I had intended simply to work out and foretell, and before I had finished I was in a fine full blast of exhortation', Wells later wrote of *Anticipations*.[17] On the one hand, the utopist is communicating an imaginative vision of a perfected world, a systematized Linnaean classification of imaginative possibilities; on the other, seeking to persuade the reader of the steps necessary to transform the present and make the vision real.[18] Wells's voice is often therefore characterized in these texts by a note of impatience, of wishing, as in *The Time Machine*, for the passage of time to be accelerated; as if by force of creative imagination alone he can impose on

---

[14] *The Work, Wealth and Happiness of Mankind*, 780.

[15] Haynes, *H. G. Wells*, 22.

[16] Jameson, *Archaeologies*, 43; Károly Pintér, 'Narrative Estrangement as Method in Wells's *A Modern Utopia*', *Undying Fire*, 4 (2005), 45–69. For an excellent Blochian discussion of this tension, see Caitríona Ní Dhúill, *Sex in Imagined Spaces: Gender and Utopia from More to Bloch* (London: Legenda, 2010).

[17] *The Future in America*, 15.

[18] 'Historical and political science has still to find its Linnaeus,' Wells notes in his essay 'The Future of the British Empire', *A Year of Prophesying*, 47–62 (49). See Harvey N. Quamen, 'Unnatural Interbreeding: H. G. Wells's *A Modern Utopia* as Species and Genre', *Victorian Literature and Culture*, 33/1 (2005), 67–84.

the future a level of system and organization that he perceives the present to be lacking, thereby 'creating imaginatively and bringing into being a new state'.[19] Humanity may be progressing, but in too slow and disorganized a way: Wells's utopian writing constitutes a catalytic intervention to ensure that the progress is faster and better organized.

Wells's authority for his interventions is, characteristically, founded on scientific principles. In Plato's *Republic*, the purpose of education is to enable its recipients to know good, and thus to do good; consequently, to do nothing towards the creation of the perfect state is evil. For Wells, to know truly is, in essence, to know scientifically, and therefore scientific education is the essential foundation of the ideal society (all the more so since Wells sees science as essentially trans-national).[20] As the passage from *A Modern Utopia* cited above indicates, Wells saw the paradigm shift occasioned by Darwinism as giving scientists the task of establishing a scientific foundation for politics, sociology, and, later, history. Wells's intellectual mentor, T. H. Huxley, when rejecting Comtean positivism as no more than a secularized Catholicism, had announced that 'the organization of society upon a new and purely scientific basis is not only practicable, but is the only political object much worth fighting for'.[21] Wells himself insisted on 'the imperative necessity of scientific method in public affairs', seeking to bring about, in Haynes's words, 'the acceptance of achieved science as the basis of a new social order'.[22] Wells thus reformulates notions of world government as if conducting a scientific experiment: according to Thomas Kuhn, 'Verification is like natural selection: it picks out the most viable among the actual alternatives in a particular historical situation.'[23] As with the formulation of laws of science, subsequent discoveries might modify or even overthrow Wells's prognostications, but at the present state of knowledge they possess the status of truth.

Science is not only the means by which his utopia will be brought into being, but also by which the purpose and direction of utopia are made intelligible to its inhabitants. Wells wrote in 1908, using the word 'socialism' for the organizational principle of his programme:

---

[19] *The Future in America*, 180–1. On Wells's impatience, see Edward Shanks, 'The Work of Mr. H. G. Wells', *London Mercury*, 5 (1922), 506–18, *Critical Heritage*, ed. Parrinder, 255–7.
[20] On nominalism and idealism in Wells's relationship to Plato, see Michael Draper, 'Wells, Plato and the Ideal State', *Wellsian: Selected Essays*, ed. Partington, 189–98.
[21] T. H. Huxley, 'The Scientific Aspects of Positivism', *Lay Sermons, Addresses and Reviews* 5th edn (London: Macmillan, 1874), 147–73 (149).
[22] *What is Coming*, 101; Haynes, *H. G. Wells*, 7.
[23] Thomas Kuhn, *The Structure of Scientific Revolutions*, 2nd edn (Chicago: University of Chicago Press, 1970), 146.

The fundamental idea upon which Socialism rests is the same fundamental idea as that upon which all real scientific work is carried on. [...] While Science gathers knowledge, Socialism in an entirely harmonious spirit criticizes and develops a general plan of social life. Each seeks to replace disorder by order.[24]

Science is Wells's basis both for the authority claimed by his writing, and the authority that the state will hold over the individual. For Plato, to know good is to do good; the scientific occupies a place in Wells's thought equivalent to the good in Plato's. Wells's favoured strategy for forestalling objection to his programme is thus to appeal to a greater truth, which, if it fails to convince his audience, does so not because of a failure of rhetoric or innate lack of value, but because it has not yet been perceived correctly. 'Most of the troubles of mankind are really misunderstandings', Wells asserts confidently in *First and Last Things*.[25] The episteme of 'scientific truth' thus gives Wells the right to overrule political objection as well as individual desires that are at odds with his interpretation of the collective will, enabling what John Huntington identifies as 'the logical shifts by which Wells evades the crucial issues of justice and translates the evolution and ethics conflict into the easy and undebatable issue of efficiency'.[26]

If the real present is an imperfect image of an ideal future, the reader is thus like a prisoner in Plato's cave and Wells the escapee whose (scientifically trained) vision is still imperfect, but clearer than that of his audience (although they may, of course, not believe him).[27] Departing from Plato's collocation of the true and the good, however, Wells stresses that his ideal society is, like all societies, in essence artificial, rather than natural: 'the modern utopia is to be, before all things, synthetic' (*A Modern Utopia*, ch. 6, 6). If individual members of species are in reproductive competition against each other, it is a good idea that members of society should restrain their violent and selfish 'natural' instincts: in *A Modern Utopia* and elsewhere, Wells uses the term 'natural man' to indicate not a blissful pre-lapsarian state, but a primitive, brutal, pre-civilized one.[28] Resorting to the natural man would result in anarchy and barbarism. If there are no

[24] *New Worlds for Old*, 22–3.
[25] *First and Last Things*, 4.
[26] Huntington, *Logic of Fantasy*, 109. See also Krishan Kumar, *Utopia and Anti-Utopia in Modern Times* (Oxford: Blackwell, 1987), 192–3.
[27] Plato, *Republic*, bk 7, part 7.
[28] 'Human Evolution: An Artificial Process', *Fortnightly Review* 60 (1896), 590–5, *Early Writings*, 211–19; *The Conquest of Time*, ed. Martin Gardner (Amherst, NY: Prometheus, 1995), 60; *Babes in the Darkling Wood*, 65. Wells writes in 'The Past and the Great State', that 'To no conceivable social state is man inherently fitted: he is a creature of jealousy and suspicion, unstable, restless, acquisitive, aggressive, intractable, and of a most subtle and nimble dishonesty', (32–3).

'natural' precepts for society, therefore, neither Wells nor any other utopian writer need feel bound by any pre-existing conditions: as Jameson puts it, 'whatever has been *constructed* at once forfeits the mesmerizing (and crippling) prestige of the natural'.[29]

Consequently, Wells's Utopia is not a lotus-eating paradise of doing as one likes, but a world that requires a substantial amount of work to construct.[30] Wells shares with Carlyle approbation of 'the habit and disposition towards industry'.[31] Individuals in utopia should not labour from compulsion, but from accurate Platonic recognition of the common good, and because their labour is of a type for which they are well fitted, and for which they have been adequately trained. The giant children in *The Food of the Gods* work hard, because they want to, and can see and benefit from their work's positive effects: in Wells's utopia, labour should always be *un*alienated. The realist novels dramatize society's failure to capitalize on the protagonists' individual qualities: the utopias are designed specifically 'to get the best from each child's individuality'.[32] Wells repeatedly stresses the need for specialization: his utopia is not the kind in which every citizen is equal-because-the-same, but rather the opposite.[33] 'The assumption that men are unclassifiable, because practically homogeneous, which underlies modern democratic methods and all the fallacies of our equal justice, is even more alien to the Utopian mind' (*A Modern Utopia*, ch. 9, 2). In this respect, both Wells and Plato are more authoritarian than liberal, Wells supporting a skilled oligarchy of specialists educated and trained to increasing specialization and complexity.

Citizens are thus more developed along specific lines, but not necessarily more free.[34] (Jameson claims that in the history of utopian writing, 'the modern concern with freedom [. . .] replaces the older Utopian preoccupation with happiness'; Wells's 'A Story of the Days to Come' and *When the Sleeper Wakes* might be seen as visions of a utopia in which no one is happy.)[35] While Wells imagines a more comfortable everyday life, this comfort may be achieved at the cost of some individual liberty:

> To have free play for one's individuality is, in the modern view, the subjective triumph of existence, as survival in creative work and offspring

[29] Jameson, *Archaeologies*, 307.
[30] William Morris, *News from Nowhere: Or An Epoch of Rest, Being some Chapters from a Utopian Romance*, ed. Stephen Arata (Peterborough: Broadview, 2003), 31–4, 66–7.
[31] *Mankind in the Making*, 184.
[32] Ibid., 235.
[33] See 'Variety in Unity: Genius and Initiative in A Socialized World', *'42 to '44*, 132–7.
[34] Haynes, *H. G. Wells*, 118–19; McLean, *Early Fiction*, 148.
[35] Jameson, *Archaeologies*, 167.

is its objective triumph. But for all men, since man is a social creature, the
play of will must fall short of absolute freedom. (*Modern Utopia*, ch. 1, 2)

Wells seeks to resolve this conflict between authority and freedom by
making, ideally, the aims of the individual and the state the same. Like
Spencer, Wells possessed a belief that the laws that govern human behaviour, as they do the physical world, might be discoverable. Wells's
substantial difference from Spencer, as Wells admits in *First and Last
Things*, is that while Spencerian evolution sees the movement from
homogeneity to heterogeneity as requiring less and less state intervention,
Wells sees the state as the authority and the guarantor of increasing
complexity and specialization.[36] The state is not an ultimately disposable
step towards utopia, but utopia's guarantor and ultimate fulfilment, the
World State the most highly adapted form of Darwinian cooperation
between members of the same species.

All utopias must confront the difficulty of placing the individual
consciousness within the generalized framework of the utopia overall:
Wells's advocacy of human rights balances the potential for authoritarianism in his ideal state.[37] If Darwinian imperatives of the betterment and
survival of the species are to be obeyed, the individual will must sometimes
be subordinated to general necessity; such a need will be recognized by the
correctly educated, and administered by the highly educated. Wells's
utopia is not a democracy: like Plato, Wells mistrusted the capacity of a
mass to choose its own best government. People do not naturally know
what is best for them, but need educating in what is best for them by the
state. Although Wells envisions the rulers of the future state as a meritocratic elite, this process is to be made collaborative and consensual through
a process of education which constitutes 'the state explaining itself to and
incorporating the will of the individual'.[38] For Oswald in *Joan and Peter*
(1918), as for Wells, 'Education is socialisation. Education is the process
of making the unsocial individual a citizen' (*Joan and Peter*, ch. 10, 3).[39]

---

[36] See *First and Last Things*, 37–8; *Early Writings*, 180n.; on Spencer, see 'The
Labour Unrest' and 'An Age of Specialisation', *An Englishman Looks at the World*, 43–94
(69), 240–4.

[37] See John S. Partington, 'Human Rights and Public Accountability in H. G. Wells's
Functional World State', in *Cosmopolitics and the Emergence of a Future*, ed. Diane Morgan
and Gary Banham (Basingstoke: Palgrave Macmillan, 2007), 163–90, and *Building Cosmopolis*, 129–40; also James Dilloway, *Human Rights and World Order* (London: H. G.
Wells Society, 1983). Leon Stover, on the other hand, sees Wells as advocating 'salvation by
force', *The Prophetic Soul: A Reading of H. G. Wells's Things to Come* (Jefferson, NC:
McFarland, 1987), 97.

[38] *Joan and Peter*, *Works*, XXIV–XXV, 262.

[39] Compare *The World Set Free*, 208.

In utopias such as Morris's Nowhere, education is undertaken voluntarily; in Wells's utopia, it is too important to be left to individual whim. Most utopian schemes imagine an ideal education for their inhabitants. In both Wells and Plato, education is something that is imposed on its inhabitants by the imagined utopia, and on its readers by the literary utopia:

> We treat the complex, difficult and honourable task of intellectual development as if it were within the capacity of any earnest but muddle-headed young lady, or any half-educated gentleman in orders; we take that for granted, and we demand in addition from them the "formation of character," moral and ethical training and supervision, aesthetic guidance, the implanting of a taste for the Best in literature, for the Best in art, for the finest conduct; we demand the clue to success in commerce and the seeds of a fine passionate patriotism from these necessarily very ordinary persons. (*Mankind in the Making*, ch. 5)

Much utopian writing, such as *News from Nowhere*, seeks to resolve difficulties of moral conduct by disposing of the notion of private property.[40] By definition, in a utopian state no individual must lack anything they need, nor must anyone possess a surplus that might deprive another of something essential to their happiness. Plato identifies pleonexia, trying to have more than your fair share, as an evil that the Republic would eliminate; More's utopia does not have a monetary economy, and thereby does not have crime.[41] Wells, however, sees the right to own property as a benefit conferred by the utopian state and also anticipates an improvement in right conduct, even inner life (see in particular *First and Last Things*) as a consequence of better accommodation and development of individual potentialities. Wells's utopian writing is never unthinkingly chiliastic, but when choosing to write utopia, rather than dystopia, Wells is by definition an optimist, making 'a plea for science and not for despair' (especially following the improvement of Wells's own health after 1900).[42] A secular amelioration of the condition of humanity is by no means certain, but with enough work it can be achieved; and achieving utopia is the highest kind of work available to humanity.

---

[40] Wagar, *World State*, 228–9.
[41] Thomas More, *Utopia: A Revised Translation, Backgrounds, Criticism*, trans. and ed. Robert M. Adams, 2nd edn (New York: Norton, 1992), 83. For Wells on More, see 'About Sir Thomas More', *An Englishman Looks at the World*, 183–7.
[42] *Mankind in the Making*, 176; Parrinder, *Shadows*, 25.

THE ART OF THE FUTURE

Wells's first explicitly futurological work, *Anticipations* (which initially outsold any of his fiction published up to that date) begins by considering neither birth, politics, nor art, but transport. Transport, like writing, is a technology of communication, and Wells's utopian texts continually stress development and movement both literal and metaphorical (albeit on directed, rather than free, lines).[43] As a realist novelist, Wells tends to chart the downward movement of his protagonists: material barriers in real life such as money, class, or social mores bar effective mobility. (The exception is *Tono-Bungay*'s George Ponderevo, who makes a successful escape by inventing two new modes of transport, thus crossing the generic boundary of realism into scientific romance.) If Wells's realist writing exposes the insufficiencies of the 'real' world on which it draws, the scientific and utopian romances in turn allow the imagining of different, better, realities. Even if these visions are dystopian, as in *The Time Machine*, they still demonstrate the possibility of a reality alternate to the existing order of things. Wells's political writing frequently figures an ideal, or at least substantially better, world that might exist in the future. When he turns to depicting the existing material world, realism thus functions as a negative image of an ideal but achievable utopian realm. The New Republic of *Anticipations* would take better care of Lewisham than the realistic world of the 1900 novel in which he appears; *Kipps* shows the social inequities that *A Modern Utopia* (both 1905) would put right; *New Worlds for Old* (1908) explicitly addresses the social concerns that also give rise to *Tono-Bungay*, which began as a serial the same year.

While Wells's visions of utopia are modified over time, certain elements remain consistent. The very first of these, *Anticipations*, prefigures many of the characteristics of Wells's later utopias: the falling-away of loyalties to national identity; technological improvement, particularly in transport; even anti-Catholicism.[44] Wells's utopian thinking is aboriginally rooted

---

[43] 'It is now a commonplace, although for many historians and scholars it is quite a recent discovery, that any change in communications involves new economic, strategic and political adjustments. For a score of centuries the horse, [...] [and] the parchment document [...] had been the limiting conditions of all statecraft.' 'The Future of the British Empire', *A Year of Prophesying*, 47–62 (52).

[44] Wells viewed Catholicism in particular as a challenge to his own historical master-narrative, and was the facet of Wells's thinking that attracted most opprobrium in the public response to *The Outline of History*. It is expressed at its most forceful in *Crux Ansata: An Indictment of the Roman Catholic Church* (Harmondsworth: Penguin, 1943). See also Lucian M. Ashworth, 'Clashing Utopias: H. G. Wells and Catholic Ireland', in *The Reception of H. G. Wells in Europe*, ed. Patrick Parrinder and John S. Partington (London: Continuum, 2005), 267–79 (273).

in the quotidian: he could describe his ideal state from a 'stratospheric' perspective that allows it to be seen in its entirety, as from a distance, but his early utopias also try to imagine everyday life in the perfect society, a 'domestic utopia'.[45] Nothing need be immune from his spirit of critical enquiry, from national identity to dusting, from the width of roads to the future of sexual monogamy. The utopian impulse in Wells springs in essence from the desire to be comfortable: consciousness perceives a lack in the material world resulting in mental unhappiness, and so turns to imagination, then to writing, for the fulfilment of that need.[46] Like Mr Polly, Wells himself is not pleased by the world, and so resolves to change it:

> I wrote [*Anticipations*] in order to clear up the muddle in my own mind about innumerable social and political questions, questions I could not keep out of my work, which it distressed me to touch upon in a stupid haphazard way, and which no one, so far as I knew, had handled in my mind to satisfy my needs.[47]

The world is imperfect, causing Wells discomfort; his 'need' is to have the nature of such imperfections satisfactorily and systematically identified, and thus, in imagination at least, to resolve the source of discomfort. After Bloch, Ruth Levitas suggests that utopia aims at 'the overcoming of antagonism between humanity and the world'.[48]

> I entertain something of the satisfaction of a man who has finished building a bridge; I feel that I have joined together things that I had never joined before. My Utopia seems real to me, very real, I can believe in it, until the metal chair-back gives to my shoulder blades, and Utopian sparrows twitter and hop before my feet. I have a pleasant moment of unhesitating self-satisfaction; I feel a shameless exultation to be there. (*A Modern Utopia*, ch. 1, 9)

Wells's very earliest utopian project was not textual but material: Spade House, the house that he designed in collaboration with architect C. A. Voysey, while writing *The Wealth of Mr. Waddy*.[49] Architectural meta-

---

[45] See Roland Barthes's discussion of Fourier, 'The Calculation of Pleasure', in *Sade, Fourier, Loyola*, trans. Richard Miller (Baltimore: Johns Hopkins University Press, 1997); 80–5; Reed, *Natural History of H. G. Wells*, 19.

[46] Sigmund Freud, 'Creative Writers and Daydreaming' (1907), *Works*, IX,141–153. In the *Autobiography*, Wells confesses to being 'tormented by a desire for achievement that overruns my capacity' (*Autobiography*, I, 20). He also discusses his first imaginative awakenings as a child when confined to bed by a broken leg (I, 76–80); see also 'My Lucky Moment', *View*, 29 April 1911, 212.

[47] *A Modern Utopia*, 1905 text, v.

[48] Ruth Levitas, *The Concept of Utopia* (London: Philip Allan, 1990), 99–101.

[49] See Martin Eastdown and Linda Sage, *The History of Spade House, Folkestone* (Folkestone: Folkestone Local History Society, [n.d.]).

phors for writing thus take on a more literal force: 'in this newly built Spade House I began a book *Anticipations* which can be considered as the keystone to the main arch of my work'.[50] Wells paid very close attention to the design of Spade House, lowering the doorknobs, for instance, so that children and the invalid he feared he might become could reach them. Wells's ideal home arises from the utopian impulse for the real world to be improved: in a letter to John Vine Milne Wells complains while house-hunting, like Ann Kipps, of 'servant-murdering basements, sanitary insanities, and not a decent bathroom anywhere'.[51]

Wells argues in *Anticipations* for the benefits of en suite bathrooms: Spade House was the first British private dwelling in which every bedroom had one (even Kipps's luxurious hotel needs servants to bring hot water). Wells suggests in *Anticipations* that houses would be easier to dust if corners were rounded off: Spade House incorporates this improvement.[52] After moving from Spade House to Easton Glebe, Wells wrote petulantly to his wife Jane from London of the 'torment that it is to an impatient man to feel the phantom home failing to realize itself. I hate things unfinished and out of place. I want things settled.'[53]

The badly designed house is an instance of relationship between social organization and social identity: the poor design of houses without central heating or running water itself produces a whole underclass of servants.[54] 'They build these 'ouses as though girls wasn't 'uman beings,' complains Ann in *Kipps* (bk 3, ch. 1, 2): the fact of servants having to live below stairs at the stately home of Uppark inspired Wells to locate the Morlocks below ground. If houses are redesigned to be like Kipps's, had it been completed, the need for the servant class disappears.

Even Spade House, in being named, was thus made a part of Wells's wider project of making art more instrumental. Voysey incorporated a distinctive heart motif in his work, but Wells 'protested at wearing my heart so conspicuously outside and we compromised on a spade. We called the house Spade House.'[55] Wells inverts art's traditional symbol of feeling to turn it into something more active and pragmatic. His preoccupation with the question of whether art should be functional or decorative is

[50] *Autobiography*, II, 643.
[51] Letter to John Vine Milne, Autumn 1898, West Yorkshire Provincial Archives, from the as yet unpublished fifth volume of Wells's *Correspondence*.
[52] *Anticipations*, 95.
[53] *Correspondence*, II, 372.
[54] In a deleted typescript passage, Kipps dreams of 'a house in which no one need drudge. [...] A house that civilises all who come into it' (Illinois Collection). In earlier versions, Masterman involves himself in the design of the house, and then goes to on plan a whole utopian city, but dies before writing the book that will describe it.
[55] *Autobiography*, II, 638.

common in much utopian writing, which often struggles with the question of whether a utopian society needs art at all.

Within the imagined utopia itself, art often occupies at best only a precarious place: if the inhabitants of utopia are uniformly happy, they are unlikely to need art as compensation or consolation. Jameson comments on Edward Bellamy's *Looking Backward* (1888), that 'readers have a right to wonder what they will read in Utopia, the unspoken thought being that a society without conflict is unlikely to produce exciting stories'.[56] As a literary genre, utopia is intrinsically non-narratable, and often needs its perfection to be disrupted to generate the text that will articulate it: even Morris's Nowhere suffers a murder part way through the text, as if an injection of plot is needed to advance Guest's, and the reader's, progress through the text.[57] The entry of the Voice and the botanist with his 'petty love story' (*A Modern Utopia*, ch. 1, 7) constitute an irruption of the narratable into *A Modern Utopia*.

Plato, famously, did not see the need for poets in the Republic: poetry runs the risk of diverting attention towards the imaginary and away from the true. Since the artist's knowledge is of representation, rather than of reality, art might mislead the self and allow humanity to over-indulge its instinctive, non-reasoning part.[58] The inhabitants of Francis Bacon's *New Atlantis* (1627), on the other hand, enjoy 'excellent poesy', but also abhor misleading images of anything untruthful.[59] Thomas More's more self-conscious and tongue-in-cheek *Utopia* is aware of itself as a (tall) story, but while Utopians are nonetheless eager consumers of books, Hylothday gives no evidence that they produce a literature of their own.[60]

William Morris shows greater commitment to aesthetic beauty, but in *News from Nowhere* (1890) he makes the creation of the beautiful so much a part of everyday life as virtually to remove the notion of 'art' altogether in favour of one of 'design'.[61] Morris's utopian art is not elevated on to a museum pedestal but a part of everyday life: instead of an aesthetic in which objects should be produced to be beautiful for their own sake, objects that are produced and used should be beautiful as a matter of course. Prefiguring the Eloi's loss of abstract nouns, the word has even

---

[56] Jameson, *Archaeologies*, 182; see also letter to the *Daily Herald*, *Correspondence*, III, 138 and cf. Bourdieu, *Distinction*, 397.

[57] On the 'narratable', see D. A. Miller, *Narrative and its Discontents: Problems of Closure in the Traditional Novel* (Princeton: Princeton University Press, 1981).

[58] Plato, *Republic*, bk 10.

[59] Francis Bacon, *The New Atlantis: A Work Unfinished*, in *Three Early Modern Utopias*, ed. Susan Bruce (Oxford: Oxford University Press, 1999), 149–86 (171).

[60] More, *Utopia*, 58–9.

[61] Levitas, *Concept of Utopia*, 110–11.

dropped out of Nowhere's language: '"what used to be called art, but which has no name amongst us now, because it has become a necessary part of the labour of every man who produces"'.[62] Morris's utopian aesthetics are also pragmatic, rather than idealist, rejecting the aestheticist isolation of the production of art from social responsibility. In a letter to Georgiana Burne-Jones, Morris even displays a moment of Wellsian iconoclasm: 'The arts have got to die, what is left of them, before they can be born again.'[63] Morris also confronts the issue of what would happen in the perfect state to the art of the pre-utopian past, here less destructive of the best that has been thought and written down:

> "You must not suppose that the new form of art was founded chiefly on the memory of the art of the past; although, strange to say, the civil war was much less destructive of art than of other things, and though what of art existed under the old forms, revived in a wonderful way during the latter part of the struggle, especially as regards music and poetry."[64]

Even so, the inhabitants of Nowhere are 'not great readers', and a taste for reading novels is no more than a harmless antiquarian eccentricity.[65]

Samuel Butler's satirical dystopia *Erewhon* (1872) has artists, but also a literally iconoclastic view towards its cultural heritage, as citizens are encouraged to destroy statues of historical figures:

> I know not why, but all the noblest arts hold in perfection but for a very little moment. They soon reach a height from which they begin to decline, and when they have begun to decline it is a pity that they cannot be knocked on the head; for an art is like a living organism—better dead than dying. There is no way of making an aged art young again; it must be born anew and grow up from infancy as a new thing, working out its own salvation from effort to effort in all fear and trembling.[66]

Walter Besant's dystopia *The Inner House* (1888) explicitly banishes its cultural residuum. The future projected in the text has been so perfected as to prevent any disruption from threatening its equilibrium. There is no ageing, no private property, no sex, no alcohol, no distinctions of class in clothing, no art or music, and no cultural memory: since the present has been perfected, the past ceases to have meaning. The narrator, Grout the Suffragan, platonically laments that:

[62] *News from Nowhere*, 176.
[63] William Morris, *The Collected Letters of William Morris*, 4 vols, ed. N. Kelvin (Princeton: Princeton University Press, 1984–96), II, 217.
[64] *News from Nowhere*, 176. For Wells's own reservations about Morris, see 'The Great State', *An Englishman Looks at the World*, 95–131 (107).
[65] *News from Nowhere*, 183.
[66] Samuel Butler, *Erewhon: Or, Over the Range* (London: A. C. Fifield, 1910).

Nothing in the whole world [...] has done so much harm to Humanity as Art. In a world of common sense which deals with nothing but fact and actuality, Art can have no place. Why imitate what we see around us? Artists cheated the world: they pretended to imitate, and they distorted or exaggerated. They put a light into the sky that never was there: they filled the human face with yearning after things impossible. [...] Why—why did we not destroy all works of Art long ago?[67]

The idea of banishing all books is likely to find sympathy from few real-life readers, and this bookless dystopia is overturned when the heroine reads books in a museum, and eventually brings about a counter-revolution.

Wells's utopias and dystopias continually recast the image of what art might be and do in his desired future. In 'A Story of the Days to Come', books are replaced by audio recordings; the state of *When the Sleeper Wakes* has a Poet Laureate but this is an honorary title and the holder no longer produces poetry (*When the Sleeper Wakes*, ch. 15). Hairdressers are considered artists; there are 'no books, no newspapers, no writing materials' (*When the Sleeper Wakes*, ch. 7). Wells's Modern Utopia needs the unpredictability of the creative, 'the poietic', in order to be in a perpetual state of improvement, but the potentialities of art itself are limited. 'There is scope for novels and the drama of life' (*A Modern Utopia*, ch. 9, 6) in the unequal marriage regulations for Utopia's Samurai ruling class, but Samurai themselves are forbidden from 'acting, singing or reciting' (*A Modern Utopia*, ch. 9, 5). Wells is very aware of the generic paradox of writing a history of the future, and his work imagines a future in which utopian writing would itself cease to exist; a state which fulfils individual potential as effectively as the New Republic would have no need of the kind of didactic art that Wells is committed to producing.[68] Wells's utopian project thus possesses a kind of death instinct, seeking to extinguish itself, to write itself out of existence.[69] When he meets a version of himself in *A Modern Utopia*, 'Wells' is not an author but a Samurai, one of the ruling elite. Most art that seeks primarily to alter the historical conditions that produced it is by its nature obsolescent: even for Plato,

---

[67] Walter Besant, *The Inner House* (Bristol: Kessinger, 1888), 78.

[68] 'The future historical perspective is [...] a kind of supplementary or lateral bonus of the Utopian dimension of the novel, full of extraordinary estrangements.' Jameson, *Archaeologies*, 76.

[69] 'One of the ways in which a literary work can be inventive is by operating at the unstable limits of the literary, and reinventing the category itself. [...] Nor can we impose in advance any limit on these reinventions of the category: there can be no guarantee that the future will have a place for the literary.' Derek Attridge, *The Singularity of Literature*, (Routledge: London, 2004), 61–2. Cf. *Mind at the End of its Tether*, 30.

before utopia is actually established, art that inspires social improvement is the highest kind of art. However, once this order is established, literature must find a new telos, or voluntarily cease to exist.[70] Wells thus imagines a cultural residuum as possibly existing in the future, but in a substantially modified form.[71]

If Homer was for Plato's Athens 'the equivalent of our Bible', Wells seeks to identify a textual corpus that would have the same degree of epistemological authority in the future.[72] *A Modern Utopia* imagines just such a compendium:

> "Our Founders made a collection of several volumes, which they called, collectively, the Book of the Samurai, a compilation of articles and extracts, poems and prose pieces, which were supposed to embody the idea of the order. It was to play the part for the *samurai* that the Bible did for the ancient Hebrews. To tell you the truth, the stuff was of very unequal merit; there was a lot of very second-rate rhetoric, and some nearly namby-pamby verse. There was also included some very obscure verse and prose that had the trick of seeming wise. But for all such defects, much of the Book, from the very beginning, was splendid and inspiring matter. From that time to this, the Book of the Samurai has been under revision, much has been added, much rejected, and some deliberately rewritten. Now, there is hardly anything in it that is not beautiful and perfect in form. The whole range of noble emotions finds expression there, and all the guiding ideas of our Modern State." (*A Modern Utopia*, ch. 9, 5)[73]

As Plato's Guardians edit Homer so that the gods do not appear foolish, the Samurai redact high culture to fit the ideological purpose they wish it

---

[70] Cf. *The Anatomy of Frustration: A Modern Synthesis* (London: Cresset, 1936), 258–60; *'42 to '44*, 137.

[71] For Wells's vision of what the future artist perhaps should be, see *The Work, Wealth and Happiness of Mankind*, 708–11.

[72] Desmond Lee, 'Translator's Introduction' to Plato, *Republic*, 11–58 (37). Cf. *Autobiography*, II, 721–2; Wells, *World Brain: H. G. Wells on the Future of World Education*, ed. Alan Mayne (London: Adamantine Press, 1994), 88; Reed, *Natural History of H. G. Wells*, 189–90. See 'The Bible of Civilisation', *The Salvaging of Civilization: The Probable Future of Mankind* (New York: Macmillan, 1921), 97–140.

[73] Cf. 'Crystal had some new fantastic fiction about the exploration of space among his books; imaginative stories that boys were reading very eagerly; they were pamphlets of thirty or forty pages printed on a beautiful paper that he said was made directly from flax and certain reeds. The librarians noted what books and papers were read and taken away, and these they replaced with fresh copies. The piles that went unread were presently reduced to one or two copies and the rest went back to the pulping mills. But many of the poets and philosophers, and story-tellers whose imaginations found no wide popularity were nevertheless treasured and their memories kept alive by a few devoted admirers.' *Men Like Gods*, *Works*, XXVIII, 276–7.

to serve.[74] The residuum survives not through the artistic authenticity and integrity of the individual work, but as fragments shaped towards an instrumental end. Indeed, this particular Utopia has taken the form it does because of the superiority of its cultural residuum:

> One might assume as an alternative to this that amidst the four-fifths of the Greek literature now lost to the world, there perished, neglected, some book of elementary significance, some earlier *Novum Organum*, that in Utopia survived to achieve the profoundest consequences. (*A Modern Utopia*, ch. 9, 1)

The Samurai 'must read aloud from the Book of the Samurai for at least ten minutes every day. Every month they must buy and read faithfully through at least one book that has been published during the past five years' (*A Modern Utopia*, ch. 9, 6). Since literature is to have the mission of perfecting society, it is important that the right kind of literature is put to this purpose. Wells claims not to be interested in discriminating between the relative claims to artistic value of different aesthetic artefacts as artefacts; but his programmatic view of art must nonetheless lead him to privileging certain types of learning and knowledge over others.[75] Wells's primary target for elimination from his curriculum for the future is classical literature.

> The literature of Rome was living reading in a sense that has suddenly passed away, it fitted all occasions, it conflicted with no essential facts in life. It was a commonplace of the thought of that time that all things recurred, all things circled back to their former seasons; there was nothing new under the sun. But now almost suddenly the circling has ceased, and we find ourselves breaking away. (*Anticipations*, ch. 3)

Wells diagnoses over-attachment to existing but archaic cultural forms as an impediment to establishing the new forms that will help bring about social revolution. In *Anticipations* and in *The Discovery of the Future*, Wells draws a distinction between two different kinds of consumers of art. The educated, specialized class are identified with the 'scientific interpretation of the universe' (*Anticipations*, ch. 4) and the future, the share-owning, non-labouring rentier class with the past, and indeed, with the arts.

> The archaic, opulently done, will appeal irresistibly to very many of these irresponsible rich as the very quintessence of art standing apart from the movement of the world as they will do to a very large extent. They will come

---

[74] Cf. also Plato, *Phaedrus* (trans. Walter Hamilton, London: Penguin, 1983), 274–7, and *World Brain*, 88.
[75] *New Worlds for Old*, 136–7.

to art with uncritical, cultured minds, full of past achievements, ignorant of present necessities. Art will be something added to life—something stuck on and richly reminiscent—not a manner pervading all real things. We may be pretty sure that very few will grasp the fact that an iron bridge or a railway engine may be artistically done—these will not be "art" objects, but hostile novelties. (*Anticipations*, ch. 4)[76]

The scientific-minded class, on the other hand:

Will not be habitually promenaders, or greatly addicted to theatrical performances; they will probably find their secondary interests [. . .] in a not too imaginative prose literature, in travel and journeys and in the less sensuous aspects of music. (*Anticipations*, ch. 4)

Art that exists only for its own sake is at best a distraction and at worst a brake on progress. Instrumental art might serve to focus and direct the energies of those who will construct the New Republic, but Wells fears that such works are failing to achieve the prominence they deserve among books both old and new. *First and Last Things*, for instance, makes a plea for a new, practical, applied form of philosophy, and argues that metaphysics has become unjustly unpopular with readers because of 'the vulgar pretensions of the learned, from their appeal to ancient names and their quotations in unfamiliar tongues, and from the easy fall into technicality of men struggling to be explicit where a high degree of explicitness is impossible'.[77]

Wells was also worried about the distribution and exchange, as well as the production, of future literature. Not only might the art of the New Republic be harmed by cherishing the wrong selection from the cultural residuum, but art's future is also threatened by the inefficiency of the present day's dissemination of literature through capitalism. As noted in chapter 2, Wells was deeply troubled by the factual and ideological sway that the periodical press appeared to have over the public, and his early political writings fret over potential citizens of the New Republic reading the periodical press or a boomed novel instead of more educative literature.[78] Literature is too important to be left to struggle for existence by itself, and Wells argues for state intervention in its production:

---

[76] Cf. the 'Genteel Whig': 'He pursued art or philosophy and literature upon their more esoteric levels, and realised more and more the general vulgarity and coarseness of the world about him, and his own detachment.' *War and the Future: Italy, France, and Britain at War* (London: Cassell, 1917), 204.

[77] *First and Last Things*, 1.

[78] *Anticipations*, 15n.

In spite of the pretentious impostors who trade upon the claim, literature, contemporary literature, is the breath of civilized life, and those who sincerely think and write the salt of the social body. To mumble over the past, to live on the classics, however splendid, is senility. The New Republic, therefore, will sustain its authors. (*Anticipations*, ch. 8)

Just as democracy is too inefficient a mechanism to bring utopia into being, so the invisible hand of market forces cannot be entrusted with production of the writing that will shape the new world: reality provides abundant evidence of capitalism's failure to administer resources capably.[79] Especially early on in his career, Wells was frustrated by the exigencies of the publishing trade, that the most important artistic activity of all might be jeopardized by the need for writers to write for money: 'almost every well-known living writer is or has been writing too much' (*Mankind in the Making*, ch. 10). So important is the production of literature in the New Republic that Wells argues for, in effect, the state supervision, even the nationalization, of literary production: the writer should be endowed by the state, paid for by a stamp tax on printed matter.[80] (In *Looking Backward*, books are published at the authors' own expense to a fully democratized and discriminating audience; newspapers are run by subscription and underwritten by the state, rather than funded by unscrupulous and partial proprietors.)

Wells even took this notion as far as to write to the Prime Minister Arthur Balfour in 1904 and 1905 asking for an endowed academic Chair so that he would not be dependent on the market for making his living.[81]

You will remember that when we met at Mrs. Webbs some time ago you talked of the problem of endowing those who made original contributions to thought. I want to ask you whether you think it might not be desirable to endow me.

I speak about £1000. I save money out & above that & my life is insured for a reasonably large sum. The only flaw in my position is that in order to keep stable and independent I have to turn out about two books a year & that even at that I have to devote a lot of intellectual energy to negotiations with editors and publishers & to the ingenious adjustment of what I have to say to what the reading public supposes it wants. I believe I could do

---

[79] In *New Worlds for Old*, 237, however, Wells refers to a book by Adam Smith, presumably *The Wealth of Nations*, as 'richly suggestive'. Cf. also 'I wish I could catch the soul of Herbert Spencer and tether it in Chicago awhile to gather fresh evidence upon the superiority of unfettered individualist enterprise to things managed by the State.' *The Future in America*, 82.

[80] Cf. *The Shape of Things to Come*, 110.

[81] *Correspondence*, II, 71–4; British Library MSS, 49856 Balfour papers 973B, ff. 223–4.

something more worthy of the name of literature if I could disregard these adjustments.[82]

Wells's hopes that he might produce 'better and more significant work than under existing conditions' were, of course, eventually dashed. Balfour wrote to the First Sea Lord that 'a pension to a writer like Wells who makes over £1000 a year wd. I think raise a howl [...] I sympathise entirely with the principle: in practice, one must be very sure that one selects genius for endowment.'[83]

A PERFECT WORLD: *THE FIRST MEN IN THE MOON*

As shown in chapter 2, Wells's experiments in scientific romance reshape perception, combating the reader's sense of things as they are towards a new perception of things as they might be. As Wells puts it in *First and Last Things*, 'I have tried to render my sense of our human possibility by monstrous images.'[84] Wells's later scientific romances further challenge established perceptions, not only of specific phenomena, but of the entire world, hinting perhaps at what that world might become:

> Just at this point, unhappily, this message broke off. Fragmentary and tantalising as the matter constituting this chapter is, it does nevertheless give a vague, broad impression of an altogether strange and wonderful world—a world with which our own may have to reckon sooner or later. This intermittent trickle of messages, this whispering of a record needle in the stillness of the mountain slopes, is the first warning of such a change in human conditions as mankind has scarcely imagined heretofore. In that satellite of ours there are new elements, new appliances, traditions, an overwhelming avalanche of new ideas. (*First Men*, ch. 24)

In *The First Men in the Moon*, Bedford is disorientated by his 'perception of the impossible' (*First Men*, ch. 5): facts which the protagonists believed to be as certain as the ground beneath their feet float free when they travel towards the Moon. Wells's utopian writing periodically downplays the importance of the essential unit of liberal thought, the self; in *Christina Alberta's Father* (1925), he claims that, 'our race has reached, and is now receding from, a maximum of *individuation*'.[85] Wells's stratospheric

---

[82] *Correspondence*, II, 71–2.

[83] A. J. Balfour to First Lord of the Treasury, British Library, Balfour Papers 49857 974B and 251–2.

[84] *First and Last Things*, 76.

[85] *Christina Alberta's Father*, 384. See also Wells's BBC broadcast of 21 October 1929, 'Points of View', *Listener*, 30 October 1929, 565–6, 592–4.

vantage in his utopian writing alters his notions about everyday life, as George Bernard Shaw complained.[86] An alteration in how Bedford perceives the world alters his perspective towards, and estranges him, even from his own self:

> I can't profess to explain the things that happened in my mind. No doubt they could all be traced directly or indirectly to the curious physical conditions under which I was living. [...] The most prominent quality of it was a pervading doubt of my own identity. I became, if I may so express it, dissociate from Bedford; I looked down on Bedford as a trivial, incidental thing with which I chanced to be connected. I saw Bedford in many relations—as an ass or as a poor beast, where I had hitherto been inclined to regard him with a quiet pride as a very spirited or rather forcible person. I saw him not only as an ass, but as the son of many generations of asses. I reviewed his school-days and his early manhood, and his first encounter with love, very much as one might review the proceedings of an ant in the sand. Something of that period of lucidity I regret still hangs about me, and I doubt if I shall ever recover the full-bodied self satisfaction of my early days. But at the time the thing was not in the least painful, because I had that extraordinary persuasion that, as a matter of fact, I was no more Bedford than I was any one else, but only a mind floating in the still serenity of space. Why should I be disturbed about this Bedford's shortcomings? I was not responsible for him or them. (*First Men*, ch. 20)

As previously noted, Wells's early scientific romances frequently call attention to the difficulty of conventional linguistic expression in representing something alien to previous human experience. The narration of *The First Men in the Moon* is as self-conscious and unreliable as those of the earlier romances; Cavor feels that he is 'casting back to the fable-hearing period of childhood again' (*First Men*, ch. 24). Both narrators are aware of themselves as characters who appear in each other's telling of the story and quarrel over their representation by the other, inviting the reader to regard these narratives sceptically. The version of Cavor's narrative that Bedford, the text's victorious redactor, eventually presents is partial, edited, and still lacking the scholarly annotations that he lazily promises in a future edition.

The First Men in the Moon is a transitional text between the scientific romances and the utopias, preoccupied with forms of social interaction, contrasting the different social models of competition and cooperation. On the Earth, Bedford schemes against his fellow-man for his own advantage; the building of the sphere is marred by disputes in labour relations; all three of Cavor's labourers have abandoned previous careers

---

[86] *Bernard Shaw and H. G. Wells*, 124.

doing something different.[87] The narrators differ like *Anticipations'* future consumers of art—Cavor is scientific, factual, looking to the future and Bedford, rather dubiously 'artistic', focused on the present and wilfully unreliable, even deceitful. Earthly government is disorganized by competition; lunar government, like Wells's ideal of science, 'is systematic, co-operative and organised'.[88] Every element of Moon society is biologically, even perfectly, adapted, to its role. Peter Kemp, amongst others, has drawn attention to the similarity between Selenite society and Wells's own utopian programmes.[89] Bedford's sympathy for a Selenite still, like Lewisham or Kipps, in the maturing process of social formation—'that wretched-looking hand sticking out of its jar seemed to have a sort of limp appeal for lost possibilities; it haunts me still'—is followed by the rhetorical observation 'although, of course it is really in the end a far more humane proceeding than our earthly method of leaving children to grow into human beings, and then making machines of them' (*First Men*, ch. 24). Cavor also speculates whether it is crueller to put an unwanted worker to sleep or out on the streets to starve.

Selenite super-evolution appears to fit each individual body into its designated role without the need for cultural adaptations such as education, or indeed art. The degeneration of the Eloi means they no longer need books; the super-adaptation of the Selenites produces a similar result. The Selenites have a type described as an 'artist' (*First Men*, ch. 25), but his role is purely one of instrumental communication, rather than aesthetics.[90] (In Lucian's *Icaromennipus*, which provides the *First Men's* epigraph, Zeus orders the execution of all philosophers, since they make no contribution to social progress.) Within a perfected social body, there is no longer any need for cultural memory in the form of artefacts, since the archive is now inscribed into perfected bodies:

> With regard to these latter, it is a curious little thing to note that the unlimited growth of the lunar brain has rendered unnecessary the invention of all those mechanical aids to brain work which have distinguished the career of man. There are no books, no records of any sort, no libraries nor inscriptions. All knowledge is stored in distended brains much as the honey-ants of Texas store honey in their distended abdomens. The lunar Somerset

---

[87] Haynes, *H. G. Wells*, 24–5.

[88] This phrase appears in the revised and enlarged edition of *First and Last Things* (London: Cassell and Company, 1917), 41.

[89] Kemp, *H. G. Wells and the Culminating Ape*, 187–214.

[90] For a discussion of the significance of this figure, see McLean, *Early Fiction*, 132–4. In 'The Empire of the Ants' (1905), the similarly terrifyingly super-adapted ants have 'an organised and detailed method of record and communication analogous to our books' (*Short Stories*, 585–97 (597)).

House and the lunar British Museum Library are collections of living brains . . . (*First Men*, ch. 24)

The Selenites also appear to have perfected language. The Grand Lunar is surprised that humanity puts itself to 'the inconvenience of diverse tongues' (*First Men*, ch. 25); Wells himself was happy for English to become the world language, and even to see regional accent, which might hamper universal communication, eradicated.[91] Science fiction's imagining of the Selenites' materialized form of language without text here provides further grounds for Wells's ironizing of the written. Bedford writes a play out of a desire neither to improve the world nor even to produce great art, but to make money for paying debts incurred by his earlier pleonexia:

> I knew there was nothing a man can do outside legitimate business transactions that has such opulent possibilities, and very probably that biased my opinion. I had, indeed, got into the habit of regarding this unwritten drama as a convenient little reserve put by for a rainy day. (*First Men*, ch. 1).

In a final irony, Bedford will make his fortune from writing: not his own, but in appropriating Cavor's productions (in some editions of this romance, this fraudulent literary producer then changes his name to 'Wells').[92] Cavor is 'not a reader of fiction' (*First Men*, ch. 3), but, in order to make himself better cultured, takes a *Complete Shakespeare* as reading matter for his journey to the Moon. The book, however, remains unread and is ultimately ejected into space with the boy who steals the sphere. When Bedford's bodily debility prevents him from concentrating on more elevated literature, he turns instead to the most debased form of printed matter, the newspaper advertisement. His extraterrestrial perspective ironizes the quotidian uses of writing: after reading of a likely confidence trickster, and of a bicycle for sale, and that a lady in distress wished to dispose of some fish knives and forks, Bedford 'laughed and let the paper drift from my hand' (*First Men*, ch. 5).

The final communications from Cavor continue to undermine faith in the trustworthiness of language. Once he is imprisoned by the Selenites, Cavor, like the Time Traveller or Prendick, can employ neither speech nor his own physical presence to verify the truth of his narrative. Bedford's representation of lunar society will only ever be partial and fragmentary, literally untranslatable since Selenite language is 'impossible to imitate or define' (*First Men*, ch. 14). The Selenites use super-adapted bodily organs to keep records and have no need for paper; the material object that is

---

[91] *Anticipations*, 195; also *Mankind in the Making* 136–7; *The Shape of Things to Come*, 322–5; McLean, *Early Fiction*, 143–4.
[92] Reed, *Natural History of H. G. Wells*, 220.

Cavor's piece of paper, by contrast, bears markings that are insufficient linguistic representation and material evidence of his physical insufficiency:

> The rising breeze dragged something into view, something small and vividly white.
>
> It was a little piece of paper crumpled tightly, as though it had been clutched tightly. I picked it up, and on it were smears of red. My eye caught faint pencil marks. I smoothed it out, and saw uneven and broken writing ending at last in a crooked streak up on the paper.
>
> I set myself to decipher this.
>
> 'I have been injured about the knee, I think my kneecap is hurt, and I cannot run or crawl,' it began—pretty distinctly written.
>
> Then less legibly: 'They have been chasing me for some time, and it is only a question of'—the word 'time' seemed to have been written here and erased in favour of something illegible—'before they get me. They are beating all about me.'
>
> Then the writing became convulsive. 'I can hear them,' I guessed the tracing meant, and then it was quite unreadable for a space. Then came a little string of words that were quite distinct: 'a different sort of Selenite altogether, who appears to be directing the —' The writing became a mere hasty confusion again.
>
> 'They have larger brain cases—much larger, and slenderer bodies, and very short legs. They make gentle noises, and move with organized deliberation . . .
>
> 'And though I am wounded and helpless here, their appearance still gives me hope.' That was like Cavor. 'They have not shot at me or attempted . . . injury. I intend—'
>
> Then came the sudden streak of the pencil across the paper, and on the back and edges—blood! (*First Men*, ch. 19)

As the post-Cartesian consciousness fantasizes like Griffin that it is an abstract, rather than merely physical entity, so does writing dream of existing mentally, beyond its material limits. Cavor's note shows the ruin of both illusions. Cavor tries to write and think effectually, but is prevented from doing so by his injuries and by his mental distraction while being chased. The note is only partly legible because of his difficulties in writing (the erasure), because it has been damaged by flight (the crumpling), and marked by the damage to Cavor's body (the blood). At the same time, what Bedford is actually trying to communicate is the fact that the Selenites possess superior bodies to men.

HYBRID GENRES: *THE FOOD OF THE GODS*

Wells's later scientific romances aspire towards utopia; consequently their genre veers further away from fictional narrative and more towards speculative description. The *Food of the Gods* and *In the Days of the Comet* begin life as a scientific romance and a realist novel, respectively but each mutates into Wellsian utopia.

The Food of the Gods obeys the generic paradigms that Wells had established in his nineteenth-century romances: a technological or scientific innovation produces a cognitive estrangement, narrated in a frame that draws attention to the inability of conventional modes of representation, notably history and the newspaper, to represent such experiences adequately. The narrative frequently doubts its own veracity, such as in the reporting of Skinner's death, and often chooses to withdraw rather than represent events more comprehensively. Even the text's final, world-changing battle is relayed indirectly.

> For a time at least the spreading circle of residual consequences about the Experimental Farm must pass out of the focus of our narrative—how for a long time a power of bigness, in fungus and toadstool, in grass and weed, radiated from that charred but not absolutely obliterated centre. Nor can we tell here at any length how these mournful spinsters, the two surviving hens, made a wonder of and a show, spent their remaining years in eggless celebrity. The reader who is hungry for fuller details in these matters is referred to the newspapers of the period—to the voluminous, indiscriminate files of the modern Recording Angel. Our business lies with Mr. Bensington at the focus of the disturbance. (*Food of the Gods*, bk 1, ch. 4)

The tone of *The Food of the Gods* is often light-heartedly humorous, but the plot is as violent as that of *The War of the Worlds*. In a conventional adventure story, the narrative usually implies some kind of sympathetic identification with the reader's viewpoint; in Wells's more violent fictions such as *The War of the Worlds*, *The Island of Doctor Moreau*, and *The Food of the Gods*, the narrative's tone, especially when representing violence, repeatedly, even priggishly, distances the reader from the action of the plot. The narration's cold-heartedness produces a further estrangement, an alienation effect designed to stimulate the reader more cognitively than emotionally.

The First Men in the Moon imagines a remodelling of the sentient living body by a utopian state; *The Food of the Gods* projects bodies who take advantage of their superior level of evolution to reconstruct the whole world. Wells had praised Darwin and Malthus for placing the body and reproduction back at the centre of intellectual enquiry, and had criticized thinkers such as Marcus Aurelius and Schopenhauer for downplaying their importance.[93] His own utopian writings mediate between individual

---

[93] *Mankind in the Making*, 14–15.

bodily experience and the organization of the state: *The Food of the Gods* mutates into a didactic grotesque on the relationship between the body and the body politic.

The consequences of the invention of Boomfood act as a further warning, like the earlier romances, against scientific research that is unsanctioned by the state. However, *The Food of the Gods'* reproductive experiment succeeds because it becomes part of the process of natural selection, not an attempt to master it: 'The reef of Science that these little "scientists" built and are yet building is so wonderful, so portentous, so full of mysterious half-shapen promises for the mighty future of man! They do not seem to realize the things they are doing!' (*Food of the Gods*, bk 1, ch. 1). Huxley's 'Evolution and Ethics' and *The Island of Doctor Moreau* show that the cosmic process can never be entirely harnessed by the rational, but that the rational has to take the contingencies of natural and sexual selection into account. 'The old Utopias—save for the breeding schemes of Plato and Campanella—ignored that reproductive competition among individualities which is the substance of life' (*A Modern Utopia*, ch. 5, 1).[94] While his utopias are very much concerned with the social production of its future citizens, Wells recognizes limits on the extent to which human culture can shape its future biology in the short term. Wells had flirted with the idea of, then repudiated, the eugenic programming of mankind's biological future.[95] Sceptical as he is towards semantic certainty, Wells does not allow definitions of categories such as 'fitness', 'beauty', 'health', or even 'madness' to be definite enough for state-sponsored eugenics to be advisable.[96] Boomfood is a success not because, like Moreau's experiments, it tries to master the cosmic process, but because it fits within it; once they are able to do so, the super-evolved organisms Boomfood produces are able to compete with existing species successfully.[97] The giant children's victory over the rest of the world proves their greater fitness for the environment that they inhabit; the

[94] Cf. Plato, *Republic*, bk 5.
[95] *The Work, Wealth and Happiness of Mankind*, 677–80; McLean, *Early Fiction*, 154–7; Sherborne, *H. G. Wells*, 152; Partington, *Cosmopolis*, 54–7, and 'Revising *Anticipations*: Wells on Race and Class, 1901 to 1905', *Undying Fire* 4 (2005), 31–44, and 'H. G. Wells's Eugenic Thinking of the 1930s and 1940s', *Utopian Studies*, 14/1 (2003), 74–81. See Wells's letters to the *Daily Mail* and the *Daily Chronicle*, *Correspondence*, II, 348–9, 437— although also, on the other hand, to *John Bull*, III, 352.
[96] 'The Problem of the Birth Supply', *Mankind in the Making*, 34–73; Wagar, *Traversing Time*, 94. For a useful comparison, see Piers J. Hale, 'Of Mice and Men: Evolution and the Socialist Utopia: William Morris, H. G. Wells and George Bernard Shaw', *Journal of the History of Biology*, 43/1 (2010), 17–66.
[97] Giants in human shape would not, of course, be more physically adept than normal-size humans: see Arwen Spicer, 'An Ecological Ideology: The Specter of Ecological Discourse in *The Food of the Gods*', *Undying Fire*, 1 (2001), 64–75 (68).

fate of Caddles, like that of the dinosaurs, proves that size and strength alone are not sufficient for evolutionary security. Caddles is intellectually limited not by his working-class descent, but by an environment that has failed to educate him properly—he is so illiterate, he cannot even read advertising skywriting—and which has not allowed his abilities to be specialized towards the functions for which they are best suited. Literally, the giant Caddles does not fit in:

> He could not go to school; he could not go to church by virtue of the obvious limitations of its cubical content. There was some attempt to satisfy the spirit of that "most foolish and destructive law"—I quote the Vicar—the Elementary Education Act of 1870, by getting him to sit outside the open window while instruction was going on within. But his presence there destroyed the discipline of the other children. They were always popping up and peering at him, and every time he spoke they laughed together. His voice was so odd! So they let him stay away.
>
> Nor did they persist in pressing him to come to church, for his vast proportions were of little help to devotion. Yet there they might have had an easier task; there are good reasons for guessing there were the germs of religious feeling somewhere in that big carcase. The music perhaps drew him. He was often in the churchyard on a Sunday morning, picking his way softly among the graves after the congregation had gone in, and he would sit the whole service out beside the porch, listening as one listens outside a hive of bees. (*Food of the Gods*, bk 2, ch. 2, 1)

A parodic version of the protagonists of the realist novels, Caddles comes to London wanting more self-realization from the world than it currently offers, only to be defeated by modernity, here in the form of advanced weapons technology.

Although super-adapted, the brains of the giant children are still morphologically human, so unlike Selenite children, they still need educating and nurturing. Wells always maintained, unlike most other utopists, that the family remained the best institution for rearing children (as demonstrated by Wells's advocacy in *The New Machiavelli* and elsewhere of the state's endowment of motherhood).[98] Since the human race cannot accurately control the process of its own evolution, it should focus its collective will on reforming that which it does have the power to reform: its institutions of power, education, religion, and marriage. The evolutionary competition in *The Food of the Gods* gains

---

[98] See the pamphlet *Will Socialism Destroy the Home?* (London: Independent Labour Party, [1907]), reprinted as 'Would Socialism Destroy the Home?', in *New Worlds for Old*, 117–39; Partington, *Cosmopolis*, 41.

an added Oedipal edge, since the son will become literally greater than his father.[99]

> "Suppose we give up this great thing that stirs within us, repudiate this thing our fathers did for us—that *you*, Father, did for us—and pass, when our time has come, into decay and nothingness! What then? Will this little world of theirs be as it was before? They may fight against greatness in us who are the children of men, but can they conquer? Even if they should destroy us every one, what then? Would it save them? No! For greatness is abroad, not only in us, not only in the Food, but in the purpose of all things! It is in the nature of all things; it is part of space and time. To grow and still to grow: from first to last that is Being—that is the law of life. What other law can there be?" (*Food of the Gods*, bk 3, ch. 5, 3)

These articulate children are better able than Caddles to impose their will on the environment because the combination of their hyper-development with their excellent education gives them a superior perspective from which the world really does look different. They can see through 'the complex pretences upon which the social fabric of the little folks was built' (bk 3, ch. 3, 3), and how things on the ground might be arranged better instead. The children are a joint allegory of Wells's collective will, 'this huge moral, intellectual being which grows now self-conscious and purposeful, just as a child grows out of its early self-ignorance to an elusive, indefinable, indisputable sense of itself.[100] Famously, G. K. Chesterton identified them as imaginative authorial projection: 'The most interesting thing about Mr. H. G. Wells is that he is the only one of his many brilliant contemporaries who has not stopped growing. One can lie awake at night and hear him grow.'[101]

The public school-educated vicar, who 'loved a classical quotation subtly misapplied' thinks of humanity as 'aere perennius', as lasting as brass; the parish doctor cites Nordau in fearing 'grave moral and intellectual deficiencies' (*Food of he Gods*, bk 2. ch. 2, 4). Both are wrong: given the right biological and social factors, there might exist a third possibility, that mankind might become more complex and effective still.

---

[99] In *Star-Begotten* (1937), Davis fears that after the Martian's psychic invasions, 'presently our children may not prove to be our own': *Star Begotten: A Biological Fantasia*, ed. John Huntington (Middleton: Wesleyan University Press, 2006), 71.

[100] *New Worlds for Old*, 284.

[101] G. K. Chesterton, 'Mr. H. G. Wells and the Giants', *Heretics* (London: Bodley Head, 1905), 62–85 (69). According to his French translator Henry D. Davray, 'Wells is like the world: his evolution never stops': in *The Reception of H. G. Wells in Europe*, ed. Parrinder and Partington, 43. See also the very funny demolition of Wells as too large to be contained to the real world by James Gillis in *False Prophets* (New York: Macmillan, 1925), 20–44.

WISHING ON A STAR: *IN THE DAYS OF THE COMET*

In the Days of the Comet hybridizes the three genres of utopia, realism, and scientific romance. Wells's use of another retrospective narrator naturalizes this text's post-utopian, post-Comet conclusion. Any estrangement from ideas of the natural and expected is produced in the text's implied reader not by the image of utopia, but by images of the pre-utopian, unjust, dirty, sexually repressed world inhabited by the text's actual reader. (Wells adopts the same model for future histories such as *The World Set Free* (1914), *The Dream* (1924), and 1933's *The Shape of Things to Come*.) 'I find the greatest difficulty in writing down the unintelligible confusions that were matter of fact to their fathers' (*In the Days of the Comet*, bk 1, ch. 3, 4) confesses the older, utopia-dwelling Leadford. Once again, the narrative calls attention to the inadequacy of its own representations: 'thin and austere comfort in thinking that the whole is not told to us, that it cannot perhaps be told to such minds as ours' (*In the Days of the Comet*, bk 3, ch. 10, 4). The beauty of Nettie, who herself is afflicted by 'inadequacy of expression' (*In the Days of the Comet*, bk 1, 3, 6), cannot even effectively be portrayed by photography, let alone writing: 'The reality of beauty yields itself to no words. I wish that I had the sister art and could draw in my margin something that escapes description' (*In the Days of the Comet*, bk 1, ch. 1, 2). (The accomplished cartoons or 'picshuas' with which Wells embellished his manuscripts may indeed be seen as showing Wells wishing to break the boundaries of linguistic representation.)[102]

The opening of the book maintains a strict realism which, together with the novel's Potteries setting, is a homage to Arnold Bennett. Wells deploys such well-worn realist techniques as detailing interiors: the squalor of the Leadfords' dwelling, the 'air of culture' (*In the Days of the Comet*, bk 1, ch. 4, 3) of the vicar Gabbitas's room, the modish bohemianism of the holiday railway carriage.[103] Wells vividly portrays a protagonist whose development is ineluctably bounded in by the power of money and class. His melodramatic passion and rage are just as much a material product of the inequable social system as the industrial waste and mendacious advertisements that litter the novel's landscape. Before the Comet, he is on the

[102] *The Picshuas of H. G. Wells: A Burlesque Diary*, ed. Gene K. Rinkel and Margaret E. Rinkel (Urbana: University of Illinois Press, 2006).
[103] See Simon J. James, 'Some Versions of Realism: Arnold Bennett and H. G. Wells', in *Bennett and Wells*, ed. John Shapcott (Stoke: Arnold Bennett Society, 2010), 30–9.

verge of decivilizing himself altogether, even fashioning a primitive club from a flint.

The fantastic innovation of this utopian romance is the Comet which makes every inhabitant of the world spontaneously adopt the political views of H. G. Wells, the light it brings literalizing a state of perfect knowledge. Clothing, the built environment, even bodily sensations are materially improved by the Change. As the Comet passes, the novel switches genre, moving from realism through the fantastic (elliptically, while the Earth's population sleeps), towards utopia, which is not a narrative genre, as Leadford admits after a lengthy passage of future history: 'I have departed widely from my individual story' (*In the Days of the Comet*, bk 3, ch. 9, 1). This text marks the beginning of the habit of Wells's characters to be mouthpieces for Wells's own political views, in passages that begin with phrases such as 'it was clear to me that I had to think out for myself religious problems, social problems, questions of conduct, questions of expediency' (*In the Days of the Comet*, bk 1, ch. 1, 5)—a habit that then becomes endemic in Wells's first-person narrators from *The New Machiavelli*'s Remington onwards.[104]

The Comet also alters the conditions of reading and writing. Written language fails to alleviate Leadford's material condition, as it fails for so many Wells protagonists. His early literary ambitions are not a route out of his suffering, but a compensation for it:

> Long ago in my crude unhappy youth, I conceived the desire to write a book. To scribble secretly and dream of authorship was one of my chief alleviations, and I read with a sympathetic envy every scrap I could get about the world of literature and the lives of literary people. It is something, even amidst this present happiness, to find leisure and opportunity to take up and partially realise these old and hopeless dreams. (*In the Days of the Comet*, bk 1, ch. 1, 1)

His letters to Nettie, Pettigrew, and Lord Redcar all fail to achieve their intended effect, and in the case of his love letters, Leadford's reading of the nineteenth-century cultural residuum even proves a handicap:

> I began to read with avidity such writing as Carlyle, Browning, and Heine have left for the perplexity of posterity, and not only to read and admire but to imitate. My letters to Nettie, after one or two genuinely intended displays of perfervid tenderness, broke out toward theology, sociology, and the cosmos in turgid and startling expressions. No doubt they puzzled her extremely. (*In the Days of the Comet*, bk 1, ch. 1, 2)

---

[104] Haynes, *H. G. Wells*, 193–5; Loing, *H. G. Wells à L'Oeuvre*, 289.

Leadford also devotes most of a chapter to describing the haste and consequent inaccuracy attendant on producing a pre-Utopian newspaper, showing how slow to respond and partial mass communication was before the Change, that this medium's assertions prove to be as fragile as its material form:

> In my bureau I have several files of the daily papers of the old time [...]. They lie before me—queer, shriveled, incredible things; the cheap paper has already become brittle and brown and split along the creases, the ink faded or smeared, and have to handle them with the utmost care when I glance among their raging headlines. As I sit here in this serene place, their quality throughout, their arrangement, their tone, their arguments and exhortations, read as though they came from drugged and drunken men. They give one the effect of faded bawling, of screams and shouts heard faintly in a little gramophone ... (*In the Days of the Comet*, bk 1, ch. 3, 3)[105]

The first newspaper produced after the Change, 'a dead souvenir of the dead ages of the world' (*In the Days of the Comet*, bk 2, ch. 7, 3), has also decayed physically, but is at least testament to the efficacy of media now produced by willing labour and not for commercial motives. Letters between Leadford and Nettie are also more effective after the Change: the Comet produces a utopian condition of efficacious writing. In one of the most disturbing passages in the whole of Wells's work, Leadford finally repudiates his youthful misreading of Ruskin and Shelley and celebrates the destruction, since they have become unnecessary, of most of the world's books in Beltane fires:[106]

> And books, countless books, too, and bales of newspapers went also to these pyres. From the private houses in Swathinglea alone—which I had deemed, perhaps not unjustly, altogether illiterate—we gathered a whole dust-cart full of cheap ill-printed editions of the minor English classics—for the most part very dull stuff indeed and still clean—and about a truckload of thumbed and dog-eared penny fiction, watery base stuff, the dropsy of our nation's mind ... And it seemed to me that when we gathered those books and papers together, we gathered together something more than print and paper, we gathered warped and crippled ideas and contagious base suggestions, the formulae of dull tolerances and stupid impatiences, the mean defensive ingenuities of sluggish habits of thinking and timid and indolent evasions. There was more than a touch of malignant satisfaction for me in helping gather it all together. (*In the Days of the Comet*, bk 3, ch. 3, 1)

---

[105]   Cf. *The Shape of Things to Come*, 92, 229; *H. G. Wells in 'Nature'*, 437.
[106]   On the burning of bad books, see also *Crux Ansata*, 55–6.

Wells credited the Fabian Society with saving him early in his writing life from a successful, merely literary career.[107] Once Wells had exiled himself from the Fabian Society, his writing was to be his main vehicle for shaping the ways in which power would distribute itself.[108] 'The battle for Socialism is to be fought not simply at the polls and in the market-place but at the writing-desk and in the study.'[109] Writing *Tono-Bungay* and the subsequent novels leading up to the First World War, Wells's political energies were not diverted into potentially wasteful collective action, but instead focused on a polemical writing that would influence the collective mind in the right direction.[110]

---

[107] *Autobiography*, II, 601.
[108] On the relationship with Fabianism and Liberalism, see Richard Toye, 'H. G. Wells and the New Liberalism', *Twentieth Century British History*, 19/2 (2008), 156–85.
[109] *New Worlds for Old*, 222.
[110] See Hynes, *Edwardian Turn of Mind*, 87–131. Hynes also reprints Wells's speech and pamphlet 'The Faults of the Fabian', 390–409.

5

Education and Catastrophe

The War and the World

> Since the passing of Victoria the Great there had been an accumulat-
> ing uneasiness in the national life. It was as if some compact and
> dignified paperweight had been lifted from people's ideas, and as if at
> once they had begun to blow about anyhow.
>
> (*The Soul of a Bishop*, ch. 2)[1]

By 1909, Wells had formally made a break with the notion of the novel as an
autonomous work of art that exists for its own sake: the origins of his final
rupture with James and with Victorian ideals of high culture are already
present in *Tono-Bungay*. From the turn of the decade onward, Wells viewed
the different genres in which he wrote, including the novel, pre-eminently
as goads to social improvement. Literature should not exist to describe the
structures and functions of society unless it actively seeks to improve them.

Wells's novels of the 1910s onwards are documents of dissent, and
themselves tend to dramatize individuals dissenting against, or trying to
evolve past, social convention.[2] In novels such as *Ann Veronica*, *The New
Machiavelli*, *Marriage*, *The Passionate Friends*, and *The Wife of Sir Isaac
Harman* (1914), a particular social practice—at the beginning of this
phase usually marriage and sexual monogamy—impedes the development
of a strong-willed protagonist who is eventually liberated, usually by love
(although, as Rebecca West complained in her review of *Marriage*, Wells's
representations were nonetheless themselves limited in their expression by
social convention).[3] Marjorie in *Marriage*, Ann Veronica, and Lady Harman seek outlets for individual development barred to them in society as it

---

[1] Cf. Wells's late reflection on his own education, 'The Irrational Behaviour of the
Writer', *'42 to '44*, 9–11 (9–10).
[2] 'The laws and institutions of mankind came just as much within the scope of biological
generalisation as the life of any living being.' *Mr. Blettsworthy on Rampole Island*, 172.
[3] Review of *Marriage*, *Freewoman*, 19 September 1912, 356–8, *Critical Heritage*, ed.
Parrinder, 203–10.

presently exists because of their gender. Ann Veronica selects Capes's vigorous scientific and eugenically appealing masculinity over Manning's effeminate Bohemianism; Marjorie chooses Trafford's scientific clearsightedness over Magnet's and her family's pointless and fruitless aesthetic self-indulgence. (Even in this latter case, the aesthetic threatens her marriage, as her frustrated energies are turned into feminine over-consumption, creating a house beautiful that is dismissed by her husband as 'this litter and rubbish for which I am wasting my life'.)[4]

The milieu of these novels also tends to be higher in social class, placing the main characters closer to the centre of power, but also making their initial stages of development more archaic. These novels often stage acts of political, as well as sexual, infidelity. Remington (*The New Machiavelli*) is a Member of Parliament, Stratton (*The Passionate Friends*) is a would-be politician, Trafford (*Marriage*) a scientific professor, Britling in *Mr. Britling Sees it Through* (1916) and Brumley (*The Wife of Sir Isaac Harman*) both writers, Mortimer Smith (*The Dream*) a publisher, Sempack (*Meanwhile*, 1927) a 'utographer', Edward Scrope (*The Soul of a Bishop*) Bishop of Princhester. Even protagonists who appear to be lunatics (in *Christina Alberta's Father*, and *Mr. Blettsworthy on Rampole Island*) possess imaginations that are all compact with those of the poet and prophet. In such cases, Wells permits himself imaginative liberty by presenting his fictions as dreams or hallucinations: what the psychoanalyst Minchett calls an 'Interpretative Reverie', or, for *The Shape of Things to Come* 'a text within a dream within a text'.[5]

The most significant difference from the earlier realist novels is that, unlike Wells's earlier mute inglorious cockneys, these individual protagonists are sufficiently articulate to make on Wells's behalf a bespoke objection to the particular social ill that the novel is attacking. Previously, the relationship between Wells's novels and political writings was that the former would diagnose ailments which the latter then attempt to cure. After 1910, the discourse of the novels is hybridized with didactic interpolations from a character who possesses the role of an authorial spokesman. In this genre that Wells dubbed the 'discussion novel', the asseverations of the author-figure are dialogized with speech or letters from other characters.[6] In purely literary terms, such a technique is somewhat contrived, but nonetheless constitutes a kind of formal innovation designed to overcome what Wells would see as the frivolous irresponsibility

---

[4] *Marriage*, 308. Cf. *Secret Places of the Heart*, 382.

[5] *Mr. Blettsworthy on Rampole Island*, 217; Pinsky, *Future Present*, 77.

[6] *Autobiography*, II, 477. See also Wells's defence of the tradition of 'discussing fundamental human problems in dialogue form' in the Preface to *Babes in the Darkling Wood*, 5–11 (6).

of producing a self-enclosed art that chooses not to address the subject of social change. In his final letter to James, Wells declared that he 'had rather be called a journalist than an artist'; James worried to Edmund Gosse that, 'He has cut loose from literature clearly—practically altogether; he will still do a lot of writing probably—but it won't be *that*.'[7] In Wells's prose writing of this period, the terms 'literature' or 'art' tend to be bracketed into such phrases as 'art and science', as if both are equivalent fields of teleological enquiry, forms of intellectual endeavour meant to bring something material about. If disciplines such as medicine and engineering are described as applied science, Wells's preferred form of writing might constitute 'applied art'.[8] Even more emphatically than before, Wells's model for literary production would be the laboratory and the street, not the museum or the church.

FIGHTING FOR PEACE

Increasingly, Wells's writing after his 'major phase' of the 1890s and 1900s becomes dominated by forecasting, and then by responding to, the subject of war.[9] *Tono-Bungay* dramatizes how the unstable nature of capitalist economics might result in a European war; in an essay 'The Possible Collapse of Civilisation', written shortly afterwards, at New Year 1909, Wells anguished that 'there are two chief things in modern life that impress me as dangerous and incalculable. The first of these is the modern currency and financial system, and the second is the chance we take of destructive war.'[10] Ideologically, of course, Wells was opposed to warfare: 'I avow myself an extreme Pacifist', he wrote in 1917's *War and the Future*.[11] According to Martha Gellhorn, 'War drove him mad. He found it all so horrible. He was in despair for the world.'[12] However, as *The War of the Worlds*, *The Food of the Gods*, and a number of short stories

---

[7] *Henry James and H. G. Wells*, 264, 164n.

[8] In his essay, 'World Well Educated', Wells praises Leonardo da Vinci and Velasquez thus: 'they were essentially men of science who thrust aside all the flowery tricks of artificial decoration and pretentious aestheticism, and who, pursuing reality, found living and enduring beauty and new depth and profundity and mastery at every stage of their research'. *Guide to the New World: A Handbook of Constructive World Revolution* (London: Gollancz, 1941), 143–8 (147). See Reed, *Natural History of H. G. Wells*, 194–8.

[9] See Cecil Degrotte Eby, *The Road to Armageddon: The Martial Spirit in English Popular Literature, 1870–1914* (Durham, OH: Duke University Press, 1988), 38–55.

[10] 'The Possible Collapse of Civilisation', *An Englishman Looks at the World*, 330–5.

[11] *War and the Future*, 11.

[12] Interview with Andrea Lynn, quoted in Andrea Lynn, *Shadow Lovers: The Last Affairs of H. G. Wells* (Oxford: Perseus Press, 2001), 431.

such as 'The Land Ironclads' (1903) demonstrate, Wells's imagination was nonetheless powerfully attracted to scenes of destructive warfare. The contradiction, for Rebecca West, is that Wells is a 'person who runs about lighting bonfires and yet nourishes a dislike of flame'. 'Are his insights into violence,' wonders Darko Suvin, 'those of a diagnostician or a fan?'[13] The very fact that wars occur, laying massive waste to biological and economic resources, is proof enough that civilization is not ordered as efficiently as Wells thought it should be; nonetheless, war then provides an opportunity for society to be improved. 'The war was bringing the whole world back to elemental things,' opines Scrope in *The Soul of a Bishop*; 'Man grasps his problems and reconstructs,' resolves Mr Blettsworthy.[14] War is the most pronounced symptom of the failure of civilization, but if civilization in its present form were destroyed, this might at least offer the opportunity for a new civilization to be constructed in its place, such an apocalypse both the 'greatest catastrophe and the greatest opportunity in history'.[15] Thinking in particular of the Wells-influenced John Wyndham, Fredric Jameson has noticed 'in SF [. . .] the way in which global cataclysm serves as a mere pretext for the dreaming of a far more positive Utopian wish-fulfilment'.[16] Wells's paradoxical choice of title for *The World Set Free* hints at the regenerative possibilities that Wells foresees in a World War; his 1936 film *Things to Come*, as in many Wellsian narratives, shows utopia arising out of catastrophe. 'War is just the killing of things and the smashing of things,' he wrote in *Boon*. 'And when it is all over, then literature and civilization will have to begin all over again' (*Boon*, ch. 9, 5).

Wells's writings in this period include two books for children, *Floor Games* (1911) and *Little Wars* (1913), which replicate the 'stratospheric' perspective of the giant children of *The Food of the Gods*, encouraging children respectively to construct model societies and to play war games. Wells's writing for children emphasizes constructiveness: in 'Master

---

[13] *H. G. Wells and Rebecca West*, ed. Gordon N. Ray (London: Macmillan, 1974), 22; Suvin and Philmus, eds., *H. G. Wells and Modern Science Fiction*, 27; Kemp, *H. G. Wells and the Culminating Ape*, 145–86.

[14] *The Soul of a Bishop*, *Works*, XXV, 270; *Mr. Blettsworthy on Rampole Island*, 173.

[15] *Mr. Britling*, *Works*, XXII, 246; Parrinder, *H. G. Wells*, 12. 'War in the future will be a question of preparation, of long years of foresight and disciplined imagination, there will be no decisive victory, but a vast diffusion of conflict—it will depend less and less on controlling personalities and driving emotions, and more and more upon the intelligence and personal quality of a great number of skilled men. [. . .] And either before or after, but, at any rate, in the shadow of war, it will become apparent, perhaps even suddenly, that the whole apparatus of power in the country is in the hands of a new class of intelligent and scientifically-educated men.' *Anticipations*, 152–3.

[16] Jameson, *Archaeologies*, 378.

Anthony and the Zeppelin' (1916), a zeppelin is encouraged to build a nest instead of dropping bombs.[17] Wells often associated violence with immaturity, accusing those he sees as warmongers such as Leo Amery, Winston Churchill, and Adolf Hitler of being overgrown boys wanting to start fights: as Benham in *The Research Magnificent* (1915) has it, '"men of thirteen years old or thereabouts, the boy who doesn't grow up"'.[18] If Europe goes to war, this is because the individual countries that compose it have failed to grow up sufficiently.[19] The desire for peace is thus a characteristic of maturity. Wells's fiction from *Ann Veronica* onwards also shows an increasing concern about child-rearing, in particular parent–child relationships after the child has reached adulthood.

The Time Machine had served as both a prophecy and a warning: in his later career, Wells reinvented himself as both a Moses bringing the law and a Cassandra frustrated at being ignored by a world heading for self-immolation.[20] Wells declared after *Anticipations*, 'I became my own first disciple' (*Autobiography*, II, 646). *The War in the Air, and Particularly How Bert Smallways Fared while It Lasted* combines the utopian rhetoric of *In the Days of the Comet* and the sociological writings with the technological speculations of the scientific romances and the immature hero of the realist-comic works. Once actual historical events caught up with those foretold in his fiction, the tone of Wells's writing became increasingly frustrated. As new editions of his earliest vision of a European War were published, Wells also added a series of increasingly strident Prefaces. In 1917, he predicted that:

> If mankind goes on with war, the smash-up of civilization is inevitable. It is chaos or the United States of the World for mankind. There is no other choice. Ten years have but added an enormous conviction to the message of this book. It remains essentially right, a pamphlet story.[21]

For all of Wells's predictions and advocacy of a peaceful scientific future World State, at the same time—and especially in *The War in the Air*—he diagnoses war as a consequence of modernity. 'We are entering upon a

[17] 'Master Anthony and the Zeppelin', *Princess Marie-Jose's Children's Book* (London: Cassell, 1916), 13–17.
[18] 'See The Singapore Arsenal' and 'Winston', *A Year of Prophesying*, 21–6 (24), 63–8 (67); *The Shape of Things to Come*, 53; *The Research Magnificent*, *Works*, XIX, 256; *Autobiography*, 102; McConnell, *Science Fiction*, 204–5. Cf. *Autobiography*, I, 102.
[19] Wells's reflections on the war as regrettable proof of the accuracy of this theorizing can be interestingly contrasted with the comparable response of Sigmund Freud: see 'On Transience' (1915), *Works*, XIV, 303–7.
[20] See Patrick Parrinder, 'Experiments in Prophecy', in *H. G. Wells: Reality and Beyond*, ed. Mullin, 7–21.
[21] Preface to the 1917 American edition, quoted in Wagar, *Traversing Time*, 141.

period in which the invention of methods and material for war is likely to be more rapid and diversified than it has ever been before,' he wrote in his essay 'The Common Sense of Warfare'.[22] Modernity is a consequence of technology; technology accelerates the pace of material change, but civilized society does not develop at the same rate. If civilization consequently breaks down, war is the inevitable result, and war will be even more destructive than before because of, in turn, those same technological advances.[23] 'The application of science to warfare' (*War in the Air*, 6, 6) amplifies the effects, but not the efficacy of warfare. The Germans in *The War in the Air* find, like the Martians, that technological superiority guarantees a greater extent of destruction, but not necessarily victory.[24] Without technology, the war degenerates to a primitive evolutionary competition for survival first between Bert and Prince Karl Albert on Goat Island, and then between atomized communities the whole world over.

The characteristic trope for modernity in turn-of-the-century fiction is the urban crowd. Wells characteristically enlarges this vision in both time and space:

> A saner world would have perceived this patent need for a reasonable synthesis, would have discussed it temperately, achieved and gone on to organise the great civilisation that was manifestly possible to mankind. [...] Its national governments [...] were too suspicious of each other, too wanting in generous imaginations. They began to behave like ill-bred people in a crowded public car, to squeeze against one another, elbow, thrust, dispute and quarrel. (*War in the Air*, ch. 4, 1)

Wells's very earliest utopian work, *Anticipations*, begins with a discussion of technologies of transport, and the resulting 'abolition of distances' (*Anticipations*, ch. 4), a phrase that Wells regularly reuses throughout his writing. *The War in the Air*'s opening fantastically accelerates this process of cognitive estrangement, extrapolating from present-day technological innovations in transport to imagined future ones, narrating the successive developments of the motorized bicycle, automobile, zeppelin, monorail, aeroplane, and helicopter. For all his Kippsish ignorance and vulgarity, Smallways is a modern man, a post-1870 reader of *Chips* and *Comic Cuts*, a technocratic enthusiast for progress like the 'mechanics and engineers' in whom *Anticipations* (ch. 3) places such hope. This enthusiasm gets him literally carried away by a modern form of transport when he is accidentally taken up by a hot air balloon. In this novel, human effort repeatedly

---

[22] 'The Common Sense of Warfare', *An Englishman Looks at the World*, 132–47 (140).
[23] See the letter to *The Times*, *Correspondence*, II, 421–3.
[24] See Michael Paris, *Winged Warfare: The Literature and Theory of Aerial Warfare in Britain, 1859–1917* (Manchester: Manchester University Press, 1992), 33–9.

fails to match up to technological progress; the plot keeps re-emphasizing the powerlessness of the individual when made subject to modern technology, especially when technology fails, or, as so often in Wells, when the possibilities of heroic action are undermined by reminders of the body, such as hunger. Bert would not be on the beach singing for pennies in the first place if his motorized bicycle had not accidentally caught fire; airships are vulnerable; even Butteridge's new flying machine does not ultimately alter the outcome of the war to any great degree.

Like those of *Tono-Bungay* and *Boon*, the narrative arc of *The War in the Air* describes society's ultimate disintegration: there will be no fortuitous ending of the kind that rescues Bert's fellow cockneys Kipps and Polly. Money has in fact disappeared from the world, bringing Chaffery's prediction of consequent social collapse true; Wells later feared that even if civilization survived the war, it might still be destroyed by financial debt.[25] In an inverse image of the future desired by *Anticipations*, once civilization ends, so does civilized transport, and humans return to the primitive condition of barely leaving the villages in which they were born. Nor do books survive, as humanity also regresses to oral culture. Such cultural dissolution is foreshadowed in the chaotic dialogizing of the book's own discourse, initially between the initial superior narrative voice of Wells's realist fiction and the Smallways' typically Wellsian Kent-cockney, then through the airman Kurt's part-English public schoolboy slang, part-German upper-class slang, to heavily German-accented English, to a narrator from years in the future after the dystopian events narrated in the novel, who comments on the novel's action in an ironic historical pluperfect:

> Mechanical invention had gone faster than intellectual and social organisation, and the world, with its silly old flags, its silly unmeaning tradition of nationality, its cheap newspapers and cheaper passions and imperialisms, its base commercial motives and habitual insincerities and vulgarities, its race lies and conflicts, was taken by surprise. Once the war began there was no stopping it. The flimsy fabric of credit that had grown with no man foreseeing, and that had held those hundreds of millions in an economic interdependence that no man clearly understood, dissolved in panic. [...] Whatever constructive guiding intelligence there had been among the nations vanished in the passionate stresses of the time. Such newspapers and documents and histories as survive from this period all tell one universal story of towns and cities with the food supply interrupted and their streets congested with starving unemployed; of crises in administration and states of siege. (*War in the Air*, ch. 8, 1)

---

[25] See, for example, 'Scrapping the Gold Standard', *A Year of Prophesying*, 123–9.

As with *In the Days of the Comet*, Wells's narrator cannot resist a swipe at the insufficiency of the literature of his own time when seen from the perspective of this future observer:

> When now in retrospect the thoughtful observer surveys the intellectual history of this time, when one reads its surviving fragments of literature, its scraps of political oratory, the few small voices that chance has selected out of a thousand million utterances to speak to later days, the most striking thing of all this web of wisdom and error is surely that hallucination of security. (*War in the Air*, ch. 9, 1)

In the United States, the country that is the first casualty of the aerial war, books 'had become simply material for the energy of collectors' (*War in the Air*, 6, 2). America's aerial bombardment is fancifully imagined as a punishment for not reading serious newspapers, for not thinking critically enough about politics and history.

> They saw war as they saw history, through an iridescent mist, deodorised, scented indeed, with all its essential cruelties tactfully hidden away. They were inclined to regret it as something ennobling, to sigh that it could no longer come into their own private experience. [...] They did not, so far as one can judge from their contemporary literature, think that they meant anything to their personal lives at all. (*War in the Air*, ch. 6, 1)

The aerial war produces a dystopian conclusion because, even as civilization decays, the world's inhabitants insist on clinging to notions of national identity, thus continuing the war between nation states.

Wells had at times considered proportional representation and the League of Nations as legitimate remedies for the decentralization of power, but rapidly turned against the latter for its continued adherence to the category of the nation state: 'A "sovereign state" is essentially and incurably a war-making state.'[26] The destruction wrought by warfare will be fruitless unless the idea of the nation state that caused the war in the first place is jettisoned in favour of a world state. Since the war is 'a war of ideas', Wells's main target when writing around war is the very idea of nationhood:[27]

> Of all the productions of the human imagination that make the world in which Mr. Bert Smallways lived confusingly wonderful, there was none quite so strange, so headlong and disturbing, so noisy and persuasive and

---

[26] *Autobiography*, II, 667; *The Shape of Things to Come*, 76. Wells also alters the protagonists' views of the League of Nations to make them more negative in the proof of *Joan and Peter* (e.g. Illinois Collection, JP-354). See also Wells's *The P.R. Parliament* (London: Proportional Representation Society, [1924]).

[27] *In the Fourth Year: Anticipations of a World Peace* (London: Chatto & Windus, 1918), v.

dangerous, as the modernisations of patriotism produced by imperial and international politics. (*War in the Air*, ch. 4, 1)

The utopian *The World Set Free*, on the other hand, imagines a different relationship between technological innovation and national identity. Wells consistently attacked the epistemological indivisibility of categories, whether linguistic or biological; recent hypotheses in atomic theory allow him to imagine even the category of the individual atom being dissolved. The invention of the atomic bomb sees countries voluntarily disarming and themselves dissolving when faced with the prospect of a war that could result in the destruction of humanity. Wells's political and historical writing repeatedly insists on mankind's common biological origin making a nonsense of nationhood as an essential property.[28] National identity is no more essential a category than any other, even of the human being as a species; as species can evolve, so can the nature of the 'imagined communities' in which members of that species combine with each other.[29] Darwin wrote in the *Descent of Man*:

> As man advances in civilisation, and small tribes are united into larger communities, the simplest reason would tell each individual that he ought to extend his social instincts and sympathies to all the members of the same nation, though personally unknown to him. This point being once reached, there is only an artificial barrier to prevent his sympathies extending to the men of all nations and races.[30]

For world peace to prevent any war occurring again in future, patriotism and the nation state also have to be outgrown.

BEASTLY TO THE GERMANS: WELLS
AND THE GREAT WAR

Tono-Bungay, *The War in the Air*, and the journalism collected in 1914's *An Englishman Looks at the World* all prophesy that the concurrent economic, technological, and social development of Britain and Germany

---

[28] The first edition of *Anticipations* cites the influence of Archdall Reid in stressing that mankind's common evolutionary origin shows national character to be a fiction, and that education is a far greater factor in individual development than heredity: see Archdall Reid, *The Present Evolution of Man* (London: Chapman and Hall, 1896), 178–87. In *Mankind in the Making*, 41–2, 55–6, however, Wells is more sceptical about the implications of Reid's version of germ theory.

[29] See Benedict Anderson, *Imagined Communities: Reflections on the Origin and Spread of Nationalism*, rev. edn (London: Verso, 2006).

[30] Darwin, *Descent of Man*, 147.

would lead them into war against each other.[31] Wells found in the establishment of the German state a negative analogue for his own utopian educational projects.[32] (According to George Stuart, Arnold Bennett thought of Wells as himself a 'Prussian'.)[33] Established in its present form as recently as 1871, Germany had needed to create a new sense of national identity to bind its separate states together, and had reorganized its educational system accordingly.[34] Wells deplored the ends to which German *Kultur* had been directed, writing in 1916 that the Germans' 'minds have been systematically corrupted by base historical teaching, and the inculcation of a rancid patriotism. They are a people under the sway of organised suggestion.'[35] He was impressed, however, by the scale and effectiveness of a Herbartian exercise that could, in the space of a single generation, effectively write the new ideology of a whole nation state.[36] The efficiency of Germany's *Gymnasien*, like the superiority of its technological advancement, highlights the unsystematic way in which the process was carried out elsewhere:

> Germany was different; Germany was teaching and teaching in schools, colleges, press, everywhere, this new Imperialism of hers, a sort of patriotic melodrama, with Britain as Carthage and Berlin instead of Rome. They pointed the whole population to that end. They *taught* this war. All over the world a thousand other educational systems pointed in a thousand other directions. (*Joan and Peter*, ch. 14, 5)

Wells believed that Germany's emphatic commitment as a national culture to military conflict made war inevitable; and the inevitability of war thus licenses Wells's imaginative investment in it as a fit subject for his writing.[37] If war is unavoidable then it should be conducted by Britain and its Allies in a scientific, organized, and efficient fashion, particularly against an enemy who constitutes such a potent ideological threat.[38] Wells

[31] See I. F. Clarke, *Voices Prophesying War: Future War, 1763–3749*, 2nd edn (Oxford: Oxford University Press, 1992), especially 118–30.

[32] *The Shape of Things to Come*, 136; Sherman, *On Contemporary Literature*, 76.

[33] George Sturt, *The Journals of George Sturt, 1890–1927: A Selection*, ed. E. D. Mackerness, 2 vols (Cambridge: Cambridge University Press, 1967), II: *1905–1927*, 750.

[34] See Detlef K. Müller, 'The Process of Systematisation: The Case of German Secondary Education', in *The Rise of the Modern Educational System: Structural Change and Social Reproduction, 1870–1920*, ed. Detlef K. Müller, Fritz Ringer, and Brian Simon (Cambridge and Paris: Cambridge University Press and Éditions de la Maison de Sciences de L'Homme, 1987), 15–52.

[35] *What is Coming*, 272, see also 229; *Outline of History*, 693; *Boon*, 253.

[36] Johann Friedrich Herbart, *The Application of Psychology to the Science of Education*, trans. B. C. Mulliner (London: Swan Sonnenschein, 1898). Cf. *First and Last Things*, 42.

[37] Partington, *Cosmopolis*, 65–86.

[38] *The Work, Wealth and Happiness of Mankind*, 629.

wrote for *Little Wars* an appendix suggesting the book's possible use in training the military. 'If Great War is to be played at all the better it is played the more humanely it is done. I see no inconsistency in deploring the practice while perfecting the method.'[39]

In September 1914, Wells published the influential pamphlet *The War that Will End War*, which declares: 'we have not sought this reckoning, we have done our utmost to avoid it; but now that it has been forced upon us it is imperative that it should be a thorough reckoning'.[40] In this pamphlet, Wells emphasized his commitment to the effective conduct of the war, seeking to capitalize on the commonplace that the war will change everything by ensuring that such changes are organized, permanent, and beneficial rather than chaotic, transitory, and harmful:

> All the realities of this war are things of the mind. This is a conflict of cultures, and nothing else in the world. All the world-wide pain and weariness, fear and anxieties, the bloodshed and destruction, the innumerable torn bodies of men and horses, the stench of putrefaction, the misery of hundreds of millions of human beings, the waste of mankind, are but the material consequences of a false philosophy and foolish thinking. We fight not to destroy a nation but a nest of evil ideals.[41]

Wells predicts, correctly, that the war will be ended not by Germany's military defeat, but by its near-starvation, and insists that the Allies should not be vindictive in triumph. Since this is 'not just another war—it is the last war!', it should lead to the nationalizing of the arms trade and to the establishment of a more enlightened system of government.[42]

The war itself energized Wells's writing, in books such as the collection of reportage *War and the Future* (1917) and his Home Front novel *Mr. Britling Sees it Through*, Wells's most profitable novel in his own lifetime.[43] Following a visit to the Front, he submitted in 1917 to the Ministry of Munitions a system of telpherage for improving communication between trenches.[44] He responded positively, at least initially, when asked to work as a propagandist for the Ministry of Information with

---

[39] *Little Wars: A Game for Boys from Twelve Years of Age to One Hundred and Fifty and for that More Intelligent Sort of Girls who Like Boys' Games and Books: With an Appendix on Kriegspiel* (London: F. Palmer, 1913; repr. New York: Da Capo, 1977), 101. Cf. 99–100.

[40] *The War that Will End War* (London: Palmer, 1914), 8.

[41] Ibid., 90.

[42] Ibid., 11.

[43] Richard Hauer Costa, 'H. G. Wells and the Palimpsest of Time', in *H. G. Wells: Reality and Beyond*, ed. Mullin 61–78 (61). See also *The Reception of H. G. Wells in Europe*, ed. Parrinder and Partington, 105.

[44] *Autobiography*, 684–5, 690–1; H. G. Wells and G. S. Coleman, 'Description of the "Leeming" Portable and Collapsible Aerial Ropeway', Illinois Collection. In the typescript of *Joan and Peter*, a system of ropeways is developed by Oswald (Illinois Collection,

responsibility for the German section of Crewe House's Enemy Propaganda Committee. (Wells later resigned in protest at the xenophobia voiced by newspapers owned by the Minister for Propaganda, Lord Northcliffe, and at Northcliffe's sacking of one of Wells's assistants who had German ancestry.)[45]

The fact of the Great War proved to Wells the truth of his claims about the danger of patriotism combining with modern technology. Such a combination can only result in the World State or apocalypse, and the former can only be achieved through a better education system. 'War is an evil thing, but people who will not learn from reason must have an ugly teacher,' he claims in *War and the Future*. 'This war has brought home to everyone the supremacy of the public need over every sort of individual claim.'[46] His memorandum for the EPC claimed that, 'the real aim of the Allies is not only to beat the enemy, but to establish a world peace that should preclude the resumption of war'.[47] Following the end of the war, Wells's attention turned more closely to the ways in which such a peace might be established.

EDUCATING FOR THE FUTURE: THE ICONOCLAST AS PEDAGOGUE

After the end of the First World War, Wells's self-appointed role as Huxleyan teacher through literature structures his writing at every level.[48] His fiction becomes even more explicitly educational and he returns to writing textbooks as well as educational polemic, biography, and even in 1923 a proposed textbook in pedagogy:

> The Labour party must and does realize that a proper system of Education is the nearest thing to a panacea for all ills that could be devised, and also that their own future depends on a first-class and up-to-date method of education being placed within the reach of every child in the country. The present time

JP-2419). Rose Tilly, 'The Search for Wells's Ropeways', *Wellsian*, 9 (1986), 18–22, suggests that the telpherage system was actually used.

[45] *Correspondence*, II, 554–9; Partington, *Cosmopolis*, 72–3; Gary S. Messinger, 'No Room for Internationalists: H. G. Wells', *British Propaganda and the State in the First World War* (Manchester: Manchester University Press, 1992), 184–99.

[46] *War and the Future*, 254.

[47] Sir Campbell Stuart, *Secrets of Crewe House: Secrets of a Famous Campaign* (London: Hodder & Stoughton, 1920), 62. On Wells and the aims of the war, see John S. Partington, 'Seeking Victory from the Jaws of Disaster: H. G. Wells and the Great War', *Undying Fire*, 2 (2003), 65–80.

[48] Partington, *Cosmopolis*, 38–41; Wagar, *World State*, 119–63.

is propitious because, not only is the existing form of education admittedly poor, but also because new and better systems have been tried and proved. [. . .]

What is wanted is a book of practical detail but also a vision for the future.[49]

Indeed, the textbook becomes for Wells the type of the most important kind of book, representing the systematization of all human knowledge, leading in 1938 to his suggestion of a macro-encyclopaedia that he dubbed the World Brain. 'You cannot make a new world in gaols and exile, you must make it in schools and books.'[50]

Wells grew up critical of the education he had received himself, and a concern with education is present in his writing from the 1890s on-wards.[51] 'I have always as a matter of conscience insulted schoolmasters,' he wrote to George Gissing in 1898, claiming also in *Mankind in the Making* that 'scolding the schoolmaster [. . .] is an amusement so entirely congenial to my temperament that I do not for one moment propose to abandon it'.[52] The war relegitimized Wells's emphasis on writing as a means of instruction, and even allowed him to claim education as his original literary vocation: 'Long before I sank below the possibility of serious consideration by my fellow-countrymen by becoming a novelist, I was a writer on education.'[53]

Pre-First World War Germany had proved that education misapplied could indeed lead to catastrophe: 'all this vast disaster to the world was no more and no less than an educational failure' (*Joan and Peter*, ch. 14, 2). Oswald's 'intelligence told him that all the inefficiency, the confusion, the cheap and bad government by press and intrigue, were the necessary and inevitable consequences of a neglect of higher education for the past fifty years' (*Joan and Peter*, ch. 9, 8). The content and method of future education must play a key part in the period of reconstruction following the war: 'This and no other is the hour for educational reconstruction. And it is in the decisions and readjustments of schools and lectures and courses, far more than anywhere else, that the real future of Great Britain will be decided.'[54] From as early as the scientific romances, Wells

[49] *Correspondence*, III, 135.
[50] Letter to Nelson Doubleday, *Correspondence*, IV, 185–9; 'The Idea of a World Encyclopaedia', *H. G. Wells in 'Nature'*, 105–22; 'Living Through: The Truth about an Interview', *A Year of Prophesying*, 334–40 (339).
[51] Cliona Murphy, 'H. G. Wells: Educationalist, Utopian, and Feminist?', in *H. G. Wells Under Revision*, ed. Parrinder and Rolfe, 218–25.
[52] *George Gissing and H. G. Wells*, 94; *Mankind in the Making*, 222.
[53] *The New Teaching of History: With a Reply to Some Recent Criticisms of The Outline of History* (London: Cassell, 1921), 12.
[54] *What is Coming*, 152.

consistently aimed at being an 'educational' writer (or, for Rebecca West, 'a pompous schoolmaster').[55] Wells's view of himself as writing in the tradition of the public intellectual meant that he shared with his predecessors Adam Smith, Robert Owen, Mill, Ruskin, Spencer, and Arnold a vital interest in education as social policy. Since the Reformation, literacy had been closely associated with political empowerment and self-fulfilment, and particularly so for those of the post-1870 generation, who had grown up more literate than their parents.[56] W. E. Forster, in his speech on the 1870 Elementary Education Bill claimed that 'if we are to hold our own position among men of our own race or among the nations of the world we must make up the smallness of our numbers by increasing the intellectual force of the individual'.[57] Robert Lowe also famously observed that 'I believe it will be absolutely necessary that you should prevail on our future masters to learn their letters.'[58] The social cohesion necessary for a utopian state can only be achieved by education; as early as *Mankind in the Making*, Wells had noted that: 'a reading and writing class of society and the existence of an organized nation (as distinguished from a tribe) appear together. When tribes coalesce into nations, schools appear' (*Mankind in the Making*, ch. 6).

Wells was educated and became a writer in a climate in which literacy, imaginative writing, education, and political progress were closely intertwined. In Wells's mind, reading is associated with both mental and material escape, with refuge from physical discomfort, from labour, and the demands of the body. However, Wells came to see the practice of undirected solitary reading as too unsystematized on its own for writing to fulfil the function that he wanted it to. Although, as Rose repeatedly demonstrates, Wells was a popular author among autodidacts, Wells nonetheless favoured education as a collective, as opposed to an individual, enterprise.[59] Education is too important a matter to be left to lone readers: if to read is to learn, then reading should be directed by the state. As Ben Knights puts it in discussing Coleridge, 'The alternative to a recognition of the state's ethical role to humanize its citizens is the continuance of a state of affairs which will lead straight to social

[55] *H. G. Wells and Rebecca West*, 118; J. R. Hammond, 'H. G. Wells as Educationalist', *Wellsian*, 4 (1981), 1–7; F. H. Doughty, *H. G. Wells, Educationist* (London: Cape, 1926).
[56] Vincent, *Literacy and Popular Culture*, 50; Hammond, *Reading*, 13.
[57] Stuart Maclure, ed., *Educational Documents: England and Wales, 1816–1963* (London: Chapman and Hall, 1965), 105.
[58] Speech, House of Commons, 15 July 1867, *Parliamentary Debates*, 188, 1549.
[59] Rose, *Intellectual Life*, 139–40 and throughout; Robert Crossley, 'Wells's Common Readers', in *H. G. Wells Under Revision*, ed. Parrinder and Rolfe, 237–47. Cf. Bourdieu, *Distinction*, 328.

dissolution and the naked struggle of particular interests'—the latter a development often imagined in Wells's dystopian writing, such as *The War in the Air*.[60]

Public rhetoric about education and the fear of social decline predated even Wells's prescient contribution to the debate. Britain had long feared that economic rivals were outstripping her in technological advancement, a development highlighted by the poor showing of British manufactures in the International Exhibition staged in Paris in 1867.[61] Reforms such as the founding in 1853 of the Science and Art Department or Forster's 1870 Education Act tended to be instituted not as progressive per se, but in order to forestall a perceived national crisis.[62] The Royal Commission on Scientific Instruction and the Advancement of Science of 1871–5, led by the Duke of Devonshire, William Cavendish (whom Wells credited with 'unexpected breadth of sympathy') reported Britain's shortage of science teachers as 'a national misfortune'.[63] Wells inherited and amplified this strain of argument:

> The foreigner is ahead of us in education, and this is especially true of the middle and upper classes, from which invention and enterprise come. [. . .] He makes a better class of man than we do. His science is better than ours. His training is better than ours. His imagination is livelier. His mind is more active. His requirements in a novel, for example, are not kindly, sedative pap; his uncensored plays deal with reality. His schools are places for vigorous education instead of genteel athleticism, and his home has books in it, and thought and conversation.[64]

An emerging theme in Victorian writing about education was that it might, as with Wells's view of other social practices, be made more exact by the application of scientific methods.[65] To this end, like his own teacher T. H. Huxley, Wells himself advocated compulsory scientific

---

[60] Knights, *Clerisy*, 42.

[61] Harold Silver, *Education as History: Interpreting Nineteenth- and Twentieth-Century Education* (London: Methuen, 1983), 81–99; Brian Simon, 'Systematisation and Segmentation: The Case of England', in *The Rise of the Modern Educational System*, ed. Müller et al., 88–108 (104). For the state's response, see Roy M. MacLeod, 'Education: Scientific and Technical', in *The 'Creed of Science' in Victorian England* (Aldershot: Ashgate, 2000), 196–225.

[62] See the findings of the 1861 Newcastle Report in Maclure, ed., *Educational Documents*, 77–8, Matthew Arnold's report on the Revised Code, 81–2, Forster's speech on the 1870 Education Bill, 99–105.

[63] Wells, *Correspondence*, I, 251; Maclure, *Educational Documents*, 107–8. Wells had considered dedicating *Kipps* to the (presumably, tenth) Duke of Devonshire (Illinois MS Collection).

[64] 'The Coming of Blériot', *An Englishman Looks at the World*, 1–7 (5).

[65] See for instance, Alexander Bain, *Education as a Science* (London: Kegan Paul, 1879); John Lawson and Harold Silver, *A Social History of Education in England* (London:

teaching in schools, at the expense of the classics if necessary.[66] As a schoolboy, Wells may have found the learning of Latin stimulating for its systematic and regular properties, but in his ideal of education he tended to favour a creative synthesis of sciences and humanities rather than a training in one exclusive of the other.[67] He was appalled that cleverer students favouring classics, and the less able being encouraged to specialize in science, as was often the case, was hopelessly backward-looking, and even potentially threatened disaster.[68] Education should provide a necessary outlet for youthful imagination and creativity, making sure that no potential for individual development is wasted, while fashioning pupils into responsible citizens who will cooperate in forming the future commonwealth.

In his rise from unpropitious lower middle-class beginnings, Wells himself had fought off successive apprenticeships that would have curtailed his own educational progress. After achieving international literary and political celebrity, Wells remained always aware of how easily his own considerable potential might have been thrown away. Reflecting on his own education in the *Autobiography*, Wells sees his schooling, typically, in terms of broader social change. He rightly identifies the reforms that brought him a scientific education as the result of economic anxiety about other better-educated and economically developing countries, particularly Germany. He also interprets the role of the new educational reforms of the late nineteenth century as not instituting a meritocratic ladder that would surmount social divisions, but negotiating a compromise that would allow them to be perpetuated.[69]

Methuen, 1973), 353; 'Science, In School and After School', *H. G. Wells in 'Nature'*, 27 September 1894; and Wells's 1938 letter to *Nature*, Correspondence, IV, 191.

[66] On nineteenth-century education as a means of social control, see Anne Digby and Peter Searby, *Children, School and Society in Nineteenth-Century England* (London: Macmillan, 1981), 23–8.

[67] *Babes in the Darkling Wood*, 202–3, argues that Greek might have become the universal world language that Wells now sees English as becoming, but missed its chance to do so.

[68] *Mankind in the Making*, 201–10. For Wells's view of the correct relationship between science and the classics, see 'The Case against the Classical Languages', *Natural Science and the Classical System in Education*, ed. E. Ray Lankester (London: Heinemann, 1918), 183–95, the report on the eleventh annual meeting of the British Science Guild in *Nature*, 99 (1917), and the controversy around Wells's response to R. W. Livingstone's *A Defence of Classical Education* collected in *H. G. Wells in 'Nature'*, 89–96, 395–6.

[69] *Autobiography*, I, 84–7. See Brian Simon, 'Education and Citizenship in England', in *The State and Educational Change: Essays in the History of Education and Pedagogy* (London: Lawrence & Wishart, 1994), 75–83 (76) and Peter Searby, 'The Schooling of Kipps: The Education of Lower Middle-Class Boys in England', in *Educating the Victorian Middle Class*, ed. Peter Searby (Leicester: History of Education Society, 1982), 113–31.

Wells's own schooling began first at a dame school and then a small private school, Morley's Commercial Academy, where he learnt mostly arithmetic and double-entry book-keeping. 'The Education Act of 1871 was not an Act for a common universal education, it was an Act to educate the lower classes for employment on lower-class lines.'[70] Morley himself was the only teacher, 'so the primary impression left upon my brain by that Academy are not impressions of competent elucidation and guidance, of a universe being made plain to me or of skills being acquired and elaborated, but of the moods of Mr. Thomas Morley and their consequences'.[71] Wells gives his schoolmaster credit for ability in teaching mathematics, but accuses the language teaching of doing more harm than good. Throughout the first volume of the *Autobiography*, Wells emphasizes the faults of the education that he received himself in order to outline the elements a modern curriculum ought to contain: science, languages, world history, and the development of a spirit of imaginative, critical curiosity.[72]

At fourteen, Wells (like Dickens before him) felt that he was being removed from his schooling far too early; later, he would argue that this age was too young for anyone to cease organized learning.[73] Apprenticed to a draper, Wells rebelled against the restraints that were imposed by labour on the development of his imagination, reading books beneath his desk, and completing algebra exercises in his spare time. Wells was found insufficiently refined to pursue the career of a draper, and after a proposal for him to become a pupil teacher at a school run by a relative fell through, he was again apprenticed, to a chemist in Midhurst. As part of his training, Wells was required to learn Latin, and was tutored by the headmaster of Midhurst Grammar School, Horace Byatt. It was Byatt to whom Wells wrote for help before running away from his third and final apprenticeship with another draper, insisting to his mother that he should return to school. Wells, as D. H. Lawrence later would, became a pupil teacher (an experience reworked in *Love and Mr. Lewisham*), taking examinations to improve his own and the school's standing: by performing well, he would earn extra grants for the school. His results were so good, however, that instead he won a scholarship to the Normal School of Science in Kensington.

This was Wells's first direct encounter with a science more practical than that learnt at the remove of cramming and textbooks, and he credits

---

[70] *Autobiography*, I, 93.
[71] Ibid., 88–9.
[72] 'Schooling', *Mankind in the Making*, 198–237.
[73] *Autobiography*, I, 132.

this experience with instilling in him the habit of thinking in systems, and connections:

> Here were microscopes, dissections, models, diagrams close to the objects they elucidated, specimens, museums, ready answers to questions, explanations, discussions [...] an extraordinary mental enlargement as my mind passed from the printed sciences within book covers to these intimate real things and then radiated outward to a realization that the synthesis of the sciences composed a vital interpretation of the world.[74]

The excitement of studying biology under Huxley in his first year subsided, however, when he became bored by the rigours of studying physics and geology, choosing instead to develop his creative imagination by reading Carlyle and Blake in the library. (Wells had objected in particular to the waste of time in being required to make his own apparatus; later, as a science teacher, Wells would circumvent the risks to the dignity of the teacher that practical demonstration threatened by drawing the results of experiments in coloured chalks on the blackboard instead.)[75] In the *Autobiography*, Wells is severe on the truculence of his younger self, but equally critical of the impractical and primitive teaching methods used to instruct him. Wells consistently railed against the Victorian tradition of 'failed tradesmen who took up teaching as a last resort or crippled soldiers and elderly widows who were given situations as teachers as a type of pension'; the *Autobiography* reproves universities for teaching science without teaching 'educational science and method'.[76]

By the time he left the Normal School, Wells's interests had become not only scientific but socialist and literary; an exclusively scientific education was no longer sufficient to occupy his reawakened and curious speculative intelligence. After graduating in 1887, Wells worked as a teacher. As of all of the educational institutions through which he passed, Wells is critical of the curriculum at Henley House. His censure of this

---

[74] Ibid., 199–200. For Wells's ideas as to how science should be taught, see *Correspondence*, I, 161, 169–74, 180–1, 251–3, and Preface to *A Textbook of Biology*, 2 vols (London: Clive, 1893), I, vii–x.

[75] See also Wells's 'Science Teaching—An Ideal and Some Realities', *Educational Times*, 1 January 1895, 23–9.

[76] David F. Mitch, *The Rise of Popular Literacy in Victorian England: The Influence of Private Choice and Public Policy* (Philadelphia: University of Pennsylvania Press, 1992), 144; *Autobiography*, I, 231–2. The first university Chair in Education had only been established in 1876 (at Edinburgh and St Andrews) as a result of a bequest, and such teacher training as there was in the late nineteenth century tended to be exclusively for women: H. C. Barnard, *A History of English Education from 1760*, 2nd edn (London: University of London Press, 1961), 190. In *Joan and Peter*, Mackinder, the headmaster of the preparatory school White Court, makes the same complaint: *Joan and Peter*, 385.

school's teaching again provides an insight into what Wells believed the chief end of education to be:

> We were teaching some "subjects," as the times went, fairly well, we were getting more than average results in outside examinations. But collectively, comprehensively we were teaching nothing at all. We were completely ignoring the primary function of the school in society, which is to correlate the intelligence, will and conscience of the individual to the social process. [. . .] We taught no history of human origins, nothing about the structure of civilization, nothing of social or political life. We did not make, we did not even attempt to make, participating citizens.[77]

An injury from a foul in a rugby match during an earlier teaching post in Holt resulted in a lengthy illness, curtailing Wells's career as a schoolteacher. He became a correspondence tutor, standardizing and systematizing exam preparation in biology by analysing past papers. During this period, Wells's first books were written, *Honours Physiography* (with the biologist Richard Gregory), and *A Textbook of Biology* (both 1893). He was also co-founder and editor of the *Science Schools Journal*, and a reviewer for the *Educational Times*, in the course of which 'educational theory was forced upon me'.[78] In time, however, Wells earned more from journalism than he could from tutoring, thus beginning his career as an imaginative writer and self-appointed teacher to the world.

Wells's post-Great War novel *The Undying Fire* (1919) is 'Dedicated to All Schoolmasters and Schoolmistresses and every Teacher in the World', and sets out the author's intended educational programme in only barely fictionalized form. The book is intended as a present-day rewriting of the Book of Job from Wells's own peculiar theological standpoint at that time.[79] The book's central character, Job Huss, is headmaster of a progressive school, and after a wager between God and Satan, he loses his son in the war, his savings in a financial disaster, four pupils and a schoolmaster in a series of accidents, and his position at the school. Job's marriage consequently suffers, and, while staying at a seaside resort, he discovers he

---

[77] *Autobiography*, I, 325.
[78] Ibid., 350.
[79] *The Undying Fire: A Contemporary Novel*, *Works*, XI, x. Wells is surprisingly theist on the subject of God in his earlier utopian writings, since theology, if not dogma, does provide a means of systematizing knowledge in a holistic and comprehensive way. During the Great War, Wells flirted with a kind of deist religious belief, dramatized in novels such as *Mr. Britling Sees It Through* and *The Soul of a Bishop*, and the non-fictional *God the Invisible King*. These views were explicitly repudiated later in *The World of William Clissold* and the *Autobiography*. Wells, however, rejects the notion of an omniscient God, since a mind must be in constant movement to be of value, and a God that can see all before and after must therefore be static. Cf. *The Soul of a Bishop*, 120–1.

has cancer. The novel is written mostly in dialogue on matters curricular and theological between the headmaster and the school governors and colleagues who visit him. On principles of which the author evidently approves, Job has modernized the school's teaching of science, added Spanish and Russian to its language options, and vigorously promoted the teaching of history.[80] As Wells argued that ideology and politics cannot, and must not be excluded from art, so Job argues that education is also of necessity polemical. Job's doctor sides with him:

> "It's one of the things I can never understand about schoolmasters and politicians and suchlike, the way they seem to take it for granted you can educate and not bring in religion and socialism and all your beliefs. What *is* education? Teaching young people to talk and read and write and calculate in order that they may be told how they stand in the world and what we think we and the world are generally up to, and the part we expect them to play in the game. Well, how can we do that and at the same time leave it all out? What *is* the game? That is what every youngster wants to know. Answering him, is education." (*The Undying Fire*, ch. 5)

History is promoted even over science in this ideal curriculum, since, Job argues, ignorance of history results in the poor social organization which prevents the effective application of science:

> They solve the problems of material science in vain until they have solved their social and political problems. [. . .] It is no occult secret; it is a plain and demonstrable thing to-day that the world could give ample food and ample leisure to every human being, if only by a world-wide teaching the spirit of unity could be made to prevail over the impulse to dissension. (*The Undying Fire*, ch. 5)

The teaching of the origins of Man is crucial as the starting-point of this collective history. 'Human history is one history and human welfare is one whole,' Wells had written in the essay 'History is One' in 1918. 'And a saner teaching of history means a better understanding of international problems, a saner national policy, and a happier world.'[81] Just as the wider teaching of a greater number of languages will further mutual understanding, so knowledge of mankind's shared origin will deconstruct the myths of English or German racial supremacy.[82] The foundation of the World

---

[80] See *Mankind in the Making*, 208–9, on Wells's view of the poor quality of language teaching in 1903, and *What is Coming*, 124–5.

[81] 'History is One', *Works*, XXVII, 12, 16.

[82] Wells ruefully noted that even while he was teaching in the final decade of the nineteenth century, evolution was still too controversial a topic to be included on the syllabus; Man does not even enter the *Outline of History* until page 39; compare *A Modern Utopia*, 289–92, *The Undying Fire*, 112–13, *Outline of History*, I, 86, *World Brain*, 133.

State is loosely identified with God's purpose for Man, and thus a Well-sian education becomes a kind of sacred duty. Job's faith in God (or Wells) is finally rewarded. A distant relative dies, leaving him a fortune; the tumour proves to be benign; ex-pupils rally round to protect Huss's job and reforms, and a telegram brings the news that his son is not dead, but a prisoner of war.

The 1924 Preface to *Joan and Peter* claims that this novel was 'designed to review the possibilities of a liberal education in contemporary England' ('Preface'). *Joan and Peter* is less formally structured around a single issue than *The Undying Fire*; like the war whose effects the novel dramatizes, poor organization renders it unnecessarily long, 'as shamelessly unfinished as a Gothic cathedral,' Wells later confessed.[83] *Joan and Peter*'s larger scope, however, allows a much fuller dramatization of the effects of different kinds of education on its eponymous hero and heroine, and its structure attempts to mirror the processes of growing up and being educated. Following the deaths of the hero and heroine's parents, the novel dramatizes the sequence of unsatisfactory kinds of education to which they are subjected; the penultimate chapter is entitled 'Joan and Peter Graduate'. The children's care passes first to two aunts Phyllis and Phoebe, New Women aesthetes, who become more parodically out-of-date as the novel progresses, and who force on the children the wrong kind of 'progressive' education. Their physician 'had the usual general practi-tioners' view that any education whatever is a terrible strain on the young, and he was quite on the side of Rousseau in that matter' (ch. 2, 3). The narrator mocks the idea that children will develop naturally if left to their own devices; the haphazard and unsystematized nature of Wells's own education had convinced him of the dangers of too much freedom. (In 1931, Wells admitted to a 'pretty hard dislike' of A. S. Neill, the founder of the democratically run school Summerhill, thinking his method 'suited (like the Montessori system) for badly disorganized children & adoles-cents', since it disregards 'the natural anti-social instinct'.)[84] Wells's educationalism was anti-Rousseau: unsupervised development leads to chaos and, consequently, disorder and waste. Aunt Phoebe in this novel is content for Peter to play 'like a happy little animal' (*Joan and Peter*, ch. 4, 9); this is exactly what Wells's imagination fears if the child is left to develop naturally. Job warns in *The Undying Fire*: that 'an untaught man is but himself alone, as lonely in his ends and destiny as any beast; a man

---

[83] *Autobiography*, II, 500.
[84] *Correspondence*, III, 405. Sherborne, *H. G. Wells*, 261, records that Wells took Anthony West, his child with Rebecca West, out of a Montessori school in 1921 because of worries about his ability to read.

instructed is a man enlarged from that narrow prison of self' (*The Undying Fire*, ch. 3).[85]

The headmistress of the undisciplined and artistic school to which their aunts send the children has a training that is well-intentioned but unsystematic:

> She had already done the Theory and Practice of Education part of the diploma. For that she had read parts of "Leonard and Gertrude" and she had attended five lectures on Froebel. These were days long before the Montessori system which is now so popular with our Miss Millses; the prevalent educational vogues of the nineties were kindergarten and Swedish drill. (*Joan and Peter*, ch. 7, 3)

The School of St George and the Venerable Bede (so named to exemplify English education) is not all bad, but modish and disorganized, failing to reward the curiosity of its pupils. Wells's young protagonists are constantly eager for the stimulation of the new, whether supplied by play or by systematized instruction. Children grow 'as children do grow under favourable circumstances, after the manner of Nature in her better moods, that is to say after the manner of Nature ploughed and weeded and given light and air' (*Joan and Peter*, ch. 7, 2). The metaphor of agriculture is a fertile one for Wells here, an adaptation of Friedrich Froebel's image of the *kindergarten*. (Wells had written a thesis on Froebel as part of his teacher training on his return to university study.)[86] The process of education may be one of natural growth, but a growth that requires careful Huxleyan cultivation; schooling must be practical, with a definite end in view, like farming, not merely aesthetic, like gardening.[87] Uncultivated, the mind might easily fall into harmful habits, such as the Pollyish belief of the children's maths mistress that seven sevens might sometimes equal fifty-six.[88]

The children's other aunt, the tyrannical Lady Charlotte Sydenham, typifies the misapplication of politics and religion to the question of education (*Joan and Peter*, ch. 8, 17). As appalled by the secularism of Joan and Peter's upbringing as she is by the centralizing tendency of 'Mr

---

[85] Oswald agrees: 'Religion, loyalty, patriotism, those strange and wonderfully interwoven nets of superstition, fear, flattery, high reason and love, have subjugated this struggling egotistical ape into larger and larger masses of co-operation, achieved enormous temporary securities. But the ape is still there, struggling subtly' (*Joan and Peter*, XXIV, 34).

[86] West, *H. G. Wells*, 83.

[87] Barnard, *History of English Literature*, 173. Compare *The Story of a Great Schoolmaster*, *Works*, XXIV, 359.

[88] Wells's late essay 'Countless Planes and Submarines' draws an analogy between poor mathematics teaching in schools and the difficulty of understanding the cost of war. *Guide to the New World*, 23–8.

Balfour's Education Act' (*Joan and Peter*, ch 8, 1), which attempted to bring more schools into municipal control, Lady Charlotte has the children kidnapped and privately educated according to her own misguided beliefs. Lady Charlotte is the first of the children's guardians to discriminate against Joan for her illegitimacy (she is in fact the love child of Dolly's brother), and Joan is farmed out to the careless servant Mrs Pybus, under whose care she falls dangerously ill. Peter is sent to a private school that is little better than a violent examination-factory, and after one punishment too many, Peter runs away; both children then pass into the care of their uncle, the benevolent Empire-builder Oswald.

Once Oswald becomes the children's sole guardian, his agonies over the best education for his wards occupy the whole of the chapter 'A Searching of Schoolmasters' (which owes much to Wells's attempts to find a suitable school for his own teenage sons, born in 1901 and 1903). Oswald, unlike the boy's previous guardians, asks Peter what he would like to learn:

"There's a lot you don't know yet." said Oswald.

"Can't I read it out of books?" asked Peter.

"You can't read everything out of books," said Oswald. "There's things you ought to see and handle. And things you can only learn by doing."

Oswald wanted Peter to plan his own school.

Peter considered. "I'd like lessons about the insides of animals and about the people in foreign countries—and how engines work—and all that sort of thing."

"Then we must find a school for you where they teach all that sort of thing," said Oswald, as though it was merely a question of ordering goods from the Civil Service Stores.

He had much to learn yet about education. (*Joan and Peter*, ch. 9, 11)

Oswald is frustrated by the lack of any centralized source of information on schools and fails, of course, to find one that reaches all his stringent requirements of teaching world history, economics, and science. When Oswald does meet a headmaster who shares his own radicalism, he learns that even mildly progressive public schools must be run on profitable lines and still appeal to more conservative parents—this also a symptom of the world's economic disorganization.

Oswald is no more impressed by Oxford and Cambridge, even Ruskin College, which dispiritingly 'reminded him of *Jude the Obscure*' (*Joan and Peter*, ch. 10, 5).[89] He concludes that 'the real work of higher education, the discussion of God, of the state and sex, of all the great issues in life' (*Joan and Peter*, ch. 10, 6) is being evaded by the universities and carried

---

[89] Compare *What is Coming*, 149–50.

out only by politically minded writers such as Chesterton, Hilaire Belloc, and Wells. Oswald objects especially to Wells for his commercial background; this is a self-conscious joke at the author's expense, but the genuine objection on the part of both author and character is that extra-curricular reading, even of books by Wells, is too unsystematic to be a provider of true higher education. As with the utopian writing, in the kind of educational order that Wells envisions, there should ideally be no need for him to write the kinds of books that he does. As *Men Like Gods* puts it:

> Utopia has no parliament, no politics, no private wealth, no business competition, no police nor prisons, no lunatics, no defectives nor cripples, and it has none of these things because it has schools and teachers who are all that schools and teachers can be. Politics, trade and competition are the methods of adjustment of a crude society. Such methods of adjustment have been laid aside in Utopia for more than a thousand years. There is no rule nor government needed by adult Utopians because all the rule and government they need they have had in childhood and youth.
>   Said Lion: "Our education is our government." (*Men Like Gods*, ch. 5)

Oswald also comes to consider the unsatisfactory nature of women's education available for Joan, who goes to Newnham College, Cambridge. Ultimately, however, Oswald's investigations are rendered moot by the First World War, which enforces the continuation of Joan and Peter's education in a wholly different sphere. The novel ends with a 'valediction' on education delivered by their uncle to the by-now married Joan and Peter, but the world still unchanged and anxiously facing reconstruction after devastation by the war.

THE BOOKS OF THE SAMURAI

A major obstacle to the kind of teaching Wells wished to promulgate was the lack of textbooks that shared his own political world-view. Such a political transformation as that dramatized in *The World Set Free* cannot occur unless the world's populations are made to question the concept of nations, and this can only be achieved by teaching a form of history that emphasizes the community between nations, and the common origin of mankind, rather than only the history of one's own country.[90] 'Men's loyalties, the sides they take in political things, are not innate, they are educational results,' Wells wrote in the *Outline*.[91] Although by his own admission not a specialist historian, Wells took it upon himself to write for

---

[90] Cf. *Autobiography*, I, 99.   [91] *Outline of History*, 557.

the world the history its political future needed, cribbing from the *Encyclopaedia Britannica* and asking historians for expert advice.[92] *Joan and Peter* had been deeply engaged with 'history' both as a subject taught in school and as the dialectical process being enacted in the real world.[93]

Wells clearly perceived the latter as the determined consequence of the former: 'There's really nothing more to be done with our present public until its ideas about history are changed,' Wells wrote to Gilbert Murray, a collaborator on the *Outline*.[94] The world's politics and social organization were a causal product of the history its leaders had been taught at school: 'the Outline of History is going to change History,' Wells boasted to Rebecca West.[95] In his rejection of university curricula, Oswald had 'considered any history fragmentary that did not begin with the geological record and end with a clear tracing of every traceable consequence of the "period" in current affairs' (*Joan and Peter*, ch. 11, 13). This is exactly the scope of the textbook Wells went on to write. 'The book will rouse anybody in the history textbook & history teaching line to blind fury,' he proclaimed. 'It is a serious raid into various departments of special knowledge [...]. It is a necessary counter to nationalism & imperialism. There will be a sustained attempt to [represent?] me as an ignorant interloper & dispose of me in that way.'[96]

The Outline of History was published in twenty-four monthly parts from November 1919 with footnotes by six collaborators, who also helped Wells redraft the work in its numerous successive editions.[97] The *Outline* is the product of an imagination both encyclopaedic and pedagogic. Wells was strongly influenced, as he acknowledges in the *Autobiography*, by Winwood Reade's 1872 secular post-Darwinian history *The Martyrdom of Man*, in showing the material basis for civilized values, and the contingency of the nation state. It is, without apology, morally judgemental, assessing past figures of history by the canon of their helping humanity's politics, economics, and education to progress in the way Wells desires, as,

---

[92] A. B. McKillop argues in *The Spinster and the Prophet* (London: Aurum, 2001) that Wells plagiarized parts of the *Outline* from an unpublished manuscript by Florence Deeks. For a hostile account of Wells's omissions see William T. Ross, *H. G. Wells's World Reborn: The Outline of History and its Companions* (Selinsgrove: Susquehanna University Press; London: Associated University Presses, 2002); for Wells's version, *Autobiography*, II, 724–5.

[93] Cf. 'History, for her, has ceased to be a fabric of picturesque incidents; it is the study of a tragic struggle that still goes on.' *The Secret Places of the Heart*, 464. See also *The Passionate Friends*, 225–50 for Wells's thoughts along these lines, even before the First World War.

[94] Quoted in MacKenzie and MacKenzie, *Life of H. G. Wells*, 321.

[95] *H. G. Wells and Rebecca West*, 104.

[96] Unpublished letter quoted in McKillop, *Spinster and the Prophet*, 144.

[97] Smith, *Desperately Mortal*, 250–1.

for example, in his approving portrayal of Alexander the Great as the type of an educated ruler.[98] The *Outline* thus presents a Whig version of history for a present that doesn't yet exist.[99] Wells is thus impatient, even dismissive, in relating events that do not point to his telos of a world utopia, such as the Peloponnesian wars, the Catholic Church, or even Shakespeare's plays. (Historian A. L. Gomme complained of this stratospheric perspective that Wells 'dislikes small things and rejoices at large things, those that grow larger and larger'.)[100]

For all of Wells's lack of specialism in this field, he had evidently identified a need not met by extant literature: the *Outline* outsold all of Wells's other books put together, selling two million copies in Britain and the US alone, and being adopted in schools worldwide.[101] He was described by Hungarian author Frigyes Karinthy in 1927 as 'the most widely read author in the world' (for the views promulgated by *The Outline*, Wells was later blacklisted in both Italy and Germany).[102] In 1927, he claimed that it had brought him over £60,000.[103] A version for the general reader, *A Short History of the World*, followed in 1922, and two companion volumes were written (although the process of collaboration on these was more problematic): *The Science of Life* (1930), with Wells's son Gyp and T. H. Huxley's grandson Julian, on biology and physical science, and *The Work, Wealth and Happiness of Mankind* (1931), covering economics and politics.

If the *Outline* is a Whig version of history from a non-existent present, *The Science of Life* is a post-Darwinian version of natural theology,

[98] *Outline of History*, 226.

[99] 'The advent of Cosmopolis must become now the dominant thesis of any scientific, directive history', 'The Traveller Provokes his Old Friends, the Teachers, Again in a Paper Called "The Poison Called History"', *Travels of a Republican Radical in Search of Hot Water* (Harmondsworth: Penguin 1939), 89–121 (101).

[100] A. L. Gomme, *Mr Wells as Historian: An Inquiry into those Parts of Mr H.G. Wells's Outline of History which Deal with Greece and Rome* (Glasgow: MacLehose, Jackson, 1921), 39. See also Hilaire Belloc, *Mr Belloc Objects to 'The Outline of History'* (London: George H. Doran, 1926); H. Drinkwater, *Footnotes to H. G. Wells (Outline of History)* (n.p.: The Sower, 1921).

[101] MacKenzie and MacKenzie, *Life of H. G. Wells*, 431. See Matthew Skelton, 'The Paratext of Everything: Constructing and Marketing H. G. Wells's *The Outline of History*', *Book History*, 4 (2001), 237–75 and *Correspondence*, III, 377.

[102] See Katalin Csala, 'The Puzzling Connection between H. G. Wells and Frigyes Karanthy', and Elmar Schenkel, 'White Elephants and Black Machines: H. G. Wells and German Culture, 1920–45', in *The Reception of H. G. Wells in Europe*, ed. Parrinder and Partington, 195–204 (200), 91–104 (108). On the response to the *Outline of History*, see Cliona Murphy, 'H. G. Wells: His History, the People and the Historians', *Wellsian*, 19 (1996), 36–47, and Roy Shuker, 'H. G. Wells: The Novelist as Educator', *Education Research and Perspectives*, 6 (1979), 44–53.

[103] *Correspondence*, III, 255, I, xxxix. See Smith, *Desperately Mortal*, 249–59 for the enormous popular response to the *Outline*, including Hilaire Belloc's objections to the work's hostile account of Catholicism.

explaining the natural world in terms of its evolutionary history, alternating descriptive analysis with polemic in support of the Darwinian method of understanding natural history:

> There is not one single character or quality of human beings, from the construction of their skeleton to the flush on their cheeks, from their embryonic development to their moral aspirations, which does not become more comprehensible, more interesting in itself, and more significant for the future, when viewed in the light that Evolution sheds upon it.[104]

The Work, Wealth and Happiness of Mankind is, similarly, a textbook with a telos: the Great Depression proves, like the Great War, the urgent necessity of reforming social and economic structures.

Wells also became involved in the actual practice of education in collaborating on the curriculum of Oundle School, where he had sent his own sons.[105] Oundle's headmaster, F. W. Sanderson, was the acknowledged model for Henderson (named Westinghouse in the Atlantic Edition of the novel), the forward-thinking headmaster of Caxton School in *Joan and Peter*. Sanderson died suddenly in 1922 in front of Wells and an audience of the Union of Scientific Workers, shortly after delivering an address on 'The Duty and Service of Science in the New Era'. As a tribute, Wells began to compile an official volume, *Sanderson of Oundle*, whose proceeds were to be devoted to the school, but Sanderson's widow objected to Wells's portrayal, so he wrote his own account instead.[106] *The Story of a Great Schoolmaster* was published in 1923 in *The New Leader* and *The New Republic* (which had also serialized *Joan and Peter*), in book form a year later, and included in volume 24 of the Atlantic Edition, following the second part of *Joan and Peter*. The scale of the tribute Wells pays indicates the store he set by the kind of education undertaken at Oundle:

> Of all the men I have met [...] one only has stirred me to a biographical effort. This one exception is F. W. Sanderson, for many years the headmaster of Oundle School. I think him beyond question the greatest man I have ever known with any degree of intimacy. [...] To tell his story is to reflect upon all the main educational ideas of the last half-century, and to revise our

---

[104] *The Science of Life*, I, 404. Cf. the review of *The Science of Life* in *H. G. Wells in 'Nature'*, 298–303.
[105] *Outline of History*, 664.
[106] 'Difficulties arose as the work advanced, and in the end Mr Wells left the task to the staff and published his own book. The composite volume, as was natural, erred on the side of hero-worship, whereas Mr Wells's showed, as some think, characteristic lapses from good taste. Somehow, between them, the real man has got overlaid and Sanderson is on his way to becoming a legendary figure.' William George Walker, *A History of the Oundle Schools* (London: The Grocers' Company, 1956), 570; also Smith, *Desperately Mortal*, 261.

conception of the process and purpose of the modern community in relation to education. (*The Story of a Great Schoolmaster*, ch. 1, 1)

Sanderson and Wells influenced each other's ideas about education, especially in the relationship between teaching and scientific methodology. The curriculum Sanderson put into practice at Oundle and advocated elsewhere was progressive, forward-looking, cooperative, and systematic in the Wellsian manner.[107] Sanderson actually implemented a number of the reforms for which Wells had argued, reducing the amount of classical teaching, vigorously promoting the teaching of history and of Russian, building not only new science laboratories but also a foundry, as he felt that science in schools should be applied and technical, as well as theoretical and experimental. He shared with Wells an ideal of the liberal education as fostering a productive synthesis between arts and sciences, permitting individual pupils to specialize in the areas which would best fulfil their individual potential.

> Science is essentially creative and co-operative, its outlook is onwards towards change, it means searching for the truth, it demands research and experiment, and does not rest on authority. Under this new spirit all history, literature and art and even languages should be rewritten. (*The Story of a Great Schoolmaster*, ch. 8, 2)

Unusually, Sanderson saw his charges as future leaders in the worlds of science, engineering, and industry, as well as the more traditional routes for public school-educated boys. He encouraged them to work collaboratively on vocational projects that interested them outside of the classroom, seeing such an enterprise as a microcosm of the collective effort necessary to improve the world in the future. For Sanderson, as for Wells, the purpose of education was as the 'propaganda of reconstruction' (*The Story of a Great Schoolmaster*, ch. 6, 1), aimed towards the creation of a better world; in Wells's account, Sanderson:

> saw the modern teacher in university and school plainly for what he has to be, the anticipator, the planner and the foundation-maker of the new and greater order of human life that arises now vividly amidst the decaying substructures of the old. (*The Story of a Great Schoolmaster*, ch 1, 1)

Wells ruefully notes, however, that Sanderson's successor as headmaster is only barely aware of the spirit motivating his predecessor's reforms, and that much valuable work might be lost.[108]

---

[107] F. W. Sanderson, 'The Teaching of Science', in *The Modern Teacher: Essays on Educational Aims and Methods*, ed. A. Watson Bain (London: Methuen, 1921), 139–72; *Sanderson of Oundle* (London: Chatto & Windus, 1923).

[108] Wells may have been unduly pessimistic about the consolidation of Sanderson's work undertaken by Dr Kenneth Fisher, who had been a science master at Eton and Clifton

NOW PLAYING: THE END OF THE WORLD

The novels that follow Wells's work on the *Outline* are distinguished largely by the looseness, rather than formal restriction, for which George Ponderevo had pleaded in the opening of *Tono-Bungay*. Wells's straining against the limits of literature eventually takes his work into other media. Having reached at last a worldwide audience with the *Outline* by writing in yet another different genre, Wells sought to address an audience beyond readers of books. In the introduction to his unproduced treatment *The King Who Was a King*, Wells dubbed cinema 'the art form of the future', adding that 'Unhappily not one in a thousand who would see this gladly on a screen will ever read it in a book.'[109] In the 1920s he gave talks that were broadcast on the radio by the BBC.[110] Then, fifty years after the debates about fiction discussed in the first chapter, Wells collaborated in the art-form whose popularity threatened to supplant that of fiction: the cinema.[111]

A number of Wells's early short stories dramatize forms of wish-fulfilment: 'The Man Who Could Work Miracles' (1898), 'The Truth About Pyecraft' (1903), 'The Magic Shop' (1903). The cinema is itself a technology of wish fulfilment. None of Wells's efforts in this direction was bounded by cinematic realism: rather, Wells immediately showed interest in the capacities of cinematic special effects to represent the fantastic in the three silent shorts on which he collaborated with Ivor Montagu in 1928: *Bluebottles*, *The Tonic*, and *Daydreams*. The machines of *Things to Come* allow the mimesis of as yet non-existent technology. Imagination and desire alone cannot make a lamp overturn in the air and stay lit: cinema technology, however, can at least give the appearance that it might be

College, and the manager of a munitions factory. On Sanderson's legacy, see Walker, *History of the Oundle Schools*, 476–580 and Raymond Flower, *Oundle and the English Public School* (London: Stacey, 1989), 89–108.

[109] *The King Who Was a King* (London: Ernest Benn, 1929), 8, 254.

[110] *The Spoken Word: H. G. Wells* (British Library 9. 7807i1+12, 2006). Wells complained to a Mr Allen that he 'got a bigger press for ten minutes of radio talk [. . .] than I do for all that mess of work' that was *The Work, Wealth and Happiness of Mankind* and *After Democracy* (1932) (*Correspondence*, III, 457). See Barry Carman, *A Prophet at the Microphone: The Story of H. G. Wells and the BBC*, broadcast on Radio 4, 27 December 1980, TS, H. G. Wells Collection, Bromley Public Library.

[111] Smith, *Desperately Mortal*, 316–22; Waller, *Writers, Readers and Reputations*, 3–16; Sherborne, *H. G. Wells*, 287. Wells wrote to Jonathan Cape in 1938 that, 'It may be the Novel is dying—unless it can lean on a film story or something of that sort', *Correspondence*, IV, 199. For the story of Wells's earliest involvements with cinema, see Sylvia Hardy, 'H. G. Wells and British Silent Cinema: The War of the Worlds', in *Young and Innocent? The Cinema in Britain, 1896–1930*, ed. Andrew Higson (Exeter: University of Exeter Press, 2002), 242–55.

doing so.[112] (James Whale's 1933 version of *The Invisible Man*, of which Wells mostly approved, repeatedly depends on this kind of effect.)[113]

Wells's first work along such lines is the unfilmed, and probably unfilmable, *The King Who Was a King* (1929), which imagines a future along the lines of *The World Set Free*: the charismatic monarch Prince Zelnika, who has received an Oundle-ish practical and scientific education, nobly renounces his personal power for the greater cause of world peace. The imagined film uses the narrative convention of a love story and the spectacle of a staged war to convey a message of world peace. Wells's first treatment was thus a utopia, but the first feature adaptation for which he provided a script (amended before filming by an uncredited Lajos Biró) is a critique of utopian wish-fulfilment. Like *Kipps*, *The Man Who Could Work Miracles* (filmed in 1937) is a parable about the dangers of the over-fulfilment of desire, imagining a world without disease, and the utopianist Maydig encouraging the hero to use his power to found a world 'drawn by pleasure instead of by pain'.[114] Eventually, Fotheringay risks bringing the world to an end, when he is goaded into stopping the rotation of the Earth, and he renounces his power. (Wells's later unproduced treatment 'The New Faust', a version of 'The Story of the Late Mr Elvesham', is also a story of an abuse of fantastic power.)[115]

Wells's most substantial contribution to cinema followed the pattern of his later novels, in which the imaginative liberty of science fiction allows the framing of a mode of living that is emphatically, and didactically, different from the real world. In 1934, Wells was approached by producer Alexander Korda to collaborate on a feature film. The prospect of writing *Things to Come* (based on Wells's 1933 future history *The Shape of Things to Come*, which had originally been titled *Whither Mankind?*), presented Wells not only with an opportunity to reach a wider audience, but also to disseminate a more fully realized image of his desired utopian future more widely, and thus bring it closer to reality. The construction of the film's costumes and sets, to which, when he was on set, Wells gave constant if not always welcome attention, constituted in itself an act towards successful utopian wish fulfilment. The more real the film appeared, the more

---

[112] Christian Metz, 'On the Impression of Reality in the Cinema', *Film Language: A Semiotics of the Cinema*, trans. Michael Taylor (New York: Oxford University Press, 1964), 3–15.
[113] *Autobiography*, II, 561. This was also presumably the case for the now lost very earliest Wells film adaptation, the French-made *The Invisible Thief* (Charles Pathé, 1909). See Alan Wykes, *H. G. Wells in the Cinema* (London: Jupiter, 1977), 28–9.
[114] *Two Film Stories*, 74
[115] 'The New Faust', *Nash's Pall Mall*, December 1936, 120–45.

achievable its displayed utopian future seems.[116] 'This is essentially a spectacular film,' Wells declares in the 'Introductory Remarks' to the film-book of *Things to Come*.[117] Cinema can produce a much stronger effect of cognitive estrangement than the written word, strikingly so in the brilliant opening of *Things to Come*, whose action begins, self-consciously, at a cinema, and which is shot in the same manner as the newsreels that would have preceded its original screenings. As *The Outline of History* is a Whig version of a history that does not yet exist, so *Things to Come* might be seen as state propaganda produced by an as yet non-existent state, 'a continuation of *The Outline of History* into the future'.[118] The beginning of the film alternates newspaper placards prophesying war with sensuous scenes of urban consumption. (Later, newspapers prematurely and inaccurately announce the end of the war.) The urban crowds of the opening serve as the cinematic equivalent of an implied reader, accused of the bourgeois complacency that fails to prevent the war. The film's anti-democratic politics are shown first in the crowd's indifference to the future, by Everytown's being swayed by the Boss's insistence on national sovereignty (played by Ralph Richardson, against Wells's wishes, as a grotesque of Mussolini), and by Theotocopulos's jeremiads against technological advancement.[119]

The film appears intoxicated with the moving image itself, with shots that constantly emphasize movement, and the plot is propelled by Wells's characteristic preoccupation with technologies of transport, from the children's toys at the opening, to the tanks of the war, to the horse-drawn Rolls - Royce of its dystopian aftermath, to Wings Over the World's solo aeroplanes and bombers, to the earth-tunnelling machines of the imagined utopian future, and the moon rocket of its triumphant conclusion. In the film's middle section, who controls the air controls the world: power and technologies of transport are explicitly equated.

Things to Come is also emphatically self-conscious and preoccupied with media of communication, staging both a lecture and a history lesson, as well as scenes of reading and writing, of screens being watched, and of the destruction of a cinema.[120] The film is concerned with education of and for the future; characters discuss the basis of law, or whether technological progress is an unmitigated good, or if it can be morally right to use poison gas. Wings Over the World's scientific 'freemasonry of efficiency' eventually triumphs over the Boss's sloganizing and bourgeois ' "peace of a

[116] Christopher Frayling, *Things to Come* (London: British Film Institute, 1995), 19–26.
[117] *Two Film Stories*, 9.   [118] Reed, *Natural History of H. G. Wells*, 148.
[119] Nick Cooper, *Things to Come: Viewing Notes* (Network DVD, 2007), 10.
[120] Williams, *H. G. Wells, Modernity and the Movies*, 98, also notes 62 inserted texts in the treatment for *The King Who Was a King*.

strong man armed who keepeth his house"' (68, 43 mins). Even in the utopian setting of the film's final section, however, the archaic still threatens mankind's future development. The Boss had been simply an anti-intellectual: 'We don't print books anymore. Who wants books to muddle their thoughts and their ideas?', adding joyfully that, 'We can't travel any more.'[121] Theotocopulos, however, is named in the treatment as a 'rebel artist'. He alludes in the written version to Shakespeare and Tennyson, '"I shall call my talks *Art and Life*. That sounds harmless enough. And I *will* go for this Brave New World of theirs—tooth and claw."'[122] It takes heroic individual action by individual members of the ruling elite to ensure the next stage of mankind's development, in spite of Theotocopulos's backward-looking aestheticism.[123]

Wells was nonetheless unhappy with the finished product, writing to Beatrice Webb that 'my film is a mess of a film and & Korda ought to be more ashamed of it than I am' and to the *Spectator* that 'to express even the simplest ideas that are not entirely conventional upon the screen is like shouting through thick felt in a thunderstorm'.[124] The interwar years had seen Wells's popularity reach its greatest height and its steepest decline. Once Wells had succeeded in conveying his programme to a world audience, but the desired effect of a World State had still not come about, Wells felt compelled to repeat himself until it did. Sarnac, the narrator of *The Dream*, complains that '"There was a fractional increase in everyone's anxiety and disorder; it didn't change the nature and passions, the ignorances and bad habits of thought of the millions who remained. The World War arose out of these ignorances and misconceptions and it did nothing to alter them."'[125] Nineteen years after *The Outline*'s publication, Europe again went to war; the League of Nations, which Wells helped to found, had failed. In spite of Wells's efforts as historian, the world seemed determined to enact George Santayana's proverb that 'those who cannot remember the past are condemned to repeat it'.[126] The Second World War only proved to Wells his failure to get his message heard: writing yet another Preface to the *The War in the Air* in 1941, Wells chooses as his epitaph: 'I told you so. You *damned* fools.'[127]

---

[121] *Two Film Stories*, 48.   [122] Ibid., 93.

[123] One reviewer objected to the film's anti-aestheticism: see Michael Roberts, 'Mr Wells's Sombre World', *Spectator*, 157 (1936), 1032–3.

[124] Letter to Beatrice Webb, *Correspondence*, IV, 103 and *The Spectator* 14 December 1936, *Correspondence*, IV, 118.

[125] *The Dream*, *Works*, 566.

[126] George Santayana, *The Life of Reason: or, The Phases of Human Progress, Revised by the Author in Collaboration with David Cory* (London: Constable, 1954), 82.

[127] *War in the Air* (Harmondsworth: Penguin, 1941), 9. In *Exasperations*, Wells reflects that the enormous sale of the *Outline* was only a boom, doubting 'if more than two or three thousand were ever attentively read. It was bought because it was the thing to read. It was bought and stowed away' (*Exasperations*, Illinois Collection, 106).

CONCLUSION: A POT OF MESSAGE

While Wells's authorial perspective remained global to the end, his final writings explore the conditions by which the individual is established. His later fictional output includes the novelle *The Croquet Player* (1936), *Star-Begotten*, and *The Camford Visitation* (both 1937), which are compact explorations of different states, and of the borders of, individual consciousness. Even in his last novel, *You Can't Be Too Careful*, Wells continues to wrestle with the difficulties of presenting a global horizon through the limits of human experience, choosing a hero as wholly typical, as lacking in narratable singularity as he can make him, in order to demonstrate truths about social formations:

> Like these amusing books you find in books on Optics that will turn inside out as you look at them, it is equally the story this empty shape of a human being at the centre of it—its resultant, its creature. [...]

Here we have a picture of the modern novel. Look at it hard and alternately you see the vase, the social vessel, and nothing else, and then the social vessel vanishes and you see individuals and nothing more.

Here we have a picture of the modern novel. Look at it hard and alternately you see the vase, the social vessel, and nothing else, and then the social vessel vanishes and you see individuals and nothing more.[128]

This new emphasis on individual consciousness does not mean that Wells's writing was taking a high modernist turn, as he makes explicit in the Preface to 1940's *Babes in the Darkling Wood*.[129] Earlier Wells texts such as *Tono-Bungay* and *Boon* may share characteristics with modernist fiction, but Wells could never choose to be a modernist writer, since he wanted his books and the ideas they contain to be read by as large an audience as possible—no doubt in part out of artistic vanity, but above all so that humanity's prospects for survival and well-being might be improved. Michael Sherborne assesses the importance of this novel in literary history thus:

> *Tono-Bungay* is [. . .] a missing link occupying the supposedly empty space between two literary eras, evincing, on the one hand, a typically Edwardian ambition to apply familiar ways of thinking to unfamiliar subject matter in the interests of a new synthesis and, on the other, a modernist submersion in dissonance, depicting a wasteland that can only acquire significant form through the compositional techniques of the artist. If *Tono-Bungay* looks like a failure against traditionalist and modernist criteria, it is in large measure because its greatness resides in its refusal to conform to either set of assumptions.[130]

There would be no place for Wells in the eventual modernist hierarchy of literature, nor did he seek to occupy one.[131] The aesthetics of Joyce or Eliot require a strenuous level of knowledge of the culture that is anathema to Wells's iconoclastic dismissal of the residuum. The solipsism of much of modernism's representation of the self is similarly antithetical to Wells's increasingly collectivizing aims. The distance of his instrumental vision for art is crystallized in a disagreement with Conrad: 'The difference between us, Wells, is fundamental. You don't care for humanity but think they are to be improved. I love humanity but know they are not!'[132] Wells acknowledged this distance when portraying a modernist artist in his 1932 novel *The Bulpington of Blup*. Wells's novels often include ironic deprecations of his own work, or self-portraits such as 'Wilkins'; here, he puts into the mouth of Theodore Bulpington (a portrait of Ford Madox

128 *You Can't Be Too Careful*, 10.
129 *Babes in the Darling Wood*, 10.
130 Sherborne, *H. G. Wells*, 203.
131 Ibid., 249–50.
132 Quoted in Hart-Davis, *Hugh Walpole*, 168.

Ford) the grounds for Wells's own self-dismissal from the pantheon of high art:

> It was, he declared, an immensely exciting time that was dawning for the creative impulse, particularly in literature. [. . .] There would have to be new forms, new men, new schools. The old reputations stood up over us now like great empty hulls that had served their purpose, Hardy, Barrie, Conrad, Kipling, Galsworthy, Bennett, Wells, Shaw, Maugham, and so forth; they had all said what they had to say; they were finished. [. . .] They ought to have gone on to the bonfires of Armistice Day. The new generation was hurrying forward to express the great new things, the deeper significances, the wider outlooks, that the war had revealed. There would be new conceptions of life, new conceptions of happiness and sex, expressed in a new language, a language richer and more subtle, reforged for the new needs.[133]

Surveying his career in 1930, Wells declared, rather overstating his case, that:

> I have never taken any very great pains about writing. I am outside the hierarchy of conscious and deliberate writers altogether. I am the absolute antithesis of Mr James Joyce. That does not prevent our being very good friends, but our work is poles asunder. Long ago, living in close conversational proximity to Henry James, Joseph Conrad, and Mr Ford Madox Hueffer, I escaped from under their immense artistic preoccupations by calling myself a journalist. To that title I adhere.[134]

Wells admired Joyce's genius, and campaigned for modernist writers to be able to write free from censorship, but still thought Joyce's kind of literary modernism 'a dead end'. Wells's personal wishes to and support for Joyce are generous, but he doesn't think his work 'gets anywhere. You have turned your back on common men, on their elementary needs and their restricted time and intelligence and you have elaborated. What is the result? Vast riddles.'[135]

Ford Madox Ford states that 'in the kingdom of letters Mr. Wells and I have been leaders of opposing forces for nearly the whole of this century'; at the same time, he acclaims Wells at his peak as a novelist as 'the Dean of our Profession' and as prophet and an influence upon the thought of the world.[136]

D. H. Lawrence reviewed the first volume of *The World of William Clissold* as 'simply not good enough to be a novel', and judged Clissold's

---

[133] *The Bulpington of Blup*, 244. See Robert Bloom, *Anatomies of Egotism: A Reading of the Last Novels of H. G. Wells* (Lincoln: University of Nebraska Press, 1977), 84.

[134] Preface to Geoffrey West, *H. G. Wells*, iii–vi (v–vi). Cf. *Autobiography*, II, 623.

[135] Letter of 23 November 1928, *Literary Criticism*, ed. Parrinder and Philmus, 176; Sherborne, *H. G. Wells*, 285. Joyce is classed by Boon as a '"first-rater"' in *Boon*, 123.

[136] Ford Madox Ford, *Mightier than the Sword: Memories and Criticisms* (London: Allen & Unwin, 1938), 145, 155.

'ailment [as] a peevish, ashy indifference to *everything*, except himself, himself as centre of the universe'.[137] E. M. Forster praised *The Outline of History* as 'a great book', but in *Aspects of the Novel* judged that, 'the world of beauty [...] is entirely closed to Wells'.[138] Wells read T. S. Eliot's poems in 1934 and admitted to Constance Coolidge that 'I just don't get it if there is anything that bright & young & clear about it. And generally I find the book making me think that a classical dictionary must have been raped by the New Yorker.'[139] Eliot in turn complained that when Wells 'uses the facts for imaginative purposes he is superb; when he uses his imagination to expound facts he is deplorable.'[140]

Wells wrote that he regarded Virginia Woolf's work 'with a lack-lustre eye'.[141] In her not wholly unfavourable review of *Joan and Peter* in *The Times Literary Supplement*, Woolf reproved Wells for blurring the boundaries between fiction and educational polemic: 'He throws off the trammels of fiction as lightly as he would throw off a coat in running a race.'[142] Wells's characters frequently liberate themselves by divesting themselves of clothing, and Wells famously responded to Woolf in *The Outline of History* that, 'human history becomes more and more a race between education and catastrophe': given the scale of the threat to humanity's future, winning the race is more important than personal aesthetics.[143] Woolf closes her review by judging that 'the sacrifice, if we choose to regard it so, of his career as a novelist has been a sacrifice to the rights of youth' and that 'the roar of genuine applause which salutes every new work of his more than makes up, we are sure, for the dubious silence, and perhaps the unconcealed boredom, of posterity'.[144] The aims of education, science, and literary production are as one for Wells: the construction of a better future. In his work from *The Time Machine* to *Mind at the End of Its Tether* (1945), Wells repeatedly presented an artistic vision of the future; the future, biologically, is literally embodied

---

[137] Review of *The World of William Clissold*, *Calendar of Modern Letters*, October 1926, in D. H. Lawrence, *Selected Literary Criticism*, ed. Anthony Beal (London: Heinemann, 1955), 133–8 (133, 137).

[138] E. M. Forster, review of *The Outline of History* in the *Athenaeum*, 2 and 9 July 1920, 8–9, 42–3, *Critical Heritage*, ed. Parrinder, 248–54 (248); Forster, *Aspects of the Novel*, 24.

[139] *Correspondence*, III, 562; cf. *Babes in the Darkling Wood*, 205. See Lisa Fluet, 'Modernism and Disciplinary History: On H. G. Wells and T. S. Eliot', *Twentieth-Century Literature*, 50/3 (2004), 283–316.

[140] T. S. Eliot, 'The Idealism of Julien Benda', *Cambridge Review*, 99, 6 June 1928, 485–8 (487).

[141] *Autobiography*, II, 462.

[142] Unsigned review of *Joan and Peter* in *The Times Literary Supplement*, *Critical Heritage*, ed. Parrinder, 244–7 (246).

[143] *Outline of History*, II, 758.

[144] *Critical Heritage*, ed. Parrinder, 247.

in children, who must be educated. Wells hoped that the correct forms of education, and the best possible teaching of history and science in particular, would establish the foundations of a reformed government of the world in which poverty and war could be eradicated, along with national boundaries.[145]

Once he wished his books to constitute actual historical interventions more than autonomous artefacts, it became inevitable that Wells would 'recede into the issues of his own time'.[146] As Parrinder puts it, once Wells 'deliberately began to dilute his fictional skills' to get his message across, his prose was 'consciously made unliterary', and thus only a handful of Wells's books attain the aesthetic heights of the very best of his output.[147] Consequently, the texts which dramatize those issues in the most fantastic and imaginative ways are those which have enjoyed the most vital afterlife. To quote Parrinder again, Wells wanted 'to influence the praxis of the twentieth century, but his real contribution was to its dreams'.[148]

Nonetheless, recent attempts to rewrite the literary history of the twentieth century offer a way of evaluating Wells's significance. Even viewed solely by high modernist canons of significant form, Wells is still unarguably an experimental writer, seeking to challenge the formal limits of literature in order to make fiction a powerful agent in the world, evolving 'a theory of fiction which was coherent and responsible'.[149] The literary ecosystem of the twentieth century was far more complex than the view from a Bloomsbury window; recent evaluations have successfully challenged the canonical definition of what constitutes the 'modern' in 'modernist'.[150] Viewed in the context of the history of reading, Wells's work looms larger still, its influence on the living world of the twentieth century as significant as that of any twentieth-century writer in English. *The Outline of History* sold 436,000 copies in its dollar edition alone; the

---

[145] It is interesting to note that the *Outline of History* was published in the same year as the Newbolt Report, which, conversely, promoted the educational use of English language and literature to reinforce national self-identity. See Patrick Scott, 'English Studies and the Cultural Construction of Nationality: The Newbolt Report Reexamined', in *Culture and Education in Victorian England*, ed. Patrick Scott and Pauline Fletcher (Lewisburg: Bucknell University Press; London and Toronto: Associated University Presses, 1990), 218–32.

[146] Huntington, *Logic of Fantasy*, xiii–xiv.

[147] Bradbury, *Social Context*, 32; Parrinder, *H. G. Wells*, 89–90.

[148] 'Introduction', *Critical Heritage*, ed. Parrinder, 1–31 (3).

[149] Batchelor, *H. G. Wells*, ix.

[150] See, for instance, the approaches adopted by Kristin Bluemel in *Intermodernism: Literary Culture in Mid-Twentieth-Century Britain* (Edinburgh: Edinburgh University Press, 2009); David M. Earle in *Re-Covering Modernism: Pulps, Paperbacks and the Prejudices of Form* (London: Ashgate, 2009). Alexandra Harris, *Romantic Moderns: English Writers, Artists and the Imagination from Virginia Woolf to John Piper* (London: Thames & Hudson, 2010).

derided *William Clissold* 20,000 in Britain, *The Shape of Things to Come* 60,000.[151] By the 1920s, *Kipps* had sold a quarter of a million copies; even such a slight work as *In Search of Hot Water* enjoyed a print run of 50,000.[152] Whatever the judgements made on Wells by his modernist contemporaries, what he wrote in these books was being read by a very large number of people.

According to Ifor Evans, 'no one can well understand the twentieth century, in its hopes and its disillusionments, without studying Wells'.[153] George Orwell wrote:

> Thinking people who were born about the beginning of this century are in some sense Wells's own creation [...] I doubt whether anyone who was writing books between 1900 and 1920, at any rate in the English language, influenced the young so much. The minds of all of us, and therefore the physical world, would be perceptibly different if Wells had never existed.[154]

The received version of literary history sees Wells as an artist 'corrupted' by his political preaching. His estranged ally Sidney Webb complained that 'he is far too conscious of literary success, measured in great prices for books and articles—he has become a sort of "little god" demanding payment in flattery as well as gold'.[155] H. L. Mencken added his condemnation:

> Once a man begins to suffer from a messianic delusion his days as a serious artist are ended. [...] He has been made discontented with the business of an artist. It was not enough to display the life of his time with accuracy and understanding; it was not even enough to criticize it with a penetrating humour and sagacity. From the depths of his being, like some foul miasma, there arose the old, fatuous yearning to change it, to improve it, to set it right where it was wrong.[156]

Wells's commitment to fiction that does something more than exist beautifully is a product of the same Victorian historical conditions that had enabled him to be a success. Wells's career was brought into being by

---

[151] *Correspondence*, III, 377.

[152] Sherborne, *H. G. Wells*, 167, 327.

[153] Ifor Evans, *A Short History of English Literature* (Harmondsworth: Penguin, 1940), 181.

[154] George Orwell, 'Wells, Hitler and the World State', *The Complete Works of George Orwell*, 20 vols, ed. Peter Davison (London: Secker & Warburg, 1986–98), XIII: *A Patriot After All*, 536–41. For an acute analysis of the relationship between the two writers, see John S. Partington, 'The Pen as Sword: George Orwell, H. G. Wells and Journalistic Parricide', *Journal of Contemporary History*, 39/1 (2004), 45–56.

[155] MacKenzie and MacKenzie, *Life of H. G. Wells*, 335.

[156] H. L. Mencken, 'The Late Mr. Wells', *Prejudices: First Series* (London: Jonathan Cape, 1921), 22–35 (28–30).

educational reforms caused by a reform in the mode of establishing political government. In turn, his writing sought itself to be educational and political, bringing about a further change in government. Veneration of the work of art as epiphenomenon is for Wells a squandering of mankind's evolved potential for self-development; but the reading and writing of the right kind of literature is a matter of the highest responsibility:

> Education is being forced upon everyone by that rapid increase in the range, complexity and instability of social co-operation that is the fundamental characteristic of contemporary experience. Men have to read and write if only to understand messages, render accounts and adapt themselves to incessantly changing processes. [...] Everywhere, now, the teaching of reading and writing spreads. [...] In man educability is carried to unprecedented levels by the use of symbols and particularly by the use of words.[157]

Having come to maturity as a writer in an age that debated the ideological effect of reading fiction, and which repeatedly reimagined the circumstances of civilization's possible destruction, Wells sought to control the effect of the fiction that he wrote himself in order to bring about a better mode of existing. Wells certainly sought to achieve 'a level of public attention which went well beyond the receptiveness of a respectful readership', as his critics complained, but when Wells ultimately chooses education over aesthetics, he does so for reasons of the deepest personal conviction.[158] In the last few years of his life, Wells's attention shifted from the World State to a campaign for human rights, which continued, and continues, long after his death. If utopia can never be achieved, there will always be a need for utopian writing, and a kind of art that seeks to make the world in which it exists a better, fairer, happier world continues to deserve the attention of literary scholars and readers alike.

---

[157] *The Work, Wealth and Happiness of Mankind*, 715–16.
[158] Stefan Collini, *Absent Minds: Intellectuals in Britain* (Oxford: Oxford University Press, 2007), 481.

Bibliography

BOOKS BY WELLS

'42 to '44: A Contemporary Memoir upon the Human Behaviour during the Crisis of the World Revolution (London: Secker & Warburg, 1944).

'Advice to Grocers' Assistants', *Grocers' Assistant*, February 1900, 154.

All Aboard for Ararat (London: Secker & Warburg, 1940).

The Anatomy of Frustration: A Modern Synthesis (London: Cresset, 1936).

Arnold Bennett and H. G. Wells: A Record of a Personal and Literary Friendship, ed., Harris Wilson (London: Rupert Hart-Davis, 1960).

'Art and Life: Postcard Biographies from the National Gallery', *Independent on Sunday*, 23 February 1997; http://www.independent.co.uk/arts-entertainment/books/art–life-postcard-biographies-from-the-national-portrait-gallery-1280306.html [accessed 7 January 2011].

Babes in the Darkling Wood (London: Secker & Warburg, 1940).

Bernard Shaw and H. G. Wells: Selected Correspondence of Bernard Shaw, ed. J. Percy Smith (Toronto: University of Toronto Press, 1995).

Boon, The Mind of the Race, The Wild Asses of the Devil, and the Last Trump (London: Fisher Unwin, 1915).

The Brothers (London: Chatto & Windus, 1938).

The Bulpington of Blup (London: Hutchinson, 1932).

The Camford Visitation (London: Methuen, 1937).

'The Case against the Classical Languages', in *Natural Science and the Classical System in Education*, ed. E. Ray Lankester (London: Heinemann, 1918), 183–95.

Certain Personal Matters (London: Fisher Unwin, 1901).

Christina Alberta's Father (Toronto: Macmillan, 1925).

The Complete Short Stories of H. G. Wells, ed. John Hammond (London: Dent, 1998).

'Concerning Mr Swinnerton', in *Frank Swinnerton: Personal Sketches* (New York: George H. Doran, 1920), 17–23.

The Conquest of Time, ed. Martin Gardner (Amherst, NY: Prometheus, 1995).

The Correspondence of H. G. Wells, ed. David C. Smith (London: Pickering & Chatto, 1998).

Correspondence, vol. 5, unpublished.

The Country of the Blind (London: Golden Cockerel Press, 1959).

The Croquet Player, ed. John Hammond (Nottingham: Trent Editions, 1998).

Crux Ansata: An Indictment of the Roman Catholic Church (Harmondsworth: Penguin, 1943).

The Discovery of the Future: With The Common Sense of World Peace and The Human Adventure, ed. Patrick Parrinder (London: PNL Press for the H. G. Wells Society, 1989).

'Education of an Elizabethan Gentleman', *University Correspondent*, 14 October 1893, 4–6.

An Englishman Looks at the World: Being a Series of Unrestrained Remarks upon Contemporary Matters (London: Cassell, 1914).

Exasperations, unpublished manuscript, Illinois Collection.

Experiment in Autobiography: Discoveries and Conclusions of a Very Ordinary Brain, 2 vols (London: Gollancz, 1934).

'The Faults of the Fabian', in Samuel Hynes, *The Edwardian Turn of Mind*, (Princeton, NJ: Princeton University Press, 1968), 390–409.

First and Last Things: A Confession of Faith and Rule of Life (London: Archibald Constable, 1908).

First and Last Things: A Confession of Faith and Rule of Life (London: Cassell and Company, 1917).

The First Men in the Moon, ed. Patrick Parrinder (London: Penguin, 2005).

Floor Games: A Father's Account of Play and its Legacy of Healing, ed. Barbara A. Turner (Cloverdale: Temenos Press, 2004).

Foreword to Brian Ború Dunne, *The 70 Adventures of a Dyspeptic* (Philadelphia: Wonston, 1937), 9.

The Future in America: A Search After Realities (London: Chapman and Hall, 1906).

George Gissing and H. G. Wells: Their Friendship and Correspondence, ed. Royal A. Gettmann (London: Rupert Hart-Davis, 1961).

God the Invisible King (London: Cassell, 1917).

et al., *The Great State: Essays in Construction* (London: Harper, 1912).

Guide to the New World: A Handbook of Constructive World Revolution (London: Gollancz, 1941).

'Hard Facts about Art Treasures', *Sunday Dispatch*, 5 March 1944, Illinois Collection.

Henry James and H. G. Wells: A Record of Their Friendship, their Debate on the Art of Fiction, and their Quarrel, ed. Leon Edel and Gordon N. Ray (London: Rupert Hart-Davis, 1959).

H. G. Wells: Early Writings in Science and Science Fiction, ed. Robert M. Philmus and David Y. Hughes (Berkeley: University of California Press, 1975).

H. G. Wells: Interviews and Recollections, ed. J. R. Hammond (Totowa, NJ: Barnes and Noble, 1980).

H. G. Wells in 'Nature', 1893–1946: A Reception Reader, ed. John S. Partington (Frankfurt: Lang, 2008).

H. G. Wells and Rebecca West, ed. Gordon N. Ray (London: Macmillan, 1974).

H. G. Wells's Literary Criticism, ed. Patrick Parrinder and Robert Philmus (Brighton: Harvester; Totowa, NJ: Barnes and Noble, 1980).

The History of Mr Polly, ed. Simon J. James (London: Penguin, 2005).

'The Holiday of a Draper's Assistant: Life in a Margin', *Pall Mall Gazette*, 58, 5 June 1894, 3.

Hoopdriver's Holiday, ed. Michael Timko (Lafayette: English Literature in Transition, 1964).

'Huxley', *Royal College of Science Magazine*, 13 April 1901, 209–11.

'The Hygenic Country', *Lika Joko*, 9, 15 December 1894, 165.

In the Fourth Year: Anticipations of a World Peace (London: Chatto & Windus, 1918).

'Introduction', *The Country of the Blind* (London: Golden Cockerel Press, 1939), 5–8.

The Invisible Man, ed. Patrick Parrinder (London: Penguin, 2005).

The Island of Doctor Moreau, ed. Patrick Parrinder (London: Penguin, 2005).

The King Who Was a King (London: Ernest Benn, 1929), 8, 254.

Kipps: The Story of a Simple Soul, ed. Simon J. James (London: Penguin, 2005).

'The Lay of the Sausage Machine', *Science Schools Journal*, 2, 27 November 1890, 42–3.

'Letter to Henry Hick', n.d. [1897] H. G. Wells Collection 1203, Bromley Public Library, Kent, UK.

'Letter to Henry Hick', 16 July 1898, H. G. Wells Collection 1205, Bromley Public Library, Kent, UK.

'The Literature of the Future: The Horoscope of Books', *Pall Mall Gazette*, 57, 11 October 1893, 3.

Little Wars: A Game for Boys from Twelve Years of Age to One Hundred and Fifty and for that More Intelligent Sort of Girls who Like Boys' Games and Books: With an Appendix on Kriegspiel (London: F. Palmer, 1913; repr. New York: Da Capo, 1977).

[pseud., Walter Glockenhammer], 'Mammon', *Science Schools Journal*, 2 (1887), 53–4.

Love and Mr. Lewisham, ed. Simon James (London: Penguin, 1995).

Man Who Could Work Miracles (London: Cresset, 1940).

Mankind in the Making (London: Chapman and Hall, 1903).

'Master Anthony and the Zeppelin', *Princess Marie-Jose's Children's Book* (London: Cassell, 1916), 13–17.

Meanwhile: The Portrait of a Lady (New York: George H. Doran, 1927).

Mind at the End of its Tether (London: Heinemann, 1945).

'Modern Reviewing', *Adelphi*, 5 (1923), 150–1.

A Modern Utopia (London: Chapman and Hall, 1905).

Mr. Blettsworthy on Rampole Island (London: Ernest Benn, 1928).

'Mr Wells Explains Himself', *T.P.'s Magazine* (December 1911), author's TS, Illinois Collection.

'Mr Wells's Economies: A Reply to Sir R. K. Wilson', *Tribune*, 3 and 23 August 1906, 3.

'My Lucky Moment', *View*, 29 April 1911, 212.

'The New Faust', *Nash's Pall Mall*, December 1936, 120–45.

The New Machiavelli, ed. Simon J. James (London: Penguin, 2005).

The New Teaching of History: With a Reply to Some Recent Criticisms of The Outline of History (London: Cassell, 1921).

New Worlds for Old (London: Archibald Constable, 1908).

'The Novels of Mr George Gissing', *Contemporary Review*, 72 (1897), 192–210.

'Of the Difficulties of Reviewing', *New Budget*, 9 May 1895, 27.

'On Capital Punishment', *Science Schools Journal*, 2 (1890), 292–4.

The Open Conspiracy: H. G. Wells on World Revolution, ed. W. Warren Wagar (Westport, CT: Praeger, 2002).

——et al., *The Outline of History: Being A Plain History of Life and Mankind* (London: Newnes, 1919).

'A Perfect Gentleman on Wheels', in *The Humours of Cycling*, ed. Jerome K. Jerome (London: Bowden, 1897), 5–14.

Phoenix: A Summary of the Inescapable Conditions of World Reorganisation (London: Secker & Warburg, 1942).

The Picshuas of H. G. Wells: A Burlesque Diary, ed. Gene K. Rinkel and Margaret E. Rinkel (Urbana: University of Illinois Press, 2006).

'Points of View', *Listener*, 30 October 1929, 565–6, 592–4.

The P. R. Parliament (London: Proportional Representation Society, [1924]).

Preface to A. D. Gristwood, *The Somme: Including Also the Coward* (London: Cape, 1927), 9–12.

'The Reading of History', *John O'London's Weekly*, 5 May 1923.

The Rights of Man: Or What Are We Fighting For? (London: Penguin, 1940).

Russia in the Shadows (London: Hodder & Stoughton, 1920).

The Salvaging of Civilization: The Probable Future of Mankind (New York: Macmillan, 1921).

The Science of Life, 2 vols (New York: Doubleday, 1931).

'Science Teaching—An Ideal and Some Realities', *Educational Times*, 1 January 1895, 23–9.

Science and the World-Mind (London: New Europe, 1942).

The Sea Lady: A Tissue of Moonshine: A Critical Text of the 1902 London First Edition, with an Introduction and Appendices, ed. Leon Stover (Jefferson, NC: McFarland and Co. Inc., 2001).

'The Secrets of the Short Story', *Saturday Review*, 80 (1895), 693.

Select Conversations with an Uncle with Two Hitherto Unreprinted Conversations, ed. David C Smith and Patrick Parrinder (London: University of North London Press, 1992).

Shakespeare Day: Report of Meeting, Organised by the Shakespeare Association, Held at King's College, University of London, on May 3, 1917, to Promote an Annual Shakespeare Day in the Schools and Other Institutions (London: Chatto & Windus [1918]), 26–30.

The Shape of Things to Come: The Ultimate Revolution (London: Hutchinson, 1936).

Socialism and The Great State (New York: Harper, 1922).

'Specimen Day [From a Holiday Itinerary]', *Science Schools Journal*, 33 (1891), 17–20.

The Spoken Word: H. G. Wells (http://shop.bl.uk/mell/productpage.cfn/British-Library/ISBN-9780712305327/87323).

Star Begotten: A Biological Fantasia, ed. John S. Huntington (Middleton: Wesleyan University Press, 2006).

'A Tale of the Twentieth Century For Advanced Thinkers', *Science Schools Journal*, 6 (1887), 188–91.

'The Ten Most Important Books in the World', *John O'London's Weekly*, 26 May 1923, 210.

A Textbook of Biology, 2 vols (London: Clive, 1893).

Things to Come (Network DVD, B000GUK3RO).

This Misery of Boots: Reprinted with Alterations from the Independent Review (London: Fabian Society, 1907).

The Time Machine: An Invention, ed. Nicholas Ruddick (Peterborough, ON: Broadview Press, 2001).

The Time Machine: An Invention, ed. Patrick Parrinder (London: Penguin, 2005).

The Time Machine and The Island of Dr Moreau, ed. Patrick Parrinder (New York: Oxford University Press, 1997).

Tono-Bungay, ed. Patrick Parrinder (London: Penguin, 2005).

Travels of a Republican Radical in Search of Hot Water (Harmondsworth: Penguin 1939).

'The Truth about Gissing', *Rhythm* Literary Supplement, December 1912, i–iv.

Two Film Scenarios: Things to Come; Man Who Could Work Miracles (London: Cresset, 1940).

Two Film Stories: Things to Come; The Man Who Could Work Miracles (London: Cresset Press, 1940).

War and the Future: Italy, France, and Britain at War (London: Cassell, 1917).

The War in the Air: And Particularly How Mr. Bert Smallways Faired While It Lasted (Harmondsworth: Penguin, 1941).

The War in the Air: And Particularly How Mr. Bert Smallways Faired While It Lasted, ed. Patrick Parrinder (London: Penguin, 2005).

The War of the Worlds, ed. Patrick Parrinder (London: Penguin, 2005).

The War that Will End War (London: Palmer, 1914).

The Wealth of Mr. Waddy: A Novel, ed. Harris Wilson (Carbondale: Southern Illinois University Press, 1969).

What is Coming: A Forecast of Things After the War (London: Cassell, 1916).

'What is Cram?', *University Correspondent*, 18 March 1893, 10.

'What Everyone Should Read: The Reading of History', *John O'London's Weekly*, 5 May 1923.

'What Will England Be Like in 1930?', *Strand*, 54 (1917), 171.

The Wheels of Chance: A Bicycling Idyll (New York: Macmillan, 1896).

The Wheels of Chance: A Holiday Adventure (London: Dent, 1896).

When the Sleeper Wakes, ed. John Lawton (London: Dent, 1994).
Will Socialism Destroy the Home? (London: Independent Labour Party, [1907]).
The Work, Wealth and Happiness of Mankind (London: Heinemann, 1932).
The Works of H. G. Wells, 28 vols. (New York: Scribner's, 1924–8).
World Brain: H. G. Wells on the Future of World Education, ed. Alan Mayne (London: Adamantine Press, 1994).
The World, its Debts and the Rich Men (London: Finer, 1922).
The World of William Clissold: A Novel from a New Angle (London: Ernest Benn, 1926).
A Year of Prophesying (New York: Macmillan, 1925).
You Can't Be Too Careful: A Sample of Life (London: Secker & Warburg, 1941).

WORKS BY OTHERS

Adorno, Theodor, *Aesthetics and Politics*, ed. Fredric Jameson (London: Verso, 1977).
——*Aesthetic Theory*, ed. Gretel Adorno and Rolf Tiedemann, trans. Robert Hullot-Kentor (London: Continuum, 2004).
——and Max Horkheimer, *Dialectic of Enlightenment*, trans. John Cumming (London: Verso, 1997).
'All Brain and Little Heart', *Time Magazine*, 20 September 1926, http://www.time.com/time/magazine/article/0,9171,901208-1,00.html [accessed 7 January 2011].
Althusser, Louis, *Lenin and Philosophy and Other Essays*, trans. Ben Brewster (London: NLB, 1971).
Amigoni, David, *Colonies, Culture and Evolution: Literature, Science and Culture in Nineteenth-Century Writing* (Cambridge: Cambridge University Press, 2007).
Anderson, Benedict, *Imagined Communities: Reflections on the Origin and Spread of Nationalism*, rev. edn (London: Verso, 2006).
Anderson, Linda R., 'Self and Society in H. G. Wells's *Tono-Bungay*', *Modern Fiction Studies*, 26/2 (1980), 199–212.
'Angry Old Buffer', 'Sexomania', *Punch*, 27 April 1895, 203.
Arnold, Ken and Tilly Tansey, *Pills and Profits: The Selling of Medicines since 1870* ([London]: Wellcome Trust, 1994).
Arnold, Matthew, *The Poems of Matthew Arnold*, ed. Kenneth Allott (London: Longman, 1965).
——*The Complete Prose Works of Matthew Arnold*, 10 vols, ed. R. H. Super (Ann Arbor: University of Michigan Press, 1974).
——*Culture and Anarchy and Other Writings*, ed. Stefan Collini (Cambridge: Cambridge University Press, 1993).
Attridge, Derek, *The Singularity of Literature* (London: Routledge, 2004).
Austin, Alfred, 'The Vice of Reading', *Temple Bar*, 42 (1874), 251–7.

Bacon, Francis, *The New Atlantics: A Work Unfinished*, in *Three Early Modern Utopias*, ed. Susan Bruce (Oxford: Oxford University Press, 1999), 149–86.

——— *The Instauratio Magna Part II: Novum Organum and Associated Texts*, ed. and trans. Graham Rees with Maria Wakely, The Oxford Francis Bacon XI (Oxford: Clarendon Press, 2004).

Bain, Alexander, *Education as a Science* (London: Kegan Paul, 1879).

Bain, A. Watson, ed., *The Modern Teacher: Essays on Educational Aims and Methods* (London: Methuen, 1921).

Baker, Steve, *Picturing the Beast: Animals, Identity and Representation* (Manchester: Manchester University Press, 1993).

Balfour Papers, British Library.

Bann, Stephen, ed., *Frankenstein: Creation and Monstrosity* (London: Reaktion, 1994).

Barnard, H. C., *A History of English Education from 1760*, 2nd edn (London: University of London Press, 1961).

Barthes, Roland, *Sade, Fourier, Loyola*, trans. Richard Miller (Baltimore: Johns Hopkins University Press, 1997).

Batchelor, John, *H. G. Wells* (Cambridge: Cambridge University Press, 1985).

Baudrillard, Jean, *For A Critique of the Political Economy of the Sign*, trans. Charles Levin (St Louis, MO: Telos Press, 1981).

——— *The Consumer Society: Myths and Structures*, trans. George Ritzer (London: Sage, 1998).

Becker, George J., ed., *Documents of Modern Literary Realism* (Princeton, NJ: Princeton University Press, 1963).

Beer, Gillian, *Darwin's Plots: Evolutionary Narrative in Darwin, George Eliot, and Nineteenth-Century Fiction* (London: Routledge, 1983).

Bellamy, William, *The Novels of Wells, Bennett and Galsworthy* (London: Routledge & Kegan Paul, 1971).

Belloc, Hilaire, *Mr. Belloc Objects to 'The Outline of History'* (London: George H. Doran, 1926).

Belsey, Catherine, *Critical Practice* (London: Methuen, 1980).

Benjamin, Walter, *Illuminations*, ed. Hannah Arendt, trans. Harry Zohn (London: Jonathan Cape, 1970).

Bennett, Arnold, *Literary Taste: How to Form it, with Detailed Instructions for Collecting a Complete Library of English Literature* (London: Hodder, 1916).

Beresford, J. D., *H. G. Wells* (New York: Henry Holt, 1915).

Bergonzi, Bernard, 'The Publication of *The Time Machine* 1894–5', *Review of English Studies*, NS 11 (1960), 42–51.

——— *The Early H. G. Wells: A Study of the Scientific Romances* (Manchester: Manchester University Press, 1961).

——— ed., *H. G. Wells: A Collection of Critical Essays* (Englewood Cliffs, NJ: Prentice-Hall, 1976).

Besant, Walter, *The Inner House* (Bristol: Kessinger, 1888).

Bivona, Daniel, *Desire and Contradiction: Imperial Visions and Domestic Debates in Victorian Literature* (Manchester: Manchester University Press, 1990).

Bloch, Ernst, *The Utopian Function of Art: Selected Essays*, trans. Jack Zipes and Frank Mecklenburg (Cambridge, MA: MIT Press, 1988).

Bloom, Robert, *Anatomies of Egotism: A Reading of the Last Novels of H. G. Wells* (Lincoln: University of Nebraska Press, 1977).

Bluemel, Kristin, *Intermodernism: Literary Culture in Mid-Twentieth-Century Britain* (Edinburgh: Edinburgh University Press, 2009).

Booth, Martin, *The Doctor, the Detective and Arthur Conan Doyle: A Biography of Arthur Conan Doyle* (London: Hodder & Stoughton, 1997).

Born, Daniel, *The Birth of Liberal Guilt in the English Novel: Charles Dickens to H. G. Wells* (Chapel Hill: University of North Carolina Press, 1995).

Bourdieu, Pierre, *Distinction: A Social Judgement of the Critique of Taste*, trans. Richard Nice (New York: Routledge 1992).

Bowlby, Rachel, *Just Looking: Consumer Culture in Dreiser, Gissing and Zola* (London: Methuen, 1985).

Bradbury, Malcolm, *The Social Context of Modern Literature* (Oxford: Blackwell, 1971).

Brandon-Jones, John, et al., *C. F. A. Voysey: Architect and Designer* (London: Lund Humphries, 1978).

Brantlinger, Patrick, *The Reading Lesson: The Threat of Mass Literacy in Nineteenth-Century British Fiction* (Bloomington: Indiana University Press, 1998).

Brome, Vincent, *Six Studies in Quarrelling* (London: Cresset, 1958).

Brooks, Van Wyck, *The World of H. G. Wells* (New York: Mitchell Kennerley, 1915).

Bruce, Susan, ed., *Three Early Modern Utopias* (Oxford: Oxford University Press, 1999).

Brydone, James E., ed., *Centenary of H. G. Wells, 1866–1966* (Folkestone: Spade House, 1966).

Buckley, J. H., *The Triumph of Time: A Study of the Victorian Concepts of Time, History, Progress and Decadence* (Cambridge, MA: Belknap Press; London: Oxford University Press, 1967).

Bullen. J. B., ed., *The Sun is God: Painting, Literature and Mythology* (Oxford: Clarendon Press, 1989).

Butler, Samuel, *Erewhon: Or, Over the Range* (London: A. C. Fifield, 1910).

Buttenhuis, Peter, *The Great War of Words: Literature as Propaganda 1914–18 and After* (London: Batsford, 1989).

Caine, Hall, 'The New Watchwords of Fiction', *Contemporary Review*, 57 (1890), 479–88.

Campanella, Thomas, *The City of the Sun*, ed. A. L. Morton, trans. A. M. Elliott and R. Millner (London: Journeyman Press, 1981).

Cantor, Paul A., '*The Invisible Man* and the Invisible Hand: H. G. Wells's Critique of Capitalism', *American Scholar*, 68/3 (1999), 89–102.

Carlyle, Thomas, *Sartor Resartus: The Life and Opinions of Herr Teufelsdröckh in Three Books*, ed. Roger L. Tarr and Mark Engel (Berkeley: University of California Press, 2000).

——*Past and Present*, ed. Chris R. Vanden Bossche, Joel J. Brattin, and D. J. Trela (Berkeley: University of California Press, 2005).

Carman, Barry, *A Prophet at the Microphone: The Story of H. G. Wells and the BBC*, broadcast on Radio 4, 27 December 1980, TS, H. G. Wells Collection, Bromley Public Library, Kent, UK.

Carroll, Joseph, *Evolution and Literary Theory* (Columbia: University of Missouri Press, 1995).

——*Literary Darwinism: Evolution, Human Nature, and Literature* (New York: Routledge, 2004).

Caserio, Robert L., *Decolonizing Tradition: New Views of Twentieth-Century 'British' Literary Canons* (Urbana: University of Illinois Press, 1992).

Chan, Winnie, *The Economy of the Short Story in British Periodicals of the 1890s* (London: Routledge, 2007).

Chase, Stuart, *The Tyranny of Words* (London: Methuen, 1938).

Chesterton, G. K., *Heretics* (London: Bodley Head, 1905).

Choi, Yoonjoung, 'Real Romance Came Out of Dreamland into Life: H. G. Wells as a Romancer' (PhD, Durham University, 2007).

Christensen, Timothy, 'The Bestial Mark of Race in *The Island of Doctor Moreau*', *Criticism*, 46/4 (2004), 575–95.

Clarke, I. F., *Voices Prophesying War: Future War, 1763–3749*, 2nd edn (Oxford: Oxford University Press, 1992).

Cohen, Ed, *Talk on the Wilde Side: Toward a Genealogy of a Discourse on Male Sexualities* (New York: Routledge, 1993).

Collini, Stefan, *Public Moralists: Political Thought and Intellectual Life in Britain, 1850–1930* (Oxford: Clarendon Press, 1991).

——*Absent Minds: Intellectuals in Britain* (Oxford: Oxford University Press, 2007).

Connor, Steven, *Dumbstruck: A Cultural History of Ventriloquism* (Oxford: Oxford University Press, 2000).

Costa, Richard Hauer, *H. G. Wells* (Boston: Twayne, 1967).

Costantini, Mariaconcetta, Renzo D'Agnillo, Renzo and Francesco Marroni, eds, *La Letteratura Vittoriana e i Mezzi di Trasporto: Dalla Nave all'Astronave* (Rome: Aracne, 2006).

Cross, Nigel, *The Common Writer: Life in Nineteenth-Century Grub Street* (Cambridge: Cambridge University Press, 1985).

Dalzell, Tom, ed., *The Concise New Partridge Dictionary of Slang and Unconventional English* (New York: Routledge, 2008).

Damasio, Antonio, *Descartes' Error: Emotion, Reason and the Human Brain* (London: Papermac, 1996).

Dames, Nicholas, *The Physiology of the Novel: Reading Neural Science and the Form of the Victorian Novel* (Oxford: Oxford University Press, 2007).

Darwin, Charles, *Metaphysics, Materialism and the Evolution of Mind: Early Writings of Charles Darwin*, ed. Paul H. Barrett and Howard E. Gruber (Chicago: University of Chicago Press, 1980).

——*On the Origin of Species by Means of Natural Selection, or the Preservation of Favoured Races in the Struggle for Life*, ed. Gillian Beer (Oxford: Oxford University Press, 1996).

——*The Descent of Man, and Selection in Relation to Sex*, ed. James Moore and Adrian Desmond (London: Penguin, 2004).

Dawson, Gowan, 'Introduction: Science and Victorian Poetry', *Victorian Poetry*, 41/1 (2003), 1–10.

——*Darwin, Literature and Victorian Responsibility* (Cambridge: Cambridge University Press, 2007).

De Certeau, Michel, *The Practice of Everyday Life*, trans. Steven Rendall (Berkeley: University of California Press, 1984).

Delbanco, Nicholas, *Group Portrait: Joseph Conrad, Stephen Crane, Ford Madox Ford, Henry James and H. G. Wells* (London: Faber, 1982).

Dempsey, Mike, ed., *Bubbles: Early Advertising Art from A. & F. Pears Ltd* (London: Fontana, 1978).

DePaolo, Charles, 'The Time Machine and the Descent of Man', *Foundation*, 85 (2002), 66–79.

Derrida, Jacques, *Dissemination*, trans. and ed. Barbara Johnson (Chicago: University of Chicago Press, 1981).

Derry, Stephen, '*The Island of Doctor Moreau* and Stevenson's *The Ebb Tide*', *Notes and Queries*, 43 (1996), 437.

——'The Time Traveller's Utopian Books and his Reading of the Future', *Foundation*, 65 (1998), 16–24.

Dessner, Lawrence Jay, 'H. G. Wells, *Mr Polly* and the Uses of Art', *English Literature in Transition*, 16 (1973), 121–34.

Devine, Christine, *Class in Turn-of-the Century Novels of Gissing, James, Hardy and Wells* (Aldershot: Ashgate, 2005).

Dickens, Charles, *Great Expectations*, ed. Margaret Cardwell (Oxford: Clarendon Press, 1993).

Digby, Anne and Peter Searby, *Children, School and Society in Nineteenth-Century England* (London: Macmillan, 1981).

Dilloway, James, *Human Rights and World Order* (London: H. G. Wells Society, 1983).

Dobbs, Rosalind, 'Biographical Sketches', unpublished MS, London School of Economics.

Doughty, F. H., *H. G. Wells, Educationist* (London: Cape, 1926).

Dowling, Linda C., 'The Decadent and the New Woman in the 1890s', *Nineteenth-Century Fiction*, 33/4 (1979), 434–53.

——*The Vulgarization of Art: The Victorians and Aesthetic Democracy* (Charlottesville: University of Virginia Press, 1996).

Draaisma, Douwe, *Metaphors of Memory: A History of Ideas About the Mind* (Cambridge: Cambridge University Press, 2000).

Draper, Michael, *H. G. Wells* (London: Macmillan, 1987).

'Drawn from Life?: Famous Characters in Modern Fiction and How They Were Conceived: H. G. Wells and Mr Polly', *Strand*, 76 (1928), 595–6.

Drinkwater, H., *Footnotes to H. G. Wells (Outline of History)* (n.p.: The Sower, 1921).

Dryden, Linda, *The Modern Gothic and Literary Doubles: Stevenson, Wilde and Wells* (Basingstoke: Palgrave Macmillan, 2003).

Eagleton, Terry, *Literary Theory: An Introduction* (Oxford: Blackwell, 1983).

Earle, David M., *Re-Covering Modernism: Pulps, Paperbacks and the Prejudices of Form* (London: Ashgate, 2009).

Eastdown, Martin and Linda Sage, *The History of Spade House, Folkestone* (Folkestone: Folkestone Local History Society, [n.d.]).

Eby, Cecil Degrotte, *The Road to Armageddon: The Martial Spirit in English Popular Literature, 1870–1914* (Durham, OH: Duke University Press, 1988).

Edel, Leon, *The Life of Henry James*, 2 vols. (Harmondsworth: Penguin, 1977).

——and Gordan N. Ray, eds, *Henry James and H. G. Wells: A Record of their Friendship, their Debate on the Art of Fiction, and their Quarrel* (London: Hart-Davis, 1959).

——and Mark Wilson, eds, *Literary Criticism: Essays on Literature, American Writers, English Writers* (New York: Library of America, 1984), 100–110.

Edmond, Rod and Vanessa Smith, eds, *Islands in History and Representation* (London: Routledge, 2003).

Eigner, Edwin M. and George J. Worth, eds, *Victorian Criticism of the Novel* (Cambridge: Cambridge University Press, 1985).

Eliot, T. S., 'The Idealism of Julien Benda', *Cambridge Review*, 99 (6 June 1928), 485–8.

Ellmann, Richard, ed., *Edwardians and Late Victorians* (New York: Columbia University Press, 1959).

Ensor, R. C. K., *England 1870–1914* (Oxford: Clarendon Press, 1936).

Evans, Ifor, *A Short History of English Literature* (Harmondsworth: Penguin, 1940).

Falk, Pasi, *The Consuming Body* (London: Sage, 1994).

Farrell, Kirby, *Post-Traumatic Culture: Injury and Interpretation in the Nineties* (Baltimore: Johns Hopkins University Press, 1998).

Feltes, N. N., *Literary Capital and the Late Victorian Novel* (Madison: University of Wisconsin Press, 1993).

Ferguson, Christine, *Language, Science and Popular Fiction in the Victorian Fin-de-Siècle: The Brutal Tongue* (Aldershot: Ashgate, 2006).

Firchow, Peter Edgerly, *Modern Utopian Fictions: From H. G. Wells to Iris Murdoch* (Washington, DC: Catholic University Press of America, 2007).

Flanders, Judith, *Consuming Passions: Leisure and Pleasure in Victorian Britain* (London: Harper Perennial, 2007).

Flower, Raymond, *Oundle and the English Public School* (London: Stacey, 1989).

Fluet, Lisa, 'Modernism and Disciplinary History: On H. G. Wells and
    T. S. Eliot', *Twentieth-Century Literature*, 50/3 (2004), 283–316.
Fogel, Daniel Mark, *Covert Relations: James Joyce, Virginia Woolf and Henry James*
    (Charlottesville: University Press of Virginia, 1990).
Ford, Ford Madox, *Mightier than the Sword: Memories and Criticisms* (London:
    Allen & Unwin, 1938).
Forster, E. M., *Aspects of the Novel* (Harmondsworth: Penguin, 1962).
Fraser, W. Hamish, *The Coming of the Mass Market, 1850–1914* (London:
    Macmillan, 1981).
Frayling, Christopher, *Things to Come* (London: British Film Institute, 1995).
Freud, Sigmund, *The Standard Edition of the Complete Psychological Works of
    Sigmund Freud*, 24 vols, trans. James Strachey (London: Hogarth Press,
    1953–74).
Frye, Northrop, *Anatomy of Criticism: Four Essays* (Princeton, NJ: Princeton
    University Press, 1971).
Garvey, Ellen Gruber, *The Adman in the Parlor: Magazines and the Gendering of
    Consumer Culture, 1880s to 1910* (New York: Oxford University Press, 1996).
Gettmann, Royal A., *George Gissing and H. G. Wells: Their Friendship and
    Correspondence* (London: Hart-Davis, 1961), 77.
Gillis, James, *False Prophets* (New York: Macmillan, 1925).
Gissing, George, *The Collected Letters of George Gissing*, ed. Pierre Coustillas, Paul
    F. Mattheisen, and Arthur C. Young, 9 vols (Athens: Ohio University Press,
    (1990–7).
Glendening, John, 'The Track of the Sphinx: H. G. Wells, the Modern Universe,
    and the Decay of Aestheticism', *Victorians Institute Journal*, 32 (2004), 129–66.
—— *The Evolutionary Imagination in Late-Victorian Novels: An Entangled Bank*
    (Aldershot: Ashgate, 2007).
Goldhill, Simon, *Reading Greek Tragedy* (Cambridge: Cambridge University
    Press, 1986).
Gomme, A. L., *Mr Wells as Historian: An Inquiry into those Parts of
    Mr H. G. Wells's Outline of History which Deal with Greece and Rome* (Glasgow:
    MacLehose, Jackson and Co., 1921).
Gould, Stephen Jay, *Time's Arrow, Time's Cycle: Myth and Metaphor in the
    Discovery of Geological Time* (Cambridge, MA: Harvard University Press, 1987).
Graham, Kenneth, *English Criticism of the Novel, 1865–1900* (Oxford: Clarendon
    Press, 1965).
Greenslade, William, *Degeneration, Culture and the Novel: 1880–1940* (Cam-
    bridge: Cambridge University Press, 1994).
Griffiths, Trevor R., '"This Island's Mine": Caliban and Colonialism', *Yearbook of
    English Studies*, 13 (1983), 159–80.
Gross, John, *The Rise and Fall of the Man of Letters: Aspects of Literary Life since
    1800* (London: Weidenfeld and Nicolson, 1969).

Guy, Josephine, 'Aesthetics, Economics and Commodity Culture: Theorizing Value in Late Nineteenth-Century Britain', *English Literature in Transition*, 42/2 (1999), 143–71.

Haggard, Sir Henry Rider, 'About Fiction', *Contemporary Review*, 51 (1887), 172–80.

Halberstam, Judith, *Skin Shows: Gothic Horror and the Technology of Monsters* (Durham, OH: Duke University Press, 1995).

Hale, Piers J., 'Of Mice and Men: Evolution and the Socialist Utopia: William Morris, H. G. Wells and George Bernard Shaw', *Journal of the History of Biology*, 43/1 (2010), 17–66.

Hallam, Julia and Nickianne Moody, eds, *Consuming for Pleasure: Selected Essays on Popular Fiction* (Liverpool: Liverpool John Moores University Press, 2000).

Hammond, J. R., *H. G. Wells and the Modern Novel* (New York: St Martin's Press 1988).

Hammond, Mary, *Reading, Publishing and the Formation of Literary Taste, 1880–1914* (Aldershot: Ashgate, 2006).

Hardy, Sylvia, 'A Story of the Days to Come: H. G. Wells and the Language of Science Fiction', *Language and Literature*, 12/3 (2003), 199–212.

Harris, Alexandra, *Romantic Moderns: English Writers, Artists and the Imagination from Virginia Woolf to John Piper* (London: Thames & Hudson, 2010).

Harris, Mason, 'Vivisection, the Culture of Science, and Intellectual Uncertainty in *The Island of Doctor Moreau*', *Gothic Studies*, 4/2 (2002), 100–15.

Harrison, Frederic, *The Choice of Books: And Other Literary Pieces* (London: Macmillan, 1886).

Hart-Davis, Rupert, *Hugh Walpole: A Biography* (London: Macmillan, 1952).

Hassler, Donald M., ed., *Patterns of the Fantastic II* (Mercer Island, WA: Starmont House, 1984).

Haynes, Roslynn D., *H. G. Wells: Discoverer of the Future: The Influence of Science on his Thought* (New York: New York University Press, 1980).

Hendershot, Cyndy, *The Animal Within: Masculinity and the Gothic* (Ann Arbor: University of Michigan Press, 1998).

Hepburn, James G., *The Author's Empty Purse and the Rise of the Literary Agent* (London: Oxford University Press, 1968).

Herbart, Johann Friedrich, *The Application of Psychology to the Science of Education*, trans. B. C. Mulliner (London: Swan Sonnenschein, 1898).

Higson, Andrew, ed., *Young and Innocent? The Cinema in Britain, 1896–1930* (Exeter: University of Exeter Press, 2002).

Hillegas, Mark R., *The Future as Nightmare: H. G. Wells and the Anti-Utopians* (New York: Oxford University Press, 1967).

Hobsbawm, Eric, *Industry and Empire: 1750 to the Present Day* (Harmondsworth: Penguin, 1969).

Howard, David, John Goode, and John Lucas, eds, *Tradition and Tolerance in Nineteenth-Century Fiction* (London: Routledge & Kegan Paul, 1966).

Hume, Kathryn, *Fantasy and Mimesis: Responses to Reality in Western Literature* (London: Methuen, 1984).

——'Eat or be Eaten: H. G. Wells's *Time Machine*', *Philological Quarterly*, 69/2 (1990), 233–51.

Humphery, George R., 'The Reading of the Working Classes', *Nineteenth Century*, 33 (1893), 690–701.

Huntington, John, *The Logic of Fantasy: H. G. Wells and Science Fiction* (New York: Columbia University Press, 1982).

Huxley, T. H., *Lay Sermons, Addresses and Reviews*, 5th edn (London: Macmillan, 1874).

——*The Major Prose of T. H. Huxley*, ed. Alan P. Barr (Athens: University of Georgia Press, 1997).

Huyssen, Andreas, *After the Great Divide: Modernism, Mass Culture, Postmodernism* (Bloomington: Indiana University Press, 1986).

Hynes, Samuel, *The Edwardian Turn of Mind* (Princeton, NJ: Princeton University Press, 1968).

James, Henry, *The Portrait of a Lady* (New York: Riverside Press, 1882).

——*The Letters of Henry James*, ed. Percy Lubbock, 2 vols (London: Macmillan, 1920).

——*Literary Criticism: Essays on Literature, American Writers, English Writers*, ed. Leon Edel and Mark Wilson (New York: Library of America, 1984).

——*Literary Criticism: French Writers, Other European Writers, The Prefaces to the New York Edition*, ed. Leon Edel (New York: Library of America, 1984).

James, Simon J., *Unsettled Accounts: Money and Narrative Form in the Novels of George Gissing* (London: Anthem, 2003).

——and Nicholas Saul, eds, *The Evolution of Literature: Legacies of Charles Darwin in European Cultures* (Amsterdam: Rodopi, 2011).

James, William *The Varieties of Religious Experience: Being the Gifford Lectures on Natural Religion Delivered at Edinburgh in 1901–1902* (New York: Longman, 1902).

Jameson, Fredric, *The Political Unconscious: Narrative as a Socially Symbolic Act* (London: Methuen, 1981).

——*Archaeologies of the Future: The Desire Called Utopia and Other Science Fictions* (London: Verso, 2005).

Jann, Rosemary, 'Sherlock Holmes Codes the Social Body', *English Literature in Transition 1880–1920*, 57 (1990), 685–708.

Jones, Steve, *The Language of the Genes: Biology, History and the Evolutionary Future* (London: HarperCollins, 1994).

Jordan, John O. and Robert L. Patten, eds, *Literature in the Market Place: Nineteenth-Century British Publishing and Reading Practices* (Cambridge: Cambridge University Press, 1995).

Keating, P. J., *The Representation of the Working Classes in Victorian Fiction* (London: Routledge & Kegan Paul, 1971).

—— *The Haunted Study: A Social History of the English Novel, 1875–1914* (London: Secker & Warburg, 1989).

Keen, Suzanne, *Victorian Renovations of the Novel: Narrative Annexes and the Boundaries of Representation* (Cambridge: Cambridge University Press, 1998).

Keesey, Douglas, '"So Much Life with (So to Speak) So Little Living": The Literary Side of the James–Wells Debate', *Henry James Review*, 6/2 (1985), 80–8.

Kemp, Peter, *H. G. Wells and the Culminating Ape* (New York: St Martin's Press, 1982).

Ketterer, David, 'Oedipus as Time-Traveller', *Science Fiction Studies*, 9 (1982), 340–1.

Knights, Ben, *The Idea of the Clerisy in the Nineteenth Century* (Cambridge: Cambridge University Press, 1978).

Kristeva, Julia, *Powers of Horror: An Essay on Abjection*, trans. Leon S. Roudiez (New York: Columbia University Press, 1982).

Kuhn, Thomas, *The Structure of Scientific Revolutions*, 2nd edn (Chicago: University of Chicago Press, 1970).

Kumar, Krishan, *Utopia and Anti-Utopia in Modern Times* (Oxford: Blackwell, 1987).

Kupinse, William, 'Wasted Value: The Serial Logic of H. G. Wells's *Tono-Bungay*', *Novel*, 33/1 (1999), 51–72.

Lacan, Jacques, *Écrits: A Selection*, trans. Alan Sheridan (London: Routledge, 2001).

LaCapra, Dominick, *Rethinking Intellectual History* (Ithaca: Cornell University Press, 1983).

Lake, David J., 'Wells's Time Traveller: An Unreliable Narrator', *Extrapolation*, 22/2 (1981), 117–26.

Lawrence, D. H., *Selected Literary Criticism*, ed. Anthony Beal (London: Heinemann, 1955).

Lawson, John and Harold Silver, *A Social History of Education in England* (London: Methuen, 1973).

Leavis, F. R., *For Continuity* (Cambridge: Minority Press, 1933).

Levitas, Ruth, *The Concept of Utopia* (London: Philip Allan, 1990).

Lodge, David, *Language of Fiction* (London: Routledge & Kegan Paul, 1966).

—— *The Novelist at the Crossroads: And Other Essays on Fiction and Criticism* (Ithaca: Cornell University Press, 1971).

Loeb, L. A., *Consuming Angels: Advertising and Victorian Women* (Oxford: Oxford University Press, 1994).

Loing, Bernard, *H. G. Wells à L'Oeuvre: Les Débuts d'un Écrivain (1894–1900)* (Paris: Didier Erudition, 1984).

Lubbock, John, 'On the Pleasure of Reading', *Contemporary Review*, 49 (1886), 240–51.

Lyell, Charles, *The Principles of Geology*, ed. Martin Rudwick, 3 vols (Chicago: University of Chicago Press, 1990).

Lynn, Andrea, *Shadow Lovers: The Last Affairs of H. G. Wells* (Oxford: Perseus Press, 2001).

MacKenzie, Norman and Jeanne MacKenzie, *The Life of H. G. Wells: The Time Traveller* (London: Hogarth Press, 1987).

Macleod, Dianne Sachko, *Art and the Victorian Middle Class* (Cambridge: Cambridge University Press, 1996).

MacLeod, Roy M., *The 'Creed of Science' in Victorian England* (Aldershot: Ashgate, 2000).

Maclure, Stuart, ed., *Educational Documents: England and Wales, 1816–1963* (London: Chapman and Hall, 1965).

Marx, Karl, *Economic and Philosophical Manuscripts of 1844*, 5th edn (Moscow: Progress, 1977).

Maxwell, Herbert, 'The Craving for Fiction', *Nineteenth Century*, 33 (1893) 1046–61.

Mazzucco, Cecile, *A Form Foredoomed to Looseness: Henry James's Preoccupation with the Gender of Fiction* (New York: Lang, 2002).

McAdam, Paul, 'Negotiating the Real: Culture and Fantastical Fiction, 1843–1973' (PhD, Durham University, 2005).

McColl, Malcolm, 'Morality in Fiction', *Contemporary Review*, 60 (1891), 234–52.

McConnell, Frank, *The Science Fiction of H. G. Wells* (New York: Oxford University Press, 1981).

McDonald, J., *A Dictionary of Obscenity, Taboo and Euphemism* (London: Sphere, 1988).

McDonald, Peter D., *British Literary Culture and Publishing Practice, 1880–1914* (Cambridge: Cambridge University Press, 1997).

McGurn, James, *On Your Bicycle: An Illustrated History of Cycling* (London: John Murray, 1987).

McKillop, A. B., *The Spinster and the Prophet* (London: Aurum, 2001).

McLean, Steven, *The Early Fiction of H. G. Wells: Fantasies of Science* (Basingstoke: Palgrave Macmillan, 2009).

——ed., *H. G. Wells: Interdisciplinary Essays* (Newcastle: Cambridge Scholars Press, 2008).

McMillan, Gloria. 'The Invisible Friends: The Lost Worlds of Henry James and H. G. Wells', *Explicator*, 47/1 (2006), 134–47.

Mencken, H. L., *Prejudices: First Series* (London: Jonathan Cape, 1921).

Messinger, Gary S., *British Propaganda and the State in the First World War* (Manchester: Manchester University Press, 1992).

Metz, Christian, *Film Language: A Semiotics of the Cinema*, trans. Michael Taylor (New York: Oxford University Press, 1964).

Mill, John Stuart, *The Collected Works of John Stuart Mill*, 33 vols, ed. Francis E. Mineka and Dwight N. Lindley (Toronto: University of Toronto Press; London: Routledge, 1972).

Miller, D. A., *Narrative and its Discontents: Problems of Closure in the Traditional Novel* (Princeton, NJ: Princeton University Press, 1981).

Mirsky, Dmitri. *The Intelligentsia of Great Britain*, trans. Alec Brown (London: Gollancz, 1935).

Mitch, David F., *The Rise of Popular Literacy in Victorian England: The Influence of Private Choice and Public Policy* (Philadelphia: University of Pennsylvania Press, 1992).

More, Thomas, *Utopia: A Revised Translation, Backgrounds, Criticism*, trans. and ed. Robert M. Adams, 2nd edn. (New York: Norton, 1992).

Moretti, Franco, *The Way of the World: The* Bildungsroman *in European Culture* (London: Verso, 1987).

Morley, John, *Studies in Literature* (London: Macmillan, 1891).

Morris, William, *The Collected Letters of William Morris*, 4 vols, ed. N. Kelvin (Princeton, NJ: Princeton University Press, 1984–96).

——*News from Nowhere: or An Epoch of Rest, Being some Chapters from a Utopian Romance*, ed. Stephen Arata (Peterborough: Broadview, 2003).

Morton, A. L., *The English Utopia* (London: Lawrence & Wishart, 1953).

Morton, Peter, *The Vital Science: Biology and the Literary Imagination, 1860–1900* (London: Allen & Unwin, 1984).

Mozley, Ann, 'On Fiction as an Educator', *Blackwood's Magazine*, 108 (1870), 449–59.

Müller, Detlef K., Fritz Ringer, and Brian Simon, eds, *The Rise of the Modern Educational System: Structural Change and Social Reproduction, 1870–1920* (Cambridge and Paris: Cambridge University Press and Éditions de la Maison de Sciences de L'Homme, 1987).

Müller, Max, *Lectures on the Science of Language: Delivered at the Royal Institution of Great Britain in April, May and June, 1861*, 2nd rev. edn, 2 vols (London: Longman, 1862).

Mullin, Michael, ed., *H. G. Wells: Reality and Beyond: A Collection of Critical Essays Prepared in Conjunction with the Exhibition and Symposium on H. G. Wells* (Champaign: Champaign Public Library and Information Center, 1986).

Naismith, William, *A Young Draper's Guide to Success* (London: Gardner, 1901).

Lord Neaves, *On Fiction As a Means of Popular Teaching* (London: Blackwood, 1869).

Newell, Kenneth B., *Structure in Four Novels by H. G. Wells* (The Hague: Mouton, 1968).

Norman, Henry, 'Theories and Practice of Modern Fiction', *Fortnightly Review*, 34 (1883), 870–86.

Ní Dhúill, Caitríona, *Sex in Imagined Spaces: Gender and Utopia from More to Bloch* (London: Legenda, 2010).

214 *Bibliography*

Niederland, William G., 'The Birth of H. G. Wells's Time Machine', *American Imago: A Psychoanalytic Journal for Culture, Science, and the Arts*, 35 (1978), 106–12.

Nordau, Max, *Degeneration*, ed. George L. Mosse (Lincoln: University of Nebraska Press, 1993).

Olmsted, J. C., ed., *A Victorian Art of Fiction*, 3 vols (New York: Garland, 1979).

Ong, Walter J., *Orality and Literacy: The Technologizing of the Word* (London: Routledge, 1988).

Orwell, George, 'Wells, Hitler and the World State', in *The Complete Works of George Orwell*, 20 vols, ed. Peter Davison (London: Secker & Warburg, 1986–98), XIII: *A Patriot After All*, 536–41.

Otis, Laura, *Membranes: Metaphors of Invasion in Nineteenth-Century Literature, Science, and Politics* (Baltimore: Johns Hopkins University Press, 1999).

Paris, Michael, *Winged Warfare: The Literature and Theory of Aerial Warfare in Britain, 1859–1917* (Manchester: Manchester University Press, 1992).

Parrinder, Patrick, 'From Midhurst Grammar School to Cosmopolis', *H. G. Wells Society Occasional Papers*, NS 1.

——*H. G. Wells* (Edinburgh: Oliver Boyd, 1970).

——'*News from Nowhere, The Time Machine* and the Break-Up of Classical Realism', *Science Fiction Studies*, 3/3 (1976), 265–74.

——'The Roman Spring of George Gissing and H. G. Wells', *Gissing Newsletter*, 21/3 (1985), 1–12.

——*Shadows of the Future: H. G. Wells, Science Fiction and Prophecy* (Liverpool: Liverpool University Press, 1995).

——'History in the Science Fiction of H. G. Wells', *Cycnos*, 22/2 (2004), http://revel.unice.fr/cycnos/document.html?id=428 [accessed 23 July 2011].

——ed., *H. G. Wells: The Critical Heritage* (London: Routledge & Kegan Paul, 1972).

——and Warren Cherniak, eds, *Textual Monopolies and the Public Domain*, (London: Office for Humanities Communication, 1997).

——and Andrzej Gasiorek, eds, *The Oxford History of the Novel in English*, vol. IV: *The Reinvention of the British Novel, 1880–1940* (Oxford: Oxford University Press, 2011).

——and John S. Partington, eds, *The Reception of H. G. Wells in Europe* (London: Continuum, 2005).

——and Christopher Rolfe, eds, *H. G. Wells under Revision: Proceedings of the International H. G. Wells Symposium, London. July 1986* (Selinsgrove: Susquehanna University Press; London: Associated University Presses, 1990).

Parry, Benita, *Postcolonial Studies: A Materialist Critique* (London: Routledge, 2004).

Partington, John, '*The Time Machine* and *A Modern Utopia*: The Static and Kinetic Utopias of the Early H. G. Wells', *Utopian Studies*, 13/1 (2002), 57–68.

——*Building Cosmopolis: The Political Thought of H. G. Wells* (Aldershot: Ashgate, 2003).

——'H. G. Wells's Eugenic Thinking of the 1930s and 1940s', *Utopian Studies*, 14/1 (2003), 74–81.

——'The Pen as Sword: George Orwell, H. G. Wells and Journalistic Parricide', *Journal of Contemporary History*, 39/1 (2004), 45–56.

——'Human Rights and Public Accountability in H. G. Wells's Functional World State', in *Cosmopolitics and the Emergence of a Future*, ed. Diane Morgan and Gary Banham (Basingstoke: Palgrave Macmillan, 2007), 163–90.

——ed., *The Wellsian: Selected Essays on H. G. Wells* (Haren: Equilibris, 2003).

Partridge, Eric, *A Dictionary of Slang and Unconventional English*, 2 vols (London: Routledge & Kegan Paul, 1967–70).

——ed., *H. G. Wells's Fin-de-Siècle: Twenty-First Century Reflections on the Early H. G. Wells* (Frankfurt: Peter Lang, 2007).

Pearson, Richard, 'Primitive Modernity: H. G. Wells and the Prehistoric Man of the 1890s', *Yearbook of English Studies*, 37/1 (2007), 58–74.

Philmus, Robert, *Into the Unknown: The Evolution of Science Fiction from Francis Godwin to H. G. Wells* (Berkeley: University of California Press, 1970).

——*Visions and Re-Visions: (Re)constructing Science Fiction* (Liverpool: Liverpool University Press, 2005).

Pick, Daniel, *Faces of Degeneration: A European Disorder c.1948–c.1919* (Cambridge: Cambridge University Press, 1989).

Pinker, Steven, *The Language Instinct: The New Science of Language and Mind* (London: Penguin, 2000).

——*The Blank Slate: The Modern Denial of Human Nature* (London: Allen Lane, 2002).

Pinsky, Michael, *Future Present: Ethics and/as Science Fiction* (London: Associated University Presses, 2003).

Plato, *The Republic*, trans. Desmond Lee, 2nd edn (Harmondsworth: Penguin, 1974).

——*Phaedrus and Letters VII and VIII*, trans. Walter Hamilton (London: Penguin, 1983).

Poovey, Mary, 'Forgotten Writers, Neglected Histories: Charles Reade and the Nineteenth-Century Transformation of the British Literary Field', *English Literary History*, 72/2 (2004), 433–53.

Popper, Karl, *The Logic of Scientific Discovery* (London: Hutchinson, 1959).

Posnock, Ross, *The Trial of Curiosity: Henry James, William James and the Challenge of Modernity* (New York: Oxford University Press, 1991).

Proctor, Brian Waller, 'On the Reading of Books', *Temple Bar*, 72 (1884), 178–86.

Punter, David, *The Literature of Terror: A History of Gothic Fictions from 1765 to the Present Day* (London: Longman, 1980).

Quamen, Harvey N., 'Unnatural Interbreeding: H. G. Wells's *A Modern Utopia* as Species and Genre', *Victorian Literature and Culture*, 33/1 (2005), 67–84.

Raknem, Ingvald, *H. G. Wells and his Critics* (Oslo: Universitetsforlaget; London: Allen & Unwin, 1962).

Rands, W. B., 'The New Fiction', *Contemporary Review*, 37 (1880), 247–62.

Ray, Martin, 'Conrad, Wells, and *The Secret Agent*: Paying Old Debts and Settling Old Scores', *Modern Language Review*, 81/3 (1986), 560–73.

Reade, Winwood, *The Martyrdom of Man*, 15th edn (London: Kegan Paul, Trench, Trubner, 1896).

Reed, John R., *The Natural History of H. G. Wells* (Athens: Ohio University Press, 1982).

Reid, G. Archdall, *The Present Evolution of Man* (London: Chapman and Hall, 1896).

Reynolds, E. J., 'What Shall Be Read?', *Science Schools Journal*, 2 (1889), 98–108.

Richards, Thomas, *The Imperial Archive: Knowledge and the Fantasy of Empire* (London: Verso, 1993).

Robbins, Ruth, *Pater to Forster, 1873–1924* (Basingstoke: Palgrave Macmillan, 2003).

Roberts, Lewis C., 'Disciplining and Disinfecting Working-Class Readers in the Victorian Public Library', *Victorian Literature and Culture*, 26 (1998), 105–32.

Roberts, Michael, 'Mr Wells's Sombre World', *Spectator*, 157 (1936), 1032–3.

Rose, Jonathan, *The Intellectual Life of the British Working Classes* (New Haven: Yale University Press, 2001).

Ross, William T., *H. G. Wells's World Reborn: The Outline of History and its Companions* (Selinsgrove: Susquehanna University Press; London: Associated University Presses, 2002).

Ruskin, John, *The Works of John Ruskin*, 39 vols, ed. E. T. Cook and A. Wedderburn (London: George Allen, 1903–12).

Russell, D. A. and Michael Winterbottom, eds, *Classical Literary Criticism* (Oxford: Oxford University Press, 1989).

Said, Edward, *Culture and Imperialism* (London: Chatto & Windus, 1993).

Sanderson of Oundle (London: Chatto & Windus, 1923).

Santayana, George, *The Life of Reason: or, The Phases of Human Progress, Revised by the Author in Collaboration with David Cory* (London: Constable, 1954).

Saunders, Corinne, ed., *A Companion to Romance: From Classical to Contemporary* (Malden, MA: Blackwell, 2004).

Scarry, Elaine, *The Body in Pain: The Making and Unmaking of the World* (New York: Oxford University Press, 1985).

Scheick, William J., 'The De-Forming In-Struction of Wells's *The Wonderful Visit* and *The Sea Lady*', *English Literature in Transition 1880–1920*, 30/4 (1987), 397–409.

——ed., *The Critical Response to H. G. Wells* (Westport, CT: Greenwood Press, 1995).

Schenkel, Elmar and Stefan Welz, eds, *Lost Worlds and Mad Elephants: Literature, Science and Technology, 1700–1900* (Berlin: Galda & Wilch, 1999).

Schorer, Mark, 'Technique as Discovery', *Hudson Review*, 1/1 (1948), 67–87.

Scott, Patrick and Pauline Fletcher, eds, *Culture and Education in Victorian England* (Lewisburg: Bucknell University Press; London and Toronto: Associated University Presses, 1990).

Searby, Peter, ed., *Educating the Victorian Middle Class* (Leicester: History of Education Society, 1982).

Secret Remedies: What They Cost and What they Contain, Based on Analysis Made for the British Medical Association (London: British Medical Association, 1909).

Shapcott, John, ed., *Bennett and Wells: Their Friendship, Fiction and Films* (Stoke: Arnold Bennett Society, 2010).

Sherborne, Michael, *H. G. Wells: Another Kind of Life* (London: Peter Owen, 2010).

Sherman, Stuart Pratt, *On Contemporary Literature* (New York: Henry Holt, 1917).

Shippey, Tom, ed., *Fictional Space: Essays on Contemporary Science Fiction* (Oxford: Blackwell, 1991), 76–103.

Shuker, Roy, 'H. G. Wells: The Novelist as Educator', *Education Research and Perspectives*, 6 (1979), 44–53.

——'H. G. Wells, Education and the World State,' *Discourse: The Australian Journal of Education Studies*, 3/1 (1982), 57–65.

Sidgwick, Alfred, *The Use of Words in Reasoning* (London: Black, 1901).

Silver, Harold, *Education as History: Interpreting Nineteenth- and Twentieth-Century Education* (London: Methuen, 1983).

Simon, Brian, *The State and Educational Change: Essays in the History of Education and Pedagogy* (London: Lawrence & Wishart, 1994).

Sirabian, Robert, 'The Conception of Science in Wells's *The Invisible Man*', *Papers on Language and Literature*, 37/4 (2001), 383–403.

Skelton, Matthew, 'The Paratext of Everything: Constructing and Marketing H. G. Wells's *The Outline of History*', *Book History*, 4 (2001), 237–75.

Slusser, George, Patrick Parrinder, and Danièle Chatelain, eds, *H. G. Wells's Perennial Time Machine: Selected Essays from the Centenary Conference 'The Time Machine: Past, Present and Future', Imperial College, London, July 26–29, 1995* (Athens: University of Georgia Press, 2001).

Smith, Dan, 'Wells' First Utopia: Materiality and Portent', http://www.slashseconds.org/issues/002/003/articles/dsmith/index.php [accessed 25 January 2011].

Smith, David C., *H. G. Wells: Desperately Mortal—A Biography* (New Haven: Yale University Press, 1986).

Smith, Don. *H. G. Wells on Film: The Utopian Nightmare* (Jefferson, NC: McFarland, 2002).

Smith, Jonathan, *Fact and Feeling: Baconian Science and the Nineteenth-Century Literary Imagination* (Madison: University of Wisconsin Press, 1994).

Snow, C. P., *The Two Cultures and The Two Cultures: A Second Look*, ed. Stefan Collini (Cambridge: Cambridge University Press, 1993).

Sommers, Jeffrey, 'Wells's *Tono-Bungay*: The Novel Within the Novel', *Studies in the Novel*, 17/1 (1985), 69–79.

Spencer, Herbert, *Political Writings*, ed. John Offer (Cambridge: Cambridge University Press, 1994).

Stoker, Bram, *Dracula*, ed. Glennis Byron (Peterborough, ON: Broadview, 1998).

Stokes, John, ed., *Fin de Siècle/Fin du Globe* (Basingstoke: Macmillan, 1992).

Stover, Leon, *The Prophetic Soul: A Reading of H. G. Wells's Things to Come* (Jefferson, NC: McFarland, 1987).

Stuart, Sir Campbell, *Secrets of Crewe House: Secrets of a Famous Campaign* (London: Hodder & Stoughton, 1920).

Sturt, George, *The Journals of George Sturt, 1890–1927: A Selection*, ed. E. D. Mackerness, 2 vols. (Cambridge: Cambridge University Press, 1967).

Stutfield, Hugh, 'Tommyrotics', *Blackwood's Edinburgh Magazine*, 157 (1895), 858–67.

Suvin, Darko, *Metamorphoses of Science Fiction: On the Poetics and History of a Literary Genre* (New Haven: Yale University Press, 1979).

——and Robert M. Philmus, eds, *H. G. Wells and Modern Science Fiction* (Lewisburg: Bucknell University Press; London: Associated University Presses, 1977).

Symonds, J. A., 'Culture: Its Meaning and Uses', *New Review*, 7 (1892), 105–15.

Todorov, Tsvetan, *The Fantastic: A Structural Approach to Literary Genre*, trans. Richard Howard (Ithaca: Cornell University Press, 1975).

——*The Poetics of Prose*, trans. Richard Howard (Oxford: Blackwell, 1977).

——*Genres in Discourse*, trans. Catherine Porter (Cambridge: Cambridge University Press, 1990).

Toye, Richard, 'H. G. Wells and the New Liberalism', *Twentieth Century British History*, 19/2 (2008), 156–85.

Trotter, David, *The English Novel in History, 1895–1920* (London: Routledge, 1993).

Tupper, Martin, *Stephan Langton*, 2 vols (London: Hurst and Blacket, [1858]).

Turner, E. S., *The Shocking History of Advertising*, rev. edn (Harmondsworth: Penguin, 1952).

The Undying Fire, 1–4 (2001–4).

Veblen, Thorstein, *Theory of the Leisure Class* (New York: Macmillan, 1912).

Vincent, David, *Literacy and Popular Culture: England, 1750–1914* (Cambridge: Cambridge University Press, 1989).

Wagar, W. Warren, *H. G. Wells and the World State* (New Haven: Yale University Press, 1961).

—— *H. G. Wells: Traversing Time* (Middletown, CT: Wesleyan University Press, 2004).

—— ed., *The Open Conspiracy: H. G. Wells on World Revolution* (Westport, CT: Praeger, 2002).

Waller, P. J., *Writers, Readers and Reputations: Literary Life in Britain, 1870–1918* (Oxford: Oxford University Press, 2006).

Walker, Pierre A., 'Leon Edel and the "Policing" of the Henry James Letters', *Henry James Review*, 21/3 (2000), 279–89.

Walker, William George, *A History of the Oundle Schools* (London: The Grocers' Company, 1956).

Wedgewood, Julia, 'Contemporary Records: I – Fiction', *Contemporary Review*, 50 (1886), 897–905.

The Wellsian, 1–33 (1976–2010).

West, Geoffrey, *H. G. Wells: A Sketch for a Portrait* (London: Gerald Howe, 1930).

West, Rebecca, *Henry James* (London: Nisbet, 1916).

Westfahl, Gary and George Slusser, eds, *No Cure for the Future: Disease and Medicine in Science Fiction and Fantasy* (Westport, CT: Greenwood Press, 2002).

Wicke, Jennifer. *Advertising Fictions: Literature, Advertisements and Social Reading* (New York: Columbia University Press, 1988).

Wilde, Oscar, *The Complete Works of Oscar Wilde*, 4 vols (Oxford: Clarendon Press, 2000–).

Williams, Keith, *H. G. Wells, Modernity and the Movies* (Liverpool: Liverpool University Press, 2007).

Williams, Raymond, *Culture and Society, 1780–1950* (Harmondsworth: Penguin, 1963).

—— *Keywords: A Vocabulary of Culture and Society* (London: Fontana, 1988).

—— *The Country and the City* (London: Hogarth Press, 1993).

Wilson, Harris, 'The Death of Masterman: A Repressed Episode in H. G. Wells's *Kipps*', *PMLA*, 86 (1971), 63–9.

Wittgenstein, Ludwig, *Philosophical Investigations*, trans. G. E. M. Anscombe (Oxford: Blackwell, 1967).

Wykes, Alan, *H. G. Wells in the Cinema* (London: Jupiter, 1977).

Žižek, Slavoj, *Enjoy your Symptom! Jacques Lacan in Hollywood and Out*, rev. edn (New York: Routledge, 2001).

Index

228 *Index*